WOMEN AND CAREER
Themes and issues in advanced industrial societies

LONGMAN SOCIOLOGY SERIES

Series Editor:
ROBERT BURGESS, University of Warwick

Editorial Advisors:
JOE BAILEY, Kingston University
ANGELA GLASNER, Oxford Brookes University
CLAIRE WALLACE, University of Lancaster

Published Titles:
Social Europe
Joe Bailey (ed.)

Forthcoming Titles:
Poverty and Wealth
John Scott

Gender and Technology
Juliet Webster

LONGMAN SOCIOLOGY SERIES

Women and Career
Themes and issues in advanced industrial societies

edited by Julia Evetts

LONGMAN
London and New York

Longman Group UK Limited,
Longman House, Burnt Mill,
Harlow, Essex CM20 2JE, England
and Associated Companies throughout the world.

*Published in the United States of America
by Longman Publishing, New York*

First published 1994

ISBN 0582 101948 PPR

British Library Cataloguing-in-Publication Data

A catalogue record for this book is
available from the British Library

Library of Congress Cataloging-in-Publication Data
Women and career : themes and issues in advanced industrial societies
/ edited by Julia Evetts.
    p. cm. – (Longman sociology series)
  Includes bibliographical references and index.
  ISBN 0–582–10194–8
  1. Women – Employment. 2. Women in the professions. I. Evetts,
Julia. II. Series.
HD6053.W627 1993
305.43 – dc20   93–15577
                                                CIP

Set by 300 in Times
Printed in Malaysia by TCP

CONTENTS

LIST OF TABLES

SERIES EDITOR'S PREFACE

The Longman Sociology Series is a new series of books which are written specifically for first and second year undergraduate students. Each title covers one key area of sociology and aims to supplement the traditional standard text.

The series is forward looking and attempts to reflect topics that will be included in syllabuses for sociology and social policy in the 1990s. It provides a range of volumes that bring together conceptual and empirical material. In addition, volumes in the series also examine key controversies and debates drawing on commentaries using conceptual and empirical material from a range of authors.

Each volume in the series whether authored or edited, will cover an area that would be commonly found in sociology and social policy syllabuses. The focus of each volume will be upon theoretically informed empirical work with policy relatedness.

The volumes are intended for an international audience and therefore comparative material is introduced where appropriate in a form that will be suitable for first and second year students.

The papers in this volume focus on women and career. As a consequence they contribute to conceptual, methodological and substantive issues in this field. The result is a volume that is an important resource for students, teachers and researchers in sociology and related fields of study.

Robert G Burgess
University of Warwick
January 1993

ACKNOWLEDGEMENTS

A large number of people have contributed indirectly to the development and completion of this collection of papers. In particular I would like to thank Hugh Barr for his early encouragement. Colleagues in the School of Social Studies made recommendations and suggestions. Robert Burgess gave continuing support. Linda Poxon typed drafts, standardised contributions and prepared the final manuscript; her willingness, speed and accuracy have been greatly appreciated.

Julia Evetts
University of Nottingham
January 1993

THE CONTRIBUTORS

Alan Aldridge is Senior Lecturer in Social Studies at the University of Nottingham. His recent research has focused on social change in the clerical profession, and he has acted as a consultant to the Church of England on women's career development. He is currently researching francophilia and the 'enterprise culture'.

Julia Allison is Director of Midwifery Studies at Norfolk College of Nursing and Midwifery Studies. She is President of the Royal College of Midwives and has done extensive research on midwifery practice.

Lynn Ashburner is a Senior Research Fellow at the University of Warwick Business School, currently researching management issues related to the new health authorities and trusts in the NHS. Her past research was on gender and work organisation and she retains an ongoing interest in gender issues as they relate to organisations.

Alice Brown is a Lecturer in the Department of Politics at the University of Edinburgh. She has also lectured in Economics at the Universities of Edinburgh and Stirling. Her research interests include women and politics, labour market policy, industrial relations and Scottish politics. She has published articles and edited books in these areas and is currently working on a book on women and Scottish politics.

Jennifer Coates is Reader in English Language and Linguistics at Roehampton Institute, London. Her published work includes *The Semantics of the Modal Auxiliaries* (1983), *Women, Men and Language* (1986) and *Women in their Speech Communities* (1989) (co-edited with Deborah Cameron). She is currently working on a new book, *Women Talking to Women*, which is an account of her long-term research project on the talk of single-sex friendship groups.

Diane M. Dunlap is Dean of the Graduate School, Hamline University, St. Paul, Minnesota. Formerly chair of the Higher Education graduate program at the University of Oregon, Professor Dunlap's research is on women in educational leadership and theories of gender and career development.

Julia Evetts is Senior Lecturer in Sociology in the School of Social Studies at the University of Nottingham. She is author of *The Sociology of Educational Ideas* (1972) and *Women in Primary Teaching* (1990). She has been researching and writing about women's and men's careers in teaching, both primary and secondary, for a number of years. Currently she is writing about careers in engineering and science in industry and is beginning a new research project on women's careers in banking.

Clara Greed is a Senior Lecturer in the School of Planning, within the Faculty of the Built Environment, University of the West of England, Bristol. She undertook doctoral research on the position of women in surveying education and practice, resulting in *Surveying Sisters* (1991). She is now completing a sequel *Planning Persons* on women town planners, and also *Introducing Town Planning*. She is a chartered town planner, fellow of the Architects and Surveyors Institute, and a member (the only female one) of CISC (Construction Industry Standing Conference), Planning and Strategy Group, producing occupational standards for NVQ (National Vocational Qualifications) Level 5 for the assessment of professional competence levels within construction professions.

Michael King is a Senior Lecturer in Sociology at the University of Nottingham. He has published articles on the sociology of science and the professions. His current research is concerned with the architectural profession in Britain.

Gudrún Kristinsdóttir is Associate Professor at the Department of Social Welfare and board member of the Women's Studies Centre, University of Umeå in Sweden. She is co-author of *Nŷi Kvennafrædarinn* (1982), a book on women's health and of *Könsperspektiv på forskning i socialt arbete* (1992), on gender and social work research. She has written *Child Welfare and Professionalisation* (1991) and several articles on children's conditions, social policy, abortion and violence against women.

Gillian Pascall is Lecturer in Social Policy and Administration at the University of Nottingham. She has written on health and women's subjects, including *Social Policy: a Feminist Analysis* (1986) and *Women Returning to Higher Education* (1993).

Vivian Shrubsall is Professor of Law and Director of the Centre for Legal Studies at the University of Exeter. She was previously Director of Training and Recruitment with the Norton Rose M5 Group of solicitors. Her career has been spent teaching Law at undergraduate, post-graduate and professional levels. She is a Fellow of the Institute of Taxation and her major teaching and research interests are the

Law of Taxation, Employment Law and professional education and training.

Olive Stevenson is Professor of Social Work Studies at the University of Nottingham. She has previously held chairs at the Universities of Keele and Liverpool. One of her main research interests is in community care, especially in relation to frail elderly people. Publications in this field include *Age and Vulnerability* (1989) and *Community Care and Empowerment* (1993).

Annis May Timpson is a Lecturer in the Department of American and Canadian Studies at the University of Nottingham where she teaches both US and Canadian politics. She is currently working on two different research projects, one on the development of employment equity policies in Canada, the other on public attitudes to civil and political liberties in Britain and Canada.

Janette Webb is a Lecturer in the Department of Business Studies at the University of Edinburgh. She has also lectured in organisation studies at Aston University and worked as a research fellow at the University of Kent. Her research interests are gender relations and employment and the politics of organisations. She has published articles in both areas and is currently writing a book on the management of organisational change.

INTRODUCTION

JULIA EVETTS

Women's employment is currently high on political and social agendas. In Britain the report of the Hansard Society Commission (1990) was concerned about the lack of women in top positions in public service, in corporate management and in key areas of influence such as the media, universities and trade unions. In 1991 the public campaign 'Opportunity 2000' attracted a great deal of media attention for its objectives to increase the quantity and proportion of women's participation in higher levels of management in public and private work organisations. Women have entered the professions and careered occupations in larger numbers since the 1960s. The question that now needs to be addressed is what happens to women who do embark on careers in professions and in occupations with promotion ladders.

The terms 'profession' and 'careered occupation' need some preliminary elaboration in this context. In general these are non-manual occupations which have a knowledge-base usually acquired in the form of vocational qualifications, both general, academic and job-related. In addition they are occupations having promotion positions acquired either through experience, skill and/or the acquisition of further vocational qualifications. Promotion ladders can be either formalised into recognised positions or operated informally in particular places of work. Career ladders can be nationally standardised (e.g. teaching, nursing) or they can be firm or company specific (e.g. in industrial organisations). Qualifications and promotions are linked in that occupational qualifications bestow competence on practitioners which is of great significance to the ideology of professionalism (Crompton and Sanderson 1990) and qualifications also form the prerequisites for promotion and career development. Many professionals today work in organisations and even those in private practices are in occupations which have recognised career routes and promotion ladders.

In career terms the qualified individual can develop a linear career either in a profession or an organisation. Alternatively the qualified individual can remain at the practitioner level. Many qualified women develop occupational careers which might include extended periods at practitioner levels, perhaps during part-time employment. Crompton and Sanderson (1990) noted that part-time work is not considered relevant to the 'linear' careers that are developed in or-

ganisational and professional contexts. It is in respect of linear promotion that women's careers are at a disadvantage compared with
men's. Men predominate at the higher levels of organisations and
professions, and 'organisational hierarchies are not sympathetic to
women' (Crompton and Sanderson 1990: 71). Some examples
demonstrate the wide gender differences in career progression.

In medicine, the proportion of female students has risen from
about 25 per cent in the 1960s, to 35 per cent in 1975 and 46 per cent
in 1985 (Allen 1990). Yet women's careers in medicine show substantial differences to their male colleagues. Only 15 per cent of hospital
consultants are female, only 3 per cent of consultant surgeons and
less than 1 per cent of general surgeons (Walford 1991). In hospitals,
women doctors are concentrated in lower status areas such as anaes-
thetics, geriatrics, radiology and mental illness and handicap. Women
doctors are found in larger numbers working in the community and in
areas such as school health. Almost 20 per cent of general practitioners are women (Allen 1990) and they are often employed on a
part-time basis. The new GPs' contract, brought in in 1990, enabled
much more flexible working which women GPs have utilised but, in
career terms, gender differences have increased. A survey of doctors
by *General Practitioner* magazine found that nearly 20 per cent of the
women, compared with only 3 per cent of the men, earned less than
£15,000 a year. In contrast only 1 per cent of female GPs earned
more than £50,000 compared with 18 per cent of the males. Nearly
twice as many men (80 per cent) were in full-time partnerships, compared with 44 per cent of the women. Also, in terms of segmentation
of general practice labour, the men took charge of minor surgery,
outside work and practice accounts, while the women were left with
family planning and smear testing.

In law also there has been an increase in female students. In the
1980s between 25 and 33 per cent of all law students were women.
Women now account for nearly 20 per cent of independent barristers.
In 1991, 42 per cent of those called to the Bar were women compared
with 7 per cent in 1972. However, at the senior end of the profession
there are only 41 women QCs out of a total of 760. At the judicial
level the figures are even lower: no women Lords of Appeal in
Ordinary; 1 woman Lord Justice of Appeal out of 27; 3 High Court
judges (80 men) and 19 circuit judges (402 men) (Wallach 1992).
Fewer women than men practice in their preferred area. Men work in
commercial and criminal law and women in family law, reflecting a
tendency for work to be allocated, by both solicitors and chambers'
clerks, on stereotypical assumptions. This is reflected in the generally
lower earnings of women, since commercial work reaps greater
rewards than family law.

Women now qualify as solicitors in roughly equal numbers with
men, and the overall percentage of practising women solicitors has
crept up from 15 per cent in 1986 to 23 per cent in 1990. However,

they only account for 12 per cent of partners (Shuaib 1991). In addition, fewer women solicitors continue to practise, they reach partnership more slowly, retire in far greater numbers and work part-time far more than men (Working Party on Women's Careers 1988). Male solicitors were far more likely to be engaged in the prestige areas of company and commercial work and in criminal and litigation cases which involved court appearances (Podmore and Spencer 1986). Women solicitors tended to be dealing with the more routine jobs such as wills, probate, estate duty and matrimonial work. For female barristers, their 'briefs' were those concerned with juvenile and female crimes while their male colleagues dealt with the 'heavy' crimes. In this way, female solicitors and barristers are denied the appropriate experiences which are necessary for career progress, partnerships and promotion.

In teaching there is a similar shortage of women in career positions, in the higher status managerial posts and in particular sectors. The majority of primary and nursery teachers, 81 per cent, are women yet 51 per cent of primary headteachers are men (DES 1990). In secondary schools, 52 per cent of teachers and 80 per cent of headteachers are men. Women in promoted posts in schools tend to have pastoral care responsibilities rather than the curricula management which most frequently leads to higher managerial positions such as headships. The higher the status of the teaching, the more pronounced the female career differences become. In universities, women form only 3 per cent of university professors and even then are paid on average almost £2,000 a year less than their male colleagues. There are proportionately fewer women at the top of the academic career structure than at the top of almost any comparable profession. The fall-off down the academic ladder is very pronounced: 2 per cent of vice-chancellors/principals are women; 3 per cent of professors; 6 per cent of senior lecturers; 14 per cent of lecturers; yet 32 per cent of contract researchers (usually on short-term contracts) are women (AUT 1990).

In the Civil Service, although women make up 48 per cent of the nearly half a million work force, the vast majority are 'toiling in the basement' (Donaldson 1992). Out of the 38 top posts at permanent secretary rank, just three are held by women. The Association of First Division Civil Servants has claimed that there are just under 8 per cent of women in posts in the most senior three grades.

In the National Health Service, which has nearly 1 million employees, almost 80 per cent of them women, the percentage of women in general management was 18 per cent in 1991 (Donaldson 1992). The number of women chief executives was 20 per cent (160 women) in 1992. In local government women comprise 66 per cent of the total 2.3 million workforce. But there are only 10 women chief executives out of 541 local authorities and women make up about 6 per cent of the top three grades (Donaldson 1992).

In banking, career progress is clearly differentiated by gender. Even though almost 60 per cent of UK clearing bank employees are women, a tiny proportion reach middle and senior manager positions. Comparing banks is difficult because of varying job titles used: one bank's supervisor is another's junior manager. The Banking, Insurance and Finance Union estimates that 5 to 6 per cent of clearing banks' management are women. In contrast, the big UK clearers say 10 to 20 per cent of management jobs are held by women, though all agree that the percentages shrink further up the corporate hierarchy. Banks have developed schemes for career breaks, workplace nurseries, maternity leave, part-time jobs and job sharing. But while a few exceptional women have reached director level, the critical mass of women in banking is just into junior management and no further (Vaughan 1991).

Even in nursing, the supposedly female profession, there is a similar picture in terms of career promotion. Male nurses are more successful in gaining rapid promotion to administrative grades, especially since the adoption of the hierarchical career promotion system recommended by the Salmon Report in the 1960s. Davies and Rosser (1986) found that men were promoted to the position of nursing officer much faster than women. On average, men reached nursing officer grade in 8.4 years while women took 17.9 years. Even women with no career break took 14.5 years. The EOC (1992: 24) reported striking differences between male and female chief nursing officers in terms of their domestic commitments. Family responsibilities did not impede men's career progress, but success for women in a nursing career was often at the expense of having a family life. The male manager was more likely to be married and have children, the female manager was more likely to be single and childless.

The statistical demonstration of women's position in terms of career seems to be similar in every professional and careered occupation. In pharmacy the majority of new qualifiers are female yet women predominate in the relatively poorly paid jobs in hospitals and in part-time positions (Crompton and Sanderson 1990). Female dentists are most likely to be found in Community Health Dental Officer positions and less likely in hospital consultancy or in principal general dental practitioner posts (Dept of Health 1992). Female accountants are concentrated in public sector employment rather than in industrial, commercial and private practice where career prospects are more numerous and varied (Crompton and Sanderson 1990). Female accountants in industry and commerce predominate at practitioner levels rather than in positions which result in organisational linear careers. Female scientists and engineers are few in terms of their numbers relative to men and they tend to be employed in public service rather than private industry (Davidson 1989, Carter and Kirkup 1990). Often female scientists and engineers who begin their careers in industry move to teaching in order more easily to combine aspects of their paid and unpaid work responsibilities.

Despite equal opportunity legislation and several years of campaigning, women are almost invisible at the top of public and private organisations. Industry is no better as a career context for women since they comprise only 0.5 per cent of directors of public companies. The Institute of Directors has seen its female membership triple to 2,600 in the past 10 years, but women still comprise only 7 per cent of its total membership.

For both women and men, the normal linear career in both public and private organisations which have a hierarchical career structure is traversed by moving into management. A career move into management, however, results in increased difficulties for women since the woman manager has to resolve contradictions in gender and work identities. It is difficult for a woman to manage other women and it is even more problematic for women to manage men since gender expectations are in conflict with managerial responsibilities. Thus, if the woman is an efficient, competent manager, she is likely to be judged as unfeminine, but if she demonstrates the supposedly female qualities of care and sensitivity in management she is likely to be assessed as an inappropriate, inefficient manager (Kanter 1977, Marshall 1984). This cultural double-bind for women in management and for women and careers has been analysed in respect of several different occupations and professions (Bourne and Wikler 1982, Marshall 1984, Gray 1987, Shakeshaft 1987). The problems which a career move into management poses for women are addressed in papers in this volume (for example those by Evetts, Dunlap and Ashburner).

In view of such differences in the career positions of women compared with men, a number of occupational associations such as medicine, law, architecture, the media and teaching, have commissioned their own research on careers. In addition, there have been edited collections which have considered women's position in a number of different occupations and professions (Silverstone and Ward 1980, Spencer and Podmore 1987). The collection by Coyle and Skinner (1988) focused on strategies and positive action for change to facilitate women's careers in a number of different occupations including the social services and the media.

Attempts to explain women's position in employment have resulted in new terms to describe the difficulties which women encounter. Hakim (1979) drew an important distinction between horizontal and vertical occupational segregation. Horizontal segregation occurs where women and men are working in different types of occupation. This kind of segregation is extensive in industrial societies but it has been reducing slightly in the later years of this century where equal opportunity legislation has had some impact on occupational choices. Vertical segregation is where men are mostly working in higher grade occupations and women in lower grade ones. This kind of occupational segregation is increasing in industrial societies, with men more often than women developing linear careers and achieving promotions in their occupations. Thus, although horizontal segregation has declined marginally, vertical segregation has increased, the end result being that occupational segregation in general has not changed very much in Britain or the USA over this century (Hakim 1979).

The current position of women in the professions has been described as one of 'marginalisation' by Spencer and Podmore (1987). The term 'marginality' has been defined as 'simultaneous membership (by ascription, self-reference, or achievement) of two or more groups whose social definitions and cultural norms are distinct from each other' (Gould and Kolb 1964: 407). The concept was developed originally by interactionist researchers of the Chicago School who focused on cultural duality and the disorganising effects of marginality (Park 1928, Stonequist 1937). In respect of women in careered occupations, cultural duality refers to women's gendered identity and membership of an occupational group where work norms and roles are not only distinct from gender roles but often in conflict. In some cases, women experience marginality because of their low numbers and hence their visibility in their work. In other cases women are marginalised through their concentration in certain kinds of work in an occupation or profession. This ghettoisation reinforces and reproduces aspects of occupational segregation both horizontal and vertical, with women's specialisms generally receiving lower status and salary recognition. Women are always marginalised in terms of their career progress and development.

In describing women's difficulties in achieving career progress and promotion, the term 'glass ceiling' has been popularly used to refer to the barriers that stand in their way. Women cannot seem to get more than halfway up most career ladders. Women usually fail to advance past mid-level, and even those who do climb beyond middle ranking positions find that they cannot get all the way to the top. A 'glass ceiling' stands between them and the highest positions (Morrison, White and Van Velsor 1987). The glass ceiling describes 'a barrier so subtle that it is transparent, yet so strong that it prevents women and minorities from moving up the management hierarchy' (Morrison and Von Glinow 1990: 200; quoted in O'Leary and Ickovics 1992).

Many of these studies have referred to women's *disadvantaged* position compared with men in terms of career progress and development. Certainly in terms of promotion, salary, status, and authority, women's careers are at a disadvantage when compared with some men's. It is important to remember, however, that some women (as indeed some men) want things other than promotion and advancement from their careers and some of these other concerns are explored in papers in this volume (see those by Stevenson, Kristinsdóttir, Aldridge, and Allison and Pascall, for example). It is necessary to begin, however, by considering the gendered aspects of the concept of career itself, since it is only in respect of a particular model of career that women's experiences are disadvantaged and are deficient.

The gendering of 'career'

It has been argued that career is a gendered concept (Dex 1985, Beechey 1987) in which some men's career patterns are regarded as the norm and other career patterns are deficient or lacking in certain respects. When the normal model of career is one of continuous service and regular and steady promotion progress to positions of greater responsibility, then careers which do not match such a model are thereby rendered 'imperfect'. For women their careers might be 'broken' or 'interrupted'; for both men and women, their careers might be 'blocked' or 'opted-out of' or 'time-serving'. Acker has argued in respect of teachers' careers (1983, 1987) that researchers have recorded what some men have done and labelled that a career. If women do the same things, then they have careers; if not, they have jobs (see also Shakeshaft 1987). Crompton and Sanderson (1990) distinguished between organisational/linear careers which involve promotion to positions of managerial responsibility and prac-titioner/occupational careers which involve doing the job and might include breaks and part-time employment. The practitioner option has constituted an important coping strategy for women in careers, although Crompton and Sanderson have argued that women are becoming less satisfied with such a strategy.

It is also important to note that individual men and women's career 'success' tends to be assessed in terms of promotions gained. Achievement is indicated and judged in terms of movements up through organisational ladders. Yet, many women and indeed many men want things other than 'advancement' from organisational career structures. There are teachers who would prefer to stay in the class-room rather than achieving promotion into managerial (non-class-room) positions. There are nurses who would rather stay on the wards and prefer patient contact to administration. There are many other examples of non-manual workers who would prefer 'to do the job' if only career (that is promotion and increased salary and status) did not require movement into management. An important conse-quence of the hierarchical model of career is the devaluation of the work and a down-grading of the salaries of those who fail to seek or fail to achieve promotion in the career.

Another significant limitation of the gendered assumptions attach-ing to the concept of career is that work careers are developed only in the paid work sphere. The concept of career has been used more generally by interactionist sociologists where career becomes the progress of an individual through a linked set of role-learning experiences. In this sense deviants (Becker 1963), psychiatric patients (Goffman 1968) and prisoners (Taylor and Cohen 1972) have careers. Hughes (1958: 64) argued that career was not confined to paid work since 'there are other points at which one's life touches the social order'. He argued that a woman may have a career in the context of the family and Finch (1983) has demonstrated how women can have 'vicarious' (or 'wife of') careers. This line of development stems from Goffman's discussion of the moral career (Goffman 1961) and of Strauss and Becker's analysis (1975) of adult socialisation as identity formation, relating changes in identity to changes in social position.

In respect of careers at work, however, models focus exclusively on developments in the paid work sphere. Careers are only constructed and developed in occupations and professions. Activities other than paid work cannot contribute to promotional skills or promotion entitlements. Of course there is an important gender differentiation in respect of this. The wider responsibilities of men (say to do military service) have been regarded as positive advantages in career terms compared with the wider responsibilities (such as to family and home) which women undertake. But, in general, personal and family responsibilities can, at most, only constitute career 'contingencies'. It is recognised that such circumstances can affect careers but they cannot constitute part of career development and career success. Personal events can influence career trajectories but they cannot be a part of career construction. Such events cannot become incorporated into organisational linear career structures except as a way of explaining the lack of promotion achievement of some career builders.

The consequences of this neglect of the personal in careers research and development has been most important for women, although the consequences are not confined to them. But when some men's career patterns (of continuous service and regular promotion progress) become the accepted and anticipated career model, then if women's careers are 'interrupted' or do not display such promotional achievements, then women's careers are 'imperfect'. Acker (1983) demonstrated the sexist assumptions in such a model where women's careers are not just different but are deficient when compared with some men's. It is, however, part of the career identity and strategy of many women to take a break from their paid work in order to have and to care for their own children. Even if the woman does not leave her employment, nevertheless for several years childcare and family concerns will be part of her developing career commitment. Thus she might postpone taking on new responsibilities, she might decline training opportunities and delay career decisions. But eventually she might also be motivated to try new things, to seek different areas of expertise and to take up new challenges. The *positive* implications of a break in paid employment and subsequent return to an occupation or entry to a new occupation, necessitated by the pursuit of mother-hood goals, have not been explored. The break has always been seen as a 'problem' because certain male career patterns have been incorporated into organisational career and promotion ladders. This has involved an assumption that careers will follow certain rather specific routes and paths, will be work-centred, have no unpaid caring responsibilities, and involve continuous work experience and orderly development and promotion up through an organisational and occupational hierarchy. Such a career model does not fit or even approximate to the developing careers of many women and men. In dual-career families personal circumstances and considerations increasingly affect men's careers also. But it is important to see such events as part of career development rather than assessing them as problems, difficulties, handicaps and interruptions to career progress. For both women and men, public and private worlds cannot be kept totally separate. The interrelationship has to become incorporated into our understanding and interpretation of career building.

The papers in this volume begin the task of de-gendering the concept of Career. The concept of work was de-gendered in the 1970s and 1980s when feminist researchers insisted on clarification of the distinction between paid and unpaid work in public and private spheres. It is now time to begin the task of clarifying the concept of career. In their different ways the papers which follow highlight the work to be done in rendering the concept of career as gender-neutral and as a tool to be used in the analysis of women's and men's adult lives.

The papers in the book are grouped into three sections. In Part One, Career Contexts and Obstacles for Women, contributors address a number of issues which are of general relevance to women in careered occupations. Social policy developments and legislative changes in Britain, Canada and Sweden are considered as providing contexts within which women's careers are being constructed. But even where policies and legislation are different, the outcome for women and promotion in their careers is remarkably similar. The career obstacles and hurdles seem to be common in most industrialised societies. Other contributors in this section describe some of these difficulties. The combination of paid and unpaid work, the work involved in caring both for children and adult dependents, starting a career late, and discourse and language are analysed as probably universal obstacles in the way of women seeking promotion in their paid work careers.

The papers in Part Two, Concepts and Explanations in Particular Careers, shift the focus from the general to the specific. The papers consider some of the issues which are perceived to be analytically significant in accounting for gender differences in particular occupations and professions. The concepts of management, service and recognition as well as issues of discrimination are examined in particular careers. Some contributors (e.g. Aldridge and Allison and Pascall) question the relevance of the concept of career in the professions (church and midwifery) which they are considering.

In Part Three, the final chapter attempts to incorporate the themes and issues identified throughout the book in order to reach some conclusions. The conceptual challenge remains the de-gendering of career in order to facilitate increased understanding of gender differences as well as improvements in organisational practices.

In identifying these themes and analysing the issues the objective is to highlight the difficulties which the concept of career itself presents for women. A number of the contributors (Brown and Webb, Stevenson, Kristinsdóttir, Aldridge) outline what, from their researches, are the limitations of applying the concept of career to women's work experiences. A wider interpretation and a clearer understanding of gender differences in careers, in research, theorising and policy-making, would promote increased flexibility for individual career builders as well as heightening awareness, responsibility and responsiveness in work organisations and professions.

References

Acker, S. (1983) 'Women and teaching: a semi-detached sociology of a semi-profession', in S. Walker and L. Barton (eds) *Gender, Class and Education*, Lewes: Falmer Press.

——(1987) 'Primary school teaching as an occupation', in S. Delamont (ed.) *The Primary School Teacher*, Lewes: Falmer Press.

Allen, I. (1990) 'Women doctors', in S. McRae (ed.) *Keeping Women In*, London: Policy Studies Institute.

AUT (1990) *Goodwill Under Stress*, London: AUT.

Becker, H. S. (1963) *Outsiders: Studies in the Sociology of Deviance*, Chicago: Free Press.

Beechey, V. (1987) *Unequal Work*, London: Verso.

Bourne, P. and Wikler, N. (1982) 'Commitment and the cultural mandate: women in medicine', in R. Kahn-Hut, A. Kaplan-Daniels and R. Colvard (eds) *Women and Work: Problems and Perspectives*, Oxford: Oxford University Press.

Carter, R. and Kirkup, G. (1990) *Women in Engineering*, Basingstoke: Macmillan.

Coyle, A. and Skinner, J. (1988) *Women and Work: Positive Action for Change*, Basingstoke: Macmillan Education.

Crompton, R. and Sanderson, K. (1990) *Gendered Jobs and Social Change*, London: Unwin Hyman.

Davidson, M. (1989) 'Restructuring women's employment in British Petroleum', in D. Elson and R. Pearson (eds) *Women's Employment and the Multinationals in Europe*, Basingstoke: Macmillan: 206–21.

Davies, C. and Rosser, J. (1986) *Processes of Discrimination: A Study of Women Working in the NHS*, London: DHSS.

Department of Health (1992) *Health and Personal Social Services Statistics for England and Wales*, London: HMSO.

DES (1990) *Statistics of Education. Teachers in Service in England and Wales*, London: HMSO.

Dex, S. (1985) *The Sexual Division of Work*, Brighton: Wheatsheaf.

Donaldson, L. (1992) 'Some women are more equal than others', *Independent* 5 November 1992: 32.

EOC (1992) *Equality Management: Women's Employment in the NHS*, Manchester: Equal Opportunities Commission.

Finch, J. (1983) *Married to the Job*, London: Allen & Unwin.

Goffman, E. (1961) 'The character of social institutions', in A. Etzioni (ed.) *A Sociological Reader on Complex Organisations*, New York: Holt, Rinehart & Winston.

Goffman, E. (1968) *Asylums*, Harmondsworth: Penguin.

Gould, J. and Kolb, W. L. (eds) (1964) *A Dictionary of the Social Sciences*, London: Tavistock.

Gray, H. L. (1987) 'Gender considerations in school management', *School Organisation*, 7(3): 297–302.

Hakim, C. (1979) 'Occupational segregation', Research Paper 9, November, London: Department of Employment.

Hansard (1990) *Women at the Top*, Report of the Hansard Society Commission, London.

Hughes, E. C. (1958) *Men and Their Work*, New York: Free Press.

Kanter, R. M. (1977) *Men and Women of the Corporation*, New York: Basic Books.

Marshall, J. (1984) *Women Managers*, Chichester: Wiley.

Morrison, A. M., White, R. P. and Van Velsor, E. (1987) *Breaking the Glass Ceiling*, Reading, MA: Addison-Wesley.

——and Von Glinow, M. A. (1990) 'Women and minorities in management', *American Psychologist*, 45(2): 200–8.

O'Leary, V. E. and Ickovics, J. R. (1992) 'Cracking the glass-ceiling', in U. Sekaran and F. T. L. Leong (eds) *Womanpower*, Newbury Park and London: Sage.

Park, R. E. (1928) 'Human migration and the marginal man', *American Journal of Sociology* 33: 892.

Podmore, D. and Spencer, A. (1986) 'Gender in the labour process – the case of women and men lawyers', in D. Knights and H. Willmott (eds) *Gender and the Labour Process*, London: Gower.

Shakeshaft, C. (1987) *Women in Educational Administration*, Beverly Hills and London: Sage.

Shuaib, S. (1991) 'Discrimination still exists', *Independent* 21 June 1991: 15.

Silverstone, R. and Ward, A. (1980) (eds) *Careers of Professional Women*, London: Croom Helm.

Spencer, A. and Podmore, D. (1987) (eds) *In a Man's World*, London: Tavistock.

Stonequist, E. V. (1937) *The Marginal Man*, New York: Charles Scribner's Sons.

Strauss, A. L. and Becker, H. S. (1975) 'Careers, personality and adult socialisation', in A. L. Strauss (ed.) *Professions, Work and Careers*, New Brunswick, NJ: Transaction Books.

Taylor, L. and Cohen, S. (1972) *Psychological Survival*, Harmondsworth: Penguin.

Vaughan, L. (1991) 'Women breach the pink-collar ghetto in banks', *Independent* 9 May 1991: 29.

Walford, D. (1991) *Women Doctors and their Careers*, Report of the Joint Working Party, Department of Health, Manchester.

Wallach, H. (1992) 'Sex discrimination at the Bar', *Independent* 27 November 1992: 25.

Working Party on Women's Careers (1988) *Equal in the Law*, London: Law Society.

Career Contexts and Obstacles for Women

PART ONE

Career Contexts and Obstacles for
Women

Career Contexts and Obstacles for Women

The papers in this section explore the career contexts and obstacles for women which are of relevance to all women's careers in industrialised societies. Social policy aims and directives and legislation provide the contexts. In Chapter 1, Pascall examines the changes in the pattern of women's working lives and certain key areas of social policy in Britain. Education and employment, childcare and family policies are discussed and the dilemmas for women's careers posed by particular policies are analysed and discussed. In Chapter 2, Shrubsall describes the changing legal framework, in respect of both UK and EC legislation, for women in careered occupations and their employers. Recent cases of sex discrimination in promotion practices, maternity rights, part-time work and pension benefits are explained and discussed. These first two chapters examine the UK and European policy and legal frameworks for women's careers. In Chapter 3, Timpson demonstrates the international similarities of the issues to do with women and career in her paper on Canadian policies. The evidence and arguments produced by Timpson suggest that the career opportunities of women working in federal sector employment in Canada are not necessarily improved by emphasising numerical targets to be achieved. Her claim is that only a clear understanding of both the procedures and prejudices that inhibit employment equality policies will result in the full realisation of such goals.

Other chapters detail the career obstacles and hurdles which seem to be common for women developing careers in industrial societies. In Chapter 4, Brown and Webb chart the experience of mature women who returned to higher education in the 1980s and the practices of employers in recruiting men and women mature graduates to professional jobs. The labour market outcomes for mature women graduates are compared with those of men in the same age group and with young students in the conventional undergraduate population. These authors argue that the problem for these mature women graduates is still that of initial *entry* into professions and careered occupations since for these women both their age and their family circumstances are limiting factors constraining their career opportunities.

Gender differences in styles of discourse in professional work are examined in Chapter 5. Coates examines the evidence which suggests that male speakers are socialised into a competitive style of discourse while female speakers are socialised into a more cooperative style. Then she considers these differences in respect of professional/client exchanges. The consequences of such differences in discourse style for promotion and progress in the professional career are explored and the difficulties for women's linear career progress in hierarchical organisations are highlighted.

In Chapters 6 and 7, the caring responsibilities of women are considered in terms of the effects on women's employment and career prospects. Stevenson examines the position of women in employment who care for dependent adults. This aspect of women's caring has received little research attention. But demographic statistics demonstrate a very big increase in numbers and proportions of elderly in the general population and large numbers of these will need care. Most carers, although not all, are women. Thus numbers of carers who are combining care with paid employment are likely to increase over the next decade. Stevenson considers how women manage emotionally, intellectually and practically their caring work and their paid employment. She considers how employers respond to women in this position as compared to women with young children. In Chapter 7 Kristinsdóttir considers parenthood and women's employment position in Sweden. Social policies and equal opportunities legislation in Sweden have gone further than in other industrialised countries to facilitate shared responsibilities for parenting and equal participation in employment. Certainly both women and men in Sweden have more or less continuous working lives. However, in terms of promotion opportunities, Swedish women still fare badly in comparison with men. This chapter considers the dilemmas for women in Sweden and discusses some of the wider implications in respect of policies for change.

CHAPTER 1

Women in professional careers: social policy developments

GILLIAN PASCALL

Working lives and professional careers?

Differences in the pattern of men's and women's working lives should lead us to re-examine the very ideas of profession and career in relation to women: ideas developed largely by men in relation to men. The themes of autonomy, control and power which identify professional work in the literature cannot be so readily applied to women, even those working in apparently the same jobs. This volume concerns women privileged by their educational qualifications, whose labour market position is much stronger than that of most women. But autonomy, control and power do not distinguish their working lives. Likewise the idea of career as lifelong dedication to enhancing skills, status, pay and authority in paid work also needs re-examination. Most women's 'careers' involve unpaid work as well as paid, commitment to family as well as to paid work, discontinuity rather than continuity, downward mobility as well as upward mobility. To understand women's working lives, we must examine unpaid work, paid employment and their interactions. This chapter, then, will consider career to involve a lifetime path trodden between paid and unpaid work as an alternative to its more traditional sense.

Women's careers in the professions must also be understood against the changing pattern of women's working lives more generally. Changes in women's employment have been one of the most dramatic features of labour market and family change over recent decades. This is true even in Britain, where mothers' paramount responsibility for children is barely questioned, there are no public childcare facilities for ordinary working mothers, most women's wages are too low to make paid childcare a viable option, and general unemployment has been high for a decade.

Despite these obstacles, women's labour market participation has steadily increased. By the late 1980s approximately two out of three women aged 16 to 59 were in paid employment (OPCS 1991: 48). In 1971, 51 per cent of married women were classified as 'economically inactive', but in 1990 this proportion was down to 29 per cent (OPCS 1992: 71). Most mothers of very young children in Britain still withdraw from the labour market – many have little alternative – but their period of absence diminishes.

This points to a major social change. Being a 'housewife' has been a major source of identity for women (as well as a lot of work). Mary Harrison has described the significance of domestic identity to an older generation of rural women – women whose only hope of paid work was domestic, and who have built their lives around the performance of domestic work for others or for their families. She describes their consequent obsession with housework routines (Harrison 1988). Younger women still do housework, but their lives are not built around it as 'housewives'. The category – in its older sense of a career for women, an identity and a life's work – is falling into disuse by younger generations, and becoming instead a temporary phase. British women are a considerable way from their Scandinavian counterparts, for whom paid work has become continuous, but the balance has shifted away from the housewife as a full-time role towards more decisive attachment to paid employment.

This attachment is greater for younger women. Higher rates of economic activity, especially in full-time work, are associated with higher educational qualifications. Young women with career prospects are the ones most likely to keep paid employment when they have children (OPCS 1991: 53).

The rewards women bring home from paid employment show more resistance to change. Evidence from the New Earnings Survey shows women's hourly earnings at 76.6 per cent of men's in 1990, with little change over the previous decade. Since women work a shorter week, their gross weekly earnings are a lower proportion still, at 68 per cent (IRS 1991: 3). Further evidence from the New Earnings Survey data on full-time workers indicates that the pay gap for non-manual workers is greater than that for manual. The non-manual group is wider than the careers which are the focus of this volume, but the figures are nevertheless interesting. Women in non-manual jobs earned 63.5 per cent of their male counterparts per hour (manual figure 72.0 per cent) and 60.7 per cent per week (manual figure 62.4 per cent) (IRS 1991: 3). It seems that women manual workers have pushed up their hourly earnings, but weekly earnings remain low compared with men who do longer hours, especially more overtime. Non-manual workers earn a low proportion per hour compared with men, but have earnings less sensitive to the length of the working week. These figures seem to reflect career pattern, with women having a flat career path contrasting with male career gradients.

Career mobility is another critical feature of employment. The traditional expectation is of a ladder going only up. Women's withdrawal from the labour market to have children is often followed by a chequered pattern of part-time work, reduction in status and earnings, combining paid and unpaid work roles. Women in careers may be more able to accrue the advantages attaching to a more 'male' working life: in particular, resources to pay for childcare with the ability to sustain continuity. But their career pattern shares features with that of less advantaged women. In some ways they meet special hurdles. If careered occupations are organised as a continuous, upwardly mobile, single-minded pathway their structures put women at a peculiar disadvantage.

Segregation of women at work has been another theme of the literature (Hakim 1979). Women work in a limited range of occupations and are more likely to be at the bottom of hierarchies. Segregation applies also to careered work, with historical patterns in medicine and nursing a long way from obliteration, and some nearly exclusive male areas, such as engineering. The Hansard Society's report on Women at the Top found that: 'In any given occupation, and in any given public office, the higher the rank, prestige or influence, the smaller the proportion of women' (Hansard Society 1990: 2).

Women's paid employment does not therefore have the same meaning as men's – does not bring the same status, capacity for independence, daily life. Lower pay, lower status in hierarchies and segregation of many women into 'women's' professions, some of which are collectively answerable to 'men's' professions – these raise a question about the nature of professionalism for women. Family obligation and position in hierarchies likewise change the meaning of career. These are serious reservations to set against genuinely radical changes in the pattern of women's working lives.

Women's continued responsibility for childcare?

Rapid labour market change has happened against a background of a distinctive family policy. Malcolm Wicks describes the social objectives of the Thatcher government:

They were to encourage people to assume greater responsibility for their own welfare (and that of their families) and thus to become less dependent on the State. For families the fulfilment of political objectives would enable and encourage 'choice'. Central to this objective was an attempt to bolster the 'traditional' family and its caring role.

(Wicks 1991: 6)

The policy was explicit and uncomplicated in the area of 'community care'. Government documents adopted the theme of the significance of caring work – highlighted by feminists who questioned its exploitative use of women's labour (for example, Finch and Groves 1983, Ungerson 1987) – and made it a policy objective. Informal care was the backbone of community care, and should remain so. Private services should also be encouraged. The government's role was to manage, to make the most efficient use of 'community' resources and the private sector: 'Helping carers to maintain their valuable contribution to the spectrum of care is both right and a sound investment' (Department of Health 1989; see also Maclean and Groves 1991 and Land 1991). Key aspects of this policy wait to be implemented, but reliance on informal care is now both project and reality. Research has complicated the claim that community care equals care by women, but has nevertheless underlined the significance of gender in patterns of care, and the predominance of women among those with the heaviest burdens (Arber and Gilbert 1989, Green 1988, Finch 1991). The significance of unpaid work in women's careers is discussed elsewhere in this volume.

If family responsibility for elders can be seen in terms of economy first and sentiment second, parental responsibility for children touches a more sensitive nerve in conservative thinking. Parental responsibility is a matter of economics too. The Child Support Act attempts to reduce the social security bill, while Britain's low levels of nursery provision place costs squarely on parents. But the need goes deeper than economics: 'we must strengthen the family. Unless we do so, we will be faced with heart-rending social problems which no Government could possibly cure – or perhaps even cope with' (Margaret Thatcher, quoted in Wicks 1991). The Child Support Act goes well beyond the costs of social security; it is also a project for family responsibility.

Concern to strengthen the family has fitted neatly with public expenditure containment. Peter Moss quotes a Department of Health memorandum from 1989: 'in the first instance it is the responsibility of the parents to make arrangements including financial arrangements, for the day-care of pre-school children' (Moss 1991: 133). He argues that economic policy and government reluctance to make demands of employers was behind its 'opposition to the adoption of a draft Directive on Parental Leave put forward by the European Commission in 1983' (Moss 1991: 133).

Pressures for change have arisen from two sources: the demographic gap among school leavers, which has left employers looking for older women workers, and the changing shape of women's working lives. The Ministerial Group on Women's Issues responded with a series of proposals:

encouragement of a 'voluntary accreditation scheme [to] provide information about the availability of childcare facilities and guarantee the quality of provision'; guidance to local education authorities and school governors 'encouraging the use of school premises for after school and holiday playschemes'; support for the voluntary sector through 'the pump-priming of projects and the encouragement of partnerships between employers and the voluntary sector'; and encouragement to employers 'to use the tax reliefs available to provide childcare facilities'.

(Moss 1991: 138)

Little legislation or public money attached to these proposals, with their emphasis on voluntarism.

Women's increased involvement in the labour market, then, has happened against a background of unchanging childcare policies. Public policy has been that family care is best, nurseries should be reserved for those children whose parental care is inadequate, and nursery education should be part-time and focused on stimulating child development.

Most women continue to leave the labour market to care for young children, leading to downward mobility in terms of job status and income on return. Here women's careers come most sharply into conflict with the traditional idea of career. The very highly structured career paths of professions such as medicine, which require intense career building in the early stages, present a special barrier to women with children. But even traditional women's occupations, such as nursing, have failed to offer a 'career' that can comfortably be combined with childcare (Mackay 1989, Buchan and Seccombe 1991).

While the pattern of full-time work, withdrawal from the labour market and later return to a more fragmented employment experience is the most common in Britain, there is a shift towards a more continuous 'Swedish' pattern. Brannen and Moss have studied women who kept their employment after childbirth. This pattern appears to improve the terms on which women combine parenthood and paid employment, by enabling women to follow a career path more like the traditional male one. The similarities should not be overplayed, however. The study found that women continued to keep responsibility for children despite their employment. The authors concluded that

Dominant ideologies about motherhood emphasise women's primary responsibility for children and remain highly ambivalent about women with very young children having full-time jobs. ... Fathers did not equally share childcare or other domestic tasks, nor did they accept equal responsibility for these areas. Support from social networks was important in some ways and for some women, but generally inadequate. Many women who returned to work experienced hostile attitudes from relatives, friends and work colleagues ... women were forced by circumstances to rely largely on personal solutions to the demands and tensions of managing the dual earner lifestyle, which fell largely upon them.

(Brannen and Moss 1991: 251–2)

Even in the apparently more sympathetic social climate of Swedish society, where women's attachment to the labour market is the norm and high quality provision for pre-school children is widespread, the impact of childcare on women's careers remains. It is primarily Swedish women who continue to balance domestic and employment responsibilities. Although the numbers are gradually changing, it is mothers rather than fathers who most often take parental leaves in Sweden, and who take them for longer periods of time. And it is predominantly mothers rather than fathers who opt for reduced work schedules while their children are young. The 'combination strategy'

(Moen 1989) that Swedish women have adopted is discussed by Kristinsdóttir in this volume.

Education

Education may not be a 'golden pathway to uncountable opportunities' (Oakley 1981: 134) but here more positive trends for women can be identified. Key areas of improvement are in qualification levels among school-leavers and access to further and higher education. Even sex-stereotyping of subject choice may be challenged through the national curriculum. All these points are relevant to women's careers, to which educational qualifications are a key.

The rise in girls' achievements in GCSE and A level is especially crucial. It was at this stage that earlier generations of girls – perhaps looking at a hostile labour market in which they expected and hoped to have small part – turned away from educational success. Currently, girl school-leavers are overtaking boys at both ends of the achievement spectrum. Fewer girls than boys are leaving school with no qualifications – 7 per cent compared with 10 per cent (UK 1988/89 (OPCS 1992)). More girls than boys have the higher levels: 17.4 per cent compared with 16.5 per cent of boys have 2 or more A levels and 12.3 per cent of girls are now achieving 3 A levels compared with 6.8 per cent in the mid-1970s (England and Wales 1989/90, DES 1992). Achievements of both sexes have been rising, but those of girls are increasing most sharply; at the higher levels, girls' results showed a dramatic rise during the latter half of the 1980s.

Participation beyond compulsory school age is another significant feature; again the position of girls and women has been changing dramatically. Since the early 1980s, the number of girls staying on at school until the age of 17 or 18 has been rising, and rising more than the proportion of boys; higher proportions of girls in the 16–18 age range are going on to FE as well. In January 1990, 39 per cent of girls in the age range 16–18 were in full-time education, compared with 34 per cent of boys (though there were more boys on Youth Training Schemes).

In further education, the number of male students dipped between the early 1970s and early 1980s; now rising again, it is still lower than the 1970/71 figure. But since 1970/71, the number of female students has risen by about 50 per cent. Increasingly, girls are qualifying to enter higher education, and access reflects this. Participation of both sexes has increased, but that of female students has risen sharply. The proportion of women amongst full-time UK students went from 41 to 42 per cent in the period 1970/71 to 1980/81, and to 48 per cent in 1989/90. Amongst these, university post-graduate students show a most surprising rise: while male figures have declined slightly since 1970/71, female ones have nearly doubled.

A more pessimistic interpretation is often drawn from analysing subject choice. It is argued that the processes of sex-role stereotyping leave girls with subjects which reduce their career prospects; and it is arguable that the drift to co-education has intensified these processes. At GCSE in 1988/89, there were more boys leaving school with A–C grades in Mathematics, Physics, Geography and Chemistry, while more girls had English, History, Biology and French. Similarly at A level, there are more boys leaving with Maths and Science qualifications, while more girls have English and Arts based subjects. The national curriculum may make a difference, though reduction of sex-stereotyping was not the legislators' prime concern (for a critical discussion, see Arnot 1989/90 and Miles and Middleton 1990). Its restriction of subject choice may ultimately change the pattern of GCSE entries, and have consequent effects at higher levels.

Occupational choice is more plainly written into subject decisions in higher education and the last decade has seen some radical change. Among full-time first degree students, medicine and dentistry now have nearly half women (46 per cent of student total) as do business and financial studies (48 per cent); but architecture has 25 per cent women and engineering and technology are nearly male preserves (12 per cent women). There are more women in education (79 per cent), allied medicine (72 per cent) and languages (72 per cent) (DES 1992, OPCS 1992). These patterns will not lead to occupational parity, but the statistics indicate improving opportunities in a number of areas for girls.

Much of the literature about girls' education in the 1970s and 1980s was concerned with under-achievement. Concern about gender differences followed concern about class differences. A classic article by Ronald King (1971) elaborated the way class and gender interacted to disadvantage working-class girls in particular. The concerns of this writing have been developed in a feminist literature about the nature of girls' educational experience and its role in turning girls towards domestic futures (see Arnot 1983).

Current levels of girls' achievement do not make the under-achievement perspective redundant. There is still room for concern about girls' educational routes, especially among the least qualified. But increases in girls' educational achievement do require us to re-think ideas about schools and girls' domesticity (Pascall and Cox 1993). The most likely explanation for girls' increasing educational success is that it goes with changes in the labour market. Current participation rates for women must make it even harder for girls and their teachers to sustain a vision of a domestic future. Teachers and pupils must be aware of the uses of educational qualifications for girls as insulation against an unfriendly labour market. Educational institutions and girls themselves are making rapid adjustments.

Education for 'women's' careers is another area of change. Rising accreditation is intended to raise their status and the service they offer. Thus teaching, social work, nursing and midwifery have joined the mainstream of higher education and developed higher educational qualifications and a graduate elite. This route to rising status may have a contradictory impact on women, because the invitation to career advancement is appealing to men too. Thus men have climbed the promotion hierarchies of teaching, nursing and social work; the same process that lifts the status of the occupation as a whole has left women out of controlling positions.

Legislating for equal opportunities and equal pay

A detailed account of equal opportunities legislation and case law appears in Chapter 2; this section offers a more general argument: that despite the theoretical possibilities inherent in our legislation, and the practical evidence of the Swedish example, British equality laws have had little impact on women's position at work, and less on women's careers.

Use of the law to enhance women's position is controversial. Male dominance of legal institutions may make law an inappropriate vehicle (Smart 1989); the existence of 'Equal Pay' legislation may disguise continuing inequalities and hinder change at other institutional levels. The alternative argument is that we should acknowledge the power and limitations of law, and seek to use it (Morris and Nott 1991: 11).

Scandinavian experience suggests that legal reform may make differences – though here equal opportunities legislation has been part of wider reforms. The British legislative environment has hindered the realisation of equal opportunities. The criticisms are well known: interpretation of the law has often been restrictive; the individual basis puts people in unequal battle with employers who can command far more resources; the complexity of cases – especially equal value cases – and consequent expense is a deterrent without legal aid; the industrial tribunals which hear cases are not specialised in equal opportunities; and finally, women who win cases may receive little compensation, and may be victimised at work. The legislation has not been widely used, reducing incentives for employers to improve practices, or even comply with the law.

British equal opportunities legislation dates from the 1970s with the Equal Pay Act, the Sex Discrimination Act and the Employment Protection Act. The British political context has not favoured major developments since. Conservative governments, mostly in office since equality legislation was enacted, have had some place for Equal Opportunities. Malcolm Wicks quotes Margaret Thatcher as arguing 'if women wish to be lawyers, doctors, engineers, scientists, we should have the same opportunities as men' (Wicks 1991: 15). But that place is limited. It is limited theoretically to equal rights – women wishing to be lawyers should be treated as men are – omitting social processes which limit women's aspirations to be lawyers and constrain the development of careers. And it is limited in practice by a preoccupation with protecting and enhancing women's caring role in the family. In contrast, forces from Europe are towards extending social rights, with a wider interpretation of equality for women at work. The European Court has forced some such changes on the national government.

The Equal Pay Act, enacted in 1970 and implemented in 1975, provided that women doing like work to men should receive the same pay. Since job segregation is a key feature of the labour market, most women were not doing like work to men's, and employers had five years to ensure that they should not be (Snell *et al.* 1981). The equal value amendment, forced by the European Court of Justice in 1984, was therefore significant in opening the Act to the majority of women whose work cannot be compared directly with a man's but requires equivalent skills and responsibility. In practice, however, the equal value amendment has brought limited change. A recent Industrial Relations Services report found evidence of casualness and ignorance among personnel staff about its application (IRS 1991). The report also argues the significance of pay structures in unequal pay. The *Enderby v. Frenchay Health Authority* (1992) case, described in the next chapter, illustrates the difficulty of using the equal value criterion in environments such as the NHS where gender has been built into the historical development of professional work, and into their pay structures. Female speech therapists are seeking equal pay with male pharmacists and clinical psychologists whose salary exceeded theirs by about 60 per cent. The failure of the law so far to override such traditional pay structures is an important measure of its limitation in practice (though this case is still at the European Court). The work of 'women's' occupations in the NHS – nursing, midwifery and most professions allied to medicine – will continue to be underpaid in comparison with that of 'men's'. Midwives and obstetricians both deliver babies, but their work is surely not of equal value!

Women with access to the same pay scales as male counterparts – academics and school teachers, for example – may still find themselves in more marginal positions, in part-time and/or less secure employment. The Equal Pay Act allows employers to pay different amounts to different employees – even when doing similar work – if there is a material difference not based on sex. It may be based on 'skill, experience, merit, seniority or any of a host of factors which indicates that, though there may be like work or work rated as equivalent or work of equal value, there is a difference between the employees so that like is not compared with like' (Morris and Nott 1991: 126). The legislation thus legitimates a male model of career with high levels of reward for those who climb the ladder and lower levels for those who simply do the work; it does not challenge the steepness of the ladder's incline. And it has not wobbled men from their position at the top.

The Sex Discrimination Act may be expected to deal with a range of working practices detrimental to women: age limits, conditions for geographical mobility, discriminatory recruitment and promotion procedures; to help women acquire qualifications through access to training; and to plan careers, through access to working conditions compatible with childcare. Its notion of indirect discrimination, where there is a requirement or condition with which a smaller proportion of women than men can comply, takes this legislation beyond equal rights, and towards acknowledging social differences such as childcare practices which may disadvantage women. This legislation is especially pertinent to career, because it covers promotion and training, and because the concept of indirect discrimination can be taken to cover key areas where women's careers diverge from men's.

Nearly twenty years of operation have brought some successful cases. Women have won cases over age limits, interview questions about marital status, and denial of part-time work to a single parent. All of these cases touch on family responsibilities and are thus relevant to women's careers. But for all the above cases, there are others where the law has been interpreted more narrowly. Much discriminatory practice is not sufficiently overt to be effectively challenged by law – old-boy networks, unexpressed prejudice against women with family responsibilities. Implementation of the law is cumbersome, and rewards from winning a sex discrimination case may not be concrete and individual. Morris and Nott – sympathetic commentators though they are – are unable to write a positive conclusion: 'one may be forced to conclude that the 1975 Act has had little practical impact ... the law does not effectively outlaw discrimination' (Morris and Nott 1991: 94).

The Employment Protection Act of 1978 gives the right not to be unfairly dismissed because of pregnancy and the right to return to the same job when the child is born, provided this is within 29 weeks of the birth: protection to women in a vital area where women's careers may be different from men's. But these rights are best earned by women who adhere to a 'male-style' career involving full-time and continuous employment. The large proportion of women whose employment is less established are not covered. Neither does British legislation offer any protection to parents caring for children over 29 weeks of age. Parental leave, flexible hours, the care of children in sickness and in health – these are all left to individuals to negotiate or manage. The widespread practice of downgrading an employee who returns to part-time employment after childbirth has not been clearly outlawed. The implication appears to be that continuing employment after childbirth is a concession allowed while caring obligations are hidden. Any strategy – such as part-time employment – to accommodate paid and unpaid work may legitimately be punished by lower grading and pay: a significant limitation to career protection.

The 1980s and early 1990s, then, have seen some widening of equality legislation in directions which could offer protection to women developing careers, and which acknowledge the different meaning and experience of career for women. This has been supported by the European Community, while going largely against the grain of British government policy. But the implementation of legislation has remained cumbersome and ineffective, to the extent that people use it at their peril.

Conclusion

Changes in paid work, the family and education have been towards a more decisive attachment to the labour market for women and the development of a more continuous career pattern. Changes in all these areas have been rapid and extensive, and have already dislodged traditional notions of women's identity being tied to the home. Changes are especially marked for those with educational qualifications at A level and above, those who have the possibility of a career rather than just a job.

All this has taken place against the background of government restraint. Among numerous central government policy innovations in education over the last decade, none has set out to reduce gender differences, though the national curriculum may do so as a by-product. The family has remained the linchpin for child support, and policies have been intended to entrench this role rather than share it with state services. Labour market policies – with privatisation as the centre-piece – have tended to undermine public sector occupations to which women have traditionally turned. And legislation for equal opportunities has been extended only through EC pressure, with overt resistance from the national government and problems of implementation untended.

Women, then, have to make their own policy. Increasingly, girls are deciding to take higher educational qualifications; with these in hand, young women are reluctant to give up the advantage which attachment to the labour market brings. The pressures on women then are to arrange their own childcare. But from this point on ideas of opportunity are not enough. They come up against cultural expectations and discriminatory practices which leave women at a disadvantage. The combination of ideas about family responsibility and male dominance of the institutional framework make career paths uncertain and even treacherous, and these are not within the power of women at present to change.

References

Arber, S. and Gilbert, G. N. (1989) 'Men: The forgotten carers', *Sociology* **23**(1): 111–18.

Arnot, M. (1983) 'Educating girls', in *The Changing Experience of Women*, The Open University, Milton Keynes: Open University Press.

Arnot, M. (1989/90), 'Consultation or legitimation: race and gender politics and the making of the national curriculum', *Critical Social Policy*. Issue 27. **9**(3): 20–38.

Brannen, J. and Moss, P. (1991) *Managing Mothers: Dual Earner Households after Maternity Leave*, London: Unwin Hyman.

Buchan, J. and Seccombe, I. (1991) *Nurses' Work and Worth: Pay, Careers and Working Patterns of Qualified Nurses*, A review for the Royal College of Nursing, Sussex, Institute of Manpower Studies Report No. 213.

Department of Health (1989) *Caring for People – Community Care in the Next Decade and Beyond*, London: HMSO.

DES (1992) *Education Statistics for the United Kingdom 1991*, London: HMSO.

Finch, J. (1991) 'Women, families and welfare in the UK', paper presented to the conference Efficiency and Justice in Social Welfare: Anglo-German Perspectives, Nottingham, 1991.

Finch, J. and Groves, D. (1983) *A Labour of Love: Women, Work and Caring*, London: Routledge and Kegan Paul.

Green, H. (1988) *Informal Carers: A Study*, London: OPCS/HMSO.

Hakim, C. (1979) 'Sexual divisions with the labour force: occupational segregation', *Department of Employment Gazette*: 1,264–8, 1,278.

Hansard Society (1990), *The Report of the Hansard Society Commission on Women at the Top*, London: The Hansard Society for Parliamentary Government.

Harrison, M. (1988) 'Domestic service between the wars – the experiences of two rural women', *Oral History* **16**(1) Spring: 48–54.

Industrial Relations Services (1991) *Pay and Gender in Britain*, A research report for the Equal Opportunities Commission, London: IRS.

Joshi, H. (1991) 'Sex and motherhood as handicaps in the labour market', in M. Maclean and D. Groves (eds) *Women's Issues in Social Policy*, London and New York: Routledge.

King, R. (1971) 'Unequal access in education – sex and social class', *Social and Economic Administration* **5**(3): 167–75.

Land, H. (1991) 'The confused boundaries of community care', in J. Gabe, M. Calnan and M. Bury (eds) *The Sociology of the Health Service*, London and New York: Routledge.

Mackay, L. (1989), *Nursing a Problem*, Milton Keynes: Open University Press.

Maclean, M. and Groves, D. (1991) *Women's Issues in Social Policy*, London and New York: Routledge.

Miles, S. and Middleton, C. (1990) 'Girls' education in the balance: the ERA and inequality', in M. Flude and M. Hammer (eds) *The Education Reform Act 1988: its origins and implications*, Basingstoke: Falmer.

Moen, P. (1989) *Working Parents: Transformations in Gender Roles and Public Policies in Sweden*, Madison and London: University of Wisconsin Press/Adamantine Press.

Morris, A. E. and Nott, S. M. (1991) *Working Women and the Law: Equality and Discrimination in Theory and Practice*, London and New York: Routledge/Sweet and Maxwell.

Moss, P. (1991) 'Day care in the UK', in E. C. Melhuish and P. Moss (eds) *Day Care for Young Children: International Perspectives*, London: Routledge.

Oakley, A. (1981) *Subject Women*, Oxford: Martin Robertson.

OPCS (1991) *General Household Survey 1989*, ch. 3 Employment and pension schemes, London: HMSO: 44–57.

OPCS (1992) *Social Trends* **22**, London: HMSO.

Pascall, G. and Cox, R. E. (1993, forthcoming) *Women Returning to Higher Education*, Buckingham: Open University Press.

Smart, C. (1989) *Feminism and the Power of Law*, London: Routledge.

Snell, M. W., Glucklich, P. and Powall, M. (1981) *Equal Pay and Opportunities: A Study of the Implementation and Effects of the Equal Pay and Sex Discrimination Acts in 26 Organizations*, London: Department of Employment, Research Paper no. 20.

Ungerson, C. (1987) *Policy is Personal: Sex, Gender and Informal Care*, London and New York: Tavistock.

Wicks, M. (1991) 'Social politics 1979–1992: families, work and welfare', a paper for the Annual Conference of the Social Policy Association.

CHAPTER 2

Equal opportunities at work: EC and UK law

VIVIAN SHRUBSALL

Introduction

Discriminatory employment practices, whether based on sex or race discrimination, are extremely difficult to combat through legal obligations and enforcement procedures. The law can encourage behaviour by setting up acceptable standards but legal action to enforce the observance of those standards is problematic. Discrimination is rarely overt and, to be effective, the law must permit the drawing of inferences and encompass covert and indirectly discriminatory treatment which has the effect in practice of putting women in a disadvantageous position in employment.

An employer is unlikely to admit that a woman was not taken on, or was not promoted or otherwise advanced, because she was female. Employment practices which impede women in career advancement are often indirect and/or the result of stereotyped assumptions. Such discrimination is never easy to establish precisely because it is based on mental attitude. Only the alleged discriminator *knows* whether or not he/she was motivated by sex discrimination. Proof of another's mental attitude is extraordinarily difficult to show, even where that proof has to satisfy the less onerous civil standard, i.e. on the balance of probabilities, rather than the criminal standard, beyond reasonable doubt. Normally, in legal actions the person initiating the litigation, the complainant or plaintiff, has to prove the case. A person complaining of sex discrimination will not be able to do so, in the absence of a concession by the defendant, unless legislation permits the drawing of inferences. For example, if there are six candidates for promotion of whom one, apparently the best qualified in terms of formal achievements and experience, is female, legislation will be effective only if it permits the drawing of an inference of sex discrimination should the female candidate not be promoted. The burden then passes to the employer to explain why the apparently most suitable candidate was not appointed and to displace the presumption of sex discrimination raised by the inference. Even then, anti-discrimination law is often criticised because, in order to have a winnable complaint, it is said that the woman has to show not that she was the equal of the man but that she was so much better than he that any

reasonable employer would have appointed/promoted her and therefore there must have been sex discrimination.

Similarly, to be effective, anti-discrimination law must deal with
indirectly unfavourable employment practices. It is no protection to
require equal treatment between the sexes if the effect *in practice* of
an apparently equal approach is to disadvantage one sex. For
example, employment advancement which is limited to those of a
certain age, or which requires mobility, or freedom from domestic
commitments, or full-time work, might be applied to all employees
equally but the effect in practice is to disadvantage women, who are
more likely to be unable to meet those requirements in practice.
However, it might be that an employer has legitimate reasons for
applying those requirements which are not sex-based, e.g. his business needs are such as to outweigh the sexually discriminatory effects
of his actions. Indirect sex discrimination is capable of justification on
non-sex grounds by the employer, i.e. the employer has the burden
of proving that, though he did discriminate on grounds of sex, he had
an acceptable reason for doing so. What then becomes crucial for
effective protection is the test adopted for that justification and the
measure against which the employer's perceived business needs are
judged.

This is the pattern adopted by national law. Direct sex discrimination which results in unfavourable treatment of women is unlawful
and actionable. But national law recognises the difficulty of establishing direct discrimination and the likely unavailability of evidence
which is overtly gender-based. Inferences of sex discrimination can
be drawn by evidence of apparently less favourable treatment.
Indeed, a complainant is assisted by a Questions and Replies procedure which allows questions to be put to the respondent employer
on a prescribed form. The employer need not reply but, provided the
applicant has put forward an apparently good case, failure to reply
will raise an inference of discriminatory conduct and so will an evas-
ive, unsatisfactory or equivocal reply. Also, national law uses the
concept of indirect discrimination and requires the employer to
justify an apparently equal employment practice which has the effect
of discriminating against women.

National and EC provisions

The main national provisions which prevent employers discriminating
on the grounds of sex in recruitment and employment practices are
contained in the Equal Pay Act 1970 and the Sex Discrimination Act
1975. Both these Acts became effective on 29 December 1975. The
delayed implementation of the 1970 Act was in the fond hope that
employers might be encouraged to move towards compliance with

the provisions of the Act gradually so that the cost of implementation could be staggered.

In the employment sphere, the enforcement mechanism under both Acts is an application to an industrial tribunal, rather than to the usual civil courts. Industrial tribunals are three-person panels with a legally qualified chairman and two lay members drawn from both sides of industry, i.e. each tribunal has one employer representative (commonly nominated through employers' federations) and one employee representative (commonly nominated by a trade union). There are considerable advantages of enforcement before industrial tribunals. Tribunals are much less formal than the courts; there are no wigs and gowns and any person can appear as representative. It is not necessary to have legal representation. (Unfortunately, Legal Aid is not available to meet the costs of legal representation before tribunal if a party does consider such representation necessary.) Cases are listed and heard more quickly and costs are only awarded against the unsuccessful side if the tribunal considers that the proceedings are frivolous, vexatious or otherwise unreasonable. Appeal lies on a matter of law to the Employment Appeal Tribunal, another specially constituted tribunal representing both sides of industry, having special expertise in industrial relations and with jurisdiction only in employment cases. Thereafter, appeal is to the normal courts at the level of the Court of Appeal and then, ultimately, to the House of Lords.

The House of Lords is the highest national court but, since the UK's accession to the EC, there is an alternative source of protection in Community law. In fact, it is in the sphere of employment law that constitutional issues about the effect of EC provisions on the individual rights of nationals of member states have been tested. Over the last decade, progress towards equal opportunities in employment has been founded much more on European law than on national provisions. Decisions of the European Court have forced the extension of national protection and the recognition of European standards.

When the United Kingdom joined the European Economic Community as it was then on 1 January 1973 provisions of Community law which were intended to be directly effective became binding within the UK without the need for national legislation. That meant that individuals in the UK could enforce Community law in UK courts even in the absence of national harmonising legislation. Articles of the Treaty of Rome itself were held very early on to be directly effective. One Article of the Treaty, Article 119, requires member states to ensure and maintain the principle that men and women should receive equal pay for equal work. It follows that UK nationals can claim the direct benefit of Article 119. If there is uncertainty over the meaning and extent of the rights enjoyed under Article 119, the individual would first have to obtain a ruling from the European Court of Justice. European 'Directives' are intended to be binding as to the result to be achieved but member states can choose the method and form of implementation. However, the European Court has gradually formulated principles which allow individuals to rely on Directives as well. Provided the date for implementation has passed, provided the language of the Directive is sufficiently precise and unconditional to create individual rights, and provided the individual is proceeding against the state or an agency of the state, an individual person can sue to enforce those rights in the courts and tribunals of the member state.

There are two main European equal opportunities Directives: the Equal Pay Directive of 1975 and the Equal Treatment Directive of 1976. As is demonstrated in the narrative which follows, those Directives, along with Article 119 of the Treaty of Rome, have had a remarkable impact on national recognition and protection of equal opportunities at work.

Equal treatment at work: the Equal Pay Act 1970

The basis of the national right to equal treatment once a woman is actually in employment is the Equal Pay Act 1970. The title of the Act is misleading since it applies not just to pay terms but to all terms and conditions of employment other than those specifically excluded such as terms providing special treatment to women in connection with pregnancy or childbirth. (For a discussion of equal entitlement to pensions see below.)

The Act achieves equal treatment by implying an equality clause wherever a woman is employed on:

1. Like work,
2. Work which has been rated equivalent,
3. Work which is of equal value,

to that of a man in the same employment as herself.

There has to be a comparable man for an application under the Equal Pay Act. The applicant has to be able to show that a male employee is receiving better treatment. It is not possible to compare with a hypothetical man.

Work is 'like' where it is the same or broadly similar and the differences, if any, between the woman's and the man's work are not of practical importance. In deciding whether work is like, the tribunal will take into account the frequency with which any differences occur in practice as well as the nature and extent of the differences.

Even if the woman is not doing the same job, she can claim equal pay (and equal treatment in respect of most other employment terms) if her job and that of a man have been rated as equivalent under a job evaluation scheme. But that entitlement depends on a job evaluation exercise having been carried out. However, if the employer did not carry out job evaluation exercises and kept women's and men's jobs strictly segregated, before the intervention of European Law there was no remedy for blatantly discriminatory pay schemes.

The inadequacy of national law was challenged by the Commission of the European Communities in 1982. It was held by the European Court of Justice that our national law was not in harmony with the relevant European provision (Article 119 of the Treaty of Rome) because no remedy was afforded to a woman who was doing work *of equal value to* a comparable man where the jobs had not actually been rated equivalent because no job evaluation scheme existed. The consequence was a change in national law and the adoption, with effect from January 1984, of a procedure for equal value claims. The best known case which was contested under that procedure was *Hayward v. Cammell Laird Shipbuilders Ltd* (1988) in which a cook in the works cafeteria at the respondents' Birkenhead shipyard claimed equal pay to that of male painters, joiners and thermal insulation engineers. The case went all the way to the House of Lords and took nearly four years to complete. The end result was that the cook was granted equal basic pay rates, despite the employers' contention that her overall package of benefits, including paid meal breaks and superior sick pay entitlement, gave her better total remuneration. The House of Lords held that a woman can point to *any* term of her contract and claim equal treatment in relation to that term irrespective of the value of the total package.

That decision was much publicised and was seen by proponents of equal opportunities in employment as a valuable landmark of advancement. However, it was also criticised as a case which damaged the cause of equality precisely because the whole package of remuneration was not being compared.

The possibility of claims for equal treatment based on work of equal value, where there is no similarity of employment between the sexes and no job evaluation schemes actually in operation, has opened up opportunities for class actions. Where jobs are performed almost entirely by women it is now possible to identify men's jobs which are of equal value and claim comparison and similar treatment. A number of such claims has been made, some of which have been backed by the Equal Opportunities Commission and the relevant trade union. However, it could be said that the trade unions have not been as vigorous in pursuing equal value pay claims as they might have been and they have been slow in mounting such claims in employment areas where women members are heavily represented. The unions' defence is always that such claims are complicated, long-drawn out and expensive.

Vital to the operation of the Equal Pay Act is the employer's defence that variation in treatment is not due to sex. This defence applies to *all three* bases of claim under the Act, i.e. the like work claim, the work rated equivalent claim and the equal value claim. Even if the work *is* like, rated equivalent or of equal value, and even if the claimant *can* show inequality in pay or other employment terms, where the employer can show that the variation in treatment is genuinely due to a material factor which is not the difference of sex the claim will fail. So, if the male comparator is doing the same job but is more experienced or better qualified than the applicant, the employer will be able to show a defence to an equal treatment claim.

But what if the man was already paid more by a previous employer and that pay had to be matched in order to recruit him into the current employment? What if the male has been head-hunted elsewhere and the employer gives him a pay rise to retain him? Can women claim equal treatment in those circumstances or is the defence of genuine material non-sex difference available? After some uncertainty over whether market forces or economic circumstances could constitute a defence, the House of Lords held in *Rainey v. Greater Glasgow Health Board* (1986) that the European standard of justification for indirect sex discrimination was the standard appropriate for the national defence, i.e., an employer must demonstrate objectively justified grounds for the difference. The result in that case was that the applicant female prosthetists who had worked for some time in the NHS could not claim equal pay with a male prosthetist who had been recruited recently into the NHS at a higher salary. The employer's defence, that it was necessary to match higher salaries paid in the private sector in order to recruit into the NHS, was accepted. That was a good and objectively justified reason for the variation. The difference in treatment was not sex-based.

The effect of market forces and the availability of the defence in the context of collectively agreed employment terms has been the subject of a recent reference to the European Court of Justice. The issue is whether the employer can defeat an equal treatment claim, relying on the defence, where the difference results from the necessity to negotiate with two or more different trade unions. In *Enderby v. Frenchay Health Authority* (1992) female senior speech therapists employed by the NHS claimed equal pay to that enjoyed by male principal pharmacists and clinical psychologists whose salary exceeded theirs by about 60 per cent. To begin with, the litigation was centred on whether or not the work was of equal value but it was then argued that, in any event, the variation in pay was genuinely due to a material factor: the separate negotiating structures by which the pay for the relevant professions was determined. Speech therapists' pay was dealt with by a different committee of the Whitley Council from that dealing with clinical psychologists. The latter had been treated as comparable to scientists such as physicists and biologists, whereas the relevant committee had considered speech therapists as a profession auxiliary to medicine. It was contended that market forces played a significant part in the salary level of pharmacists since they were much sought after in the private sector. Whilst the applicants accepted that there was no intention to discriminate on the grounds of sex, they argued that professions treated as auxiliary to medicine were overwhelmingly composed of women and salaries of speech therapists were artificially depressed in consequence. They further argued that though market forces might be *a* factor in the different pay levels enjoyed by pharmacists, the employers had not established that market forces justified the whole of the difference. The Court of Appeal has asked the European Court of Justice for guidance.

The decision of the European Court will have a significant effect on equal opportunities in employment. The *Enderby* case is crucial in determining the width of the genuine material non-sex factor defence in equal treatment claims. There will often be different negotiating structures representing holders of jobs which are predominantly female. Indeed, secretarial, clerical and junior administrative positions are commonly women-dominated and frequently have separate bargaining machinery than that for positions which are predominantly male. If the fact that there is separate bargaining machinery is sufficient justification of pay differences, a very sharp brake is placed on the efficacy of equal treatment claims.

Equal treatment at work: the Sex Discrimination Act 1975

The Equal Pay Act obliges an employer to treat men and women equally in relation to any term or condition of the contract. The Sex Discrimination Act is the Act which applies where there is no appropriate contract term. The Act applies to recruitment and offers of employment (i.e. where there is no contract at all) and to discriminatory action against employees which is not governed by any employment term, e.g. access to promotion, training, benefits or other facilities or services and dismissal or any other detriment. It is unlawful to discriminate directly on grounds of sex and indirectly, i.e. by applying a condition or requirement which appears to be equal but which adversely affects women in practice and which the employer cannot justify on grounds other than sex. Although it may be easier to succeed if she does, it is not necessary for a plaintiff to show an existing comparable male employee under the Sex Discrimination Act; comparison may be made with a hypothetical man, i.e. the applicant may argue that a man would not have been so treated or, if she had been male the employer's action would have been different.

Genuine occupational qualification

There are certain jobs which require an employee of a particular sex and in respect of which the Act does not apply. Eight such cases are listed and they are exhaustive. The Act contains no general exception which allows the employer scope for special pleading: his job must fall within one of the specific exceptions. They include employment which calls for a man for reasons of physiology or authenticity (e.g. male role in a dramatic production), of decency or privacy (male attendant in male toilet), because the only reasonably available living accommodation is communal (oil rig workers), or because the employee will be working in a private home and the job requires intimate physical or social contact. Also included are jobs in hospitals, prisons or other establishments providing persons of one sex special care, supervision or attention, and jobs abroad in countries whose laws and customs are such that the holders of the positions have to be male.

Indirect sex discrimination and justification

It has already been argued that sex discrimination is rarely overt or admitted. The efficacy of legal provisions combating sex discrimination depends on the recognition of covert discrimination and the application of gender-based assumptions. Often people who adopt such practices or make stereotyped assumptions have no intention to discriminate on grounds of sex and they might be surprised to be told that that is the effect in practice. Nevertheless, if an employer does not promote a married woman because he assumes that married women put domestic concerns above employment commitments, that is unlawful discrimination. Similarly, if an employer does not offer training to a woman of child-bearing age because of an assumption that she will not be working long enough to repay the investment, that is also unlawful discrimination. So it is if, there being redundancies, part-time employees are selected for redundancy first. Statistics show that the overwhelming majority of part-time workers are women. Any such practice constitutes indirect sex discrimination and would have to be justified.

Again, it is largely as a result of European law that part-time workers have protection under the Act. One national case in the early 1980s acknowledged the discriminatory effect of less favourable treatment of part-timers, but later cases refused to draw such an inference in the absence of clear statistical evidence presented to the court. It was the European Court which put it beyond argument that less favourable treatment of part-time employees constitutes indirect sex discrimination. However, the employer can still justify the less favourable treatment, as was done to the satisfaction of the High Court in 1991 when the Equal Opportunities Commission unsuccessfully challenged the restriction to full-time workers of national statutory unfair dismissal and redundancy rights.

In one of the part-time cases (*Bilka Kaufhaus*, 1986), the Euro-

pean Court established the test for justification of an indirectly discriminatory employment practice as requiring the employer to show
objective economic grounds for his action. The European Court said
that meant that the employer must show that 'the measures complained of correspond to a real need on the part of the undertaking,
are appropriate with a view to achieving the objectives pursued and
are necessary to that end'.

That test of justification is very different from the test which had
been formulated by our national Court of Appeal, i.e. reasons acceptable to right-thinking people as sound and tolerable reasons.
There was no element of necessity or proportionality in that test and
several critics argued that the standard would turn out to be the
subjective standard of a conservative judiciary not noted for their
enthusiasm in pushing forward the frontiers of equal opportunity law!
The European Court makes it clear that the employer must explain
why he has adopted the discriminatory measure (in *Bilka Kaufhaus*
that measure was the exclusion of part-time workers from the company pension scheme), that there was a need to do so (the employers
had argued that they had to make full-time work more attractive to
ensure the presence of adequate full-time staff in the late afternoons
and on Saturdays, periods during which part-time staff were unwilling to work) and that the measure was appropriate (i.e. suitable and
likely to achieve the objective) and necessary (i.e. the only way of
achieving the objective). In fact, the European Court remitted to the
German national court the question of whether the practice was justi-
fiable in accordance with the test established. The test suggests that a
high level of justification will be required. The same high level should
apply in UK courts and tribunals.

It should be noted that it is not possible to justify direct sex discrimination. If an employee is less favourably treated because of her
sex that is unlawful discrimination and there is no defence even
where the employer claims to have acted from a benign motive.

Sexual harassment at work

The phrase 'sexual harassment' does not appear in the Sex Discrimination Act but the type of behaviour which might be understood by
that phrase has prompted a considerable number of complaints under
the Act. So, unwelcome sexual advances or suggestive or abusive
treatment of women because they are women will be less favourable
treatment and actionable if the employee suffers any detriment.
Offensive comments about a woman's physical appearance, touching
and brushing against female employees are all capable of founding
complaint under the Act. Employers are vicariously liable if the sexual harassment takes place in the course of employment unless the

employer shows that all reasonably practicable steps were taken to prevent the conduct complained of. Indeed, if a complaint is made about another employee and it is not seriously investigated by the employer, the complainant may be able to resign and claim constructive unfair dismissal.

The climate of opinion has gradually shifted as to what is acceptable behaviour at work. Public conscience has been raised by media attention given to such cases as the investigation into allegations of sexual harassment against Clarence Thomas at the time of his nomination to the United States Supreme Court and to the Kennedy 'date-rape' trial. The European Community has promulgated a Recommendation and a Code of Practice on the Protection of the Dignity of Men and Women at Work and, nationally, the Department of Employment has issued an advisory booklet on sexual harassment.

The European Code of Practice defines sexual harassment as 'unwanted conduct of a sexual nature, or other conduct based on sex affecting the dignity of women and men at work. This can include unwelcome physical, verbal or non-verbal conduct'. The Code emphasises the largely subjective character of sexual harassment; by using the terms 'unwanted' and 'unwelcome', it makes it clear that it is for each individual to determine what behaviour is acceptable and what is regarded as offensive. The focus is on the reaction of the recipient, rather than the intention of the perpetrator. The final version of the Code does not include a list of examples contained in earlier drafts which would have made it explicit that the display of pornographic or sexually suggestive pictures does constitute 'non-verbal conduct of a sexual nature'.

The Code recommends employers to adopt a preventative policy in respect of sexual harassment, rather than reacting to complaints as they arise. Employers should issue policy statements making it clear that such behaviour will not be permitted or condoned and ensure that the statement is communicated to all levels of employees. Managers (including supervisors) should be given a particular duty to ensure that sexual harassment does not occur in work areas for which they are responsible. There should be a formal complaints procedure established and reaction to complaints of sexual harassment should be responsive and supportive. Employers should provide 'awareness' training as well as more specific training for those who operate the complaints procedure. Violation of the organisation's policy should be treated as a disciplinary offence and the disciplinary rules should make clear what is regarded as inappropriate behaviour at work.

Neither the Recommendation nor the Code is binding on employers. However, in *Grimaldi* (1990) the European Court rules that 'national courts are bound to take Recommendations into consideration in order to decide disputes submitted to them, in particular where they clarify the interpretation of national provisions adopted in order to implement them or where they are designed to supplement binding Community measures'. Since both the Recommendation and the Code annexed to it are expressly stated to supplement a binding Community measure (i.e. the Equal Treatment Directive of 1976), national industrial tribunals and higher courts should take account of these EC provisions.

Employment and pregnancy

National law gives female employees special protection in respect of pregnancy and confinement. Provided the woman has at least 2 years' service down to the expected date of confinement and that she complies with requirements for the giving of notice to the employer, she has the right to take maternity leave and to return to work at any time up to 29 weeks after confinement, on terms at least as favourable as those she would have enjoyed had she never been absent. A draft EC Directive on maternity protection proposes a right to 14 weeks' absence without the necessity of 2 years' qualifying service.

A female employee also has rights to Statutory Maternity Pay: for 18 weeks at a lower rate corresponding to the rate for statutory sick pay (£46.30 for the financial year 1992/93) and for 6 weeks of absence at a higher rate of 90 per cent of her normal week's earnings. Entitlement to the latter depends on at least 2 years' service with the employer.

If a woman is dismissed by reason of pregnancy she can bring a claim of unfair dismissal provided she has 2 years' service. Such a dismissal is automatically unfair unless, because of her pregnancy, the woman is incapable of doing adequately the work she is employed to do. Even then, the dismissal is unfair unless the employer has offered her any suitable alternative vacancy.

However, if the woman has less than 2 years' service there is no protection in unfair dismissal. The only possible remedy then is an action under the Sex Discrimination Act. Similarly, if a woman is refused employment, or promotion or other advancement, because she is pregnant the only possible action in national law is under the Sex Discrimination Act. But the difficulty with such an action is the necessity to show less favourable treatment than a man has or would have received. Early cases failed because tribunals held that, since men cannot be pregnant, it was not possible to draw the necessary comparison. (See *Turley v. Allders Department Stores Ltd* (1980).) Later national cases allowed pregnant women to compare with men subject to some medical or other disability which necessitated extended periods of absence from work.

A very different approach has been adopted at European level. In the case of *Dekker* (1991), which has been described as a decision of 'transcendent importance', the European Court of Justice held that it was breach of Community law to refuse to employ a woman found to be suitable for a job because the woman was pregnant. It was not necessary to compare with any male. As only women could be adversely affected by refusal to appoint on grounds of pregnancy, such treatment amounted to direct discrimination on grounds of sex, which could not be justified by any financial or other disadvantage to the employer during the woman's maternity leave.

The decision in *Dekker* has caused some controversy nationally and within the EC. In fact, all the candidates for the job in that case were female. The complainant had been recommended for appointment but was not taken on because, since she was pregnant at the time, the employers' insurers would not cover the employers' liability to pay her sick pay entitlement during her maternity leave. The employers argued that there was no intention to discriminate and that they would have refused to employ a man whose sick pay entitlement could not be covered by insurance. Nevertheless, the court found for the complainant: refusal to appoint because of pregnancy was direct sex discrimination.

In recent national cases attempts have been made to distinguish and limit the effect of the *Dekker* decision. In *Webb v. Emo Air Cargo Ltd* (1992) the Court of Appeal held that it did not oblige national courts to hold that it was unlawful sex discrimination to dismiss on grounds of pregnancy a woman who was engaged as a replacement for someone who was herself away on maternity leave. The Court held that the complainant in *Webb* was not suitable or capable of doing the job for which she was engaged (the temporary replacement of another worker) because of her pregnancy. She would herself have to take leave during the period in which the employer required cover. If a man had been engaged to do a job for a particular period and had then proved incapable of doing it, perhaps because of absence by illness, he also would have been dismissed. There was no sex discrimination in those circumstances. The court also held that to adopt the *Dekker* principle would distort the meaning of a national statute (the Sex Discrimination Act 1975) which pre-dated the Community measure on which the European case was based (the 1976 Equal Treatment Directive). That would be contrary to a House of Lords decision on the constitutional effect of Community law within the UK.

The decision in *Webb* was supported in another Court of Appeal decision in 1992. That case endorsed the view that a pregnant woman does need to show less favourable treatment than that of a man who suffered from some medical disability requiring a similar period of absence. However, though the House of Lords in *Webb* has upheld the Court of Appeal decision on the effect of national law, the case has been referred to the European Court so it cannot be regarded yet as settled.

Pensions and retirement

It is in relation to retirement practices and entitlement to pensions that European law has had the most radical impact on national law and the development of equal treatment as between the sexes. As originally drafted, both national Acts exempted from the obligation of equal treatment retirement ages and pension benefits. The justification was always the different state retirement ages and the different state pensionable ages for men and women. It was always said that national law could not place a higher burden on employers than the state was willing to discharge. However, cases were fought before the European Court which successfully challenged the national exemptions.

In *Marshall* (1986) a senior dietician employed by the Southampton Area Health Authority, who was compulsorily retired at the age of 62, was able to show that the practice was in breach of the European Equal Treatment Directive of 1976. Since the date for implementation by member states had passed and there was no effective implementation in the UK, the European Court held that Miss Marshall could enforce the Directive against the UK government or agencies of it. Since the result of that case would have given protection to women in public employment, but not those employed by private undertakings, and that was regarded as unacceptable, national law was amended in 1986 to outlaw discriminatory compulsory retirement for all workers. From 1986, if a woman is compulsorily retired from employment at an age at which men continue working, she has a remedy under national law. Further, any employment practice in respect of promotion, transfer or training which is related to retirement age must be the same for male and female employees.

The leading case on pension benefits is *Barber* (1990). In that case the European Court held that benefits under occupational pension schemes must be granted on equal terms to men and women alike. The case caused consternation in the pensions world since it had been understood that where entitlement to state pensions differed between the sexes, a particular provision of Community Law ousted the general obligation on employers to provide equal treatment. It was also the case that contributions to pension schemes had been made on the assumption that right to benefits accrued differently for men than women. Because of that understanding and the astounding financial consequences of the European Court's ruling, the principle in *Barber* was limited by the Court to entitlement to a pension only *after* the date of the judgment, i.e. May 1990. The effect of that limitation was not clear and, although a Protocol was agreed at the Maastricht Summit in late 1991 (which would have limited entitlement to equality to pension rights *accruing* only after May 1990), that measure has not yet been ratified and may never be ratified. Litigation is continuing before the European Court for further guidance on the temporal effect of *Barber*.

Conclusion

The narrative above has outlined legislative provisions and judicial interpretation which give some protection for women throughout their career. Whether as an applicant for employment being discriminated against on grounds of sex, as an existing employee suffering unfair treatment or being denied training or promotion opportunities merely for being female, or as a female worker whose job is terminated earlier than if she had been male, the law affords some redress. That protection is qualified; it is not easy to prove sex discrimination, nor is the process of litigation a pleasant experience. Women will not have genuine equality in career until sexually discriminatory treatment is generally considered as socially unacceptable. But at least national law has established some ground rules.

What is clear is that national provisions have been dramatically extended by the interpretation and application of European law. Nearly all the advances made in the last decade have had their basis in Community law. Without the intervention of European law, the United Kingdom would not have provisions giving rights to equal pay for work of equal value nor any objective limitation on the equal pay and indirect sex discrimination defences. There would be nothing to prevent discriminatory retirement practices, nor to require equality in entitlement to pensions. Since the UK government has resisted those extensions as far as possible and has taken every opportunity to appear before the European Court to argue for restricted application of European law, it is to be expected that future advances will also depend on a radical approach from the EC and bold interpretation by the European Court.

CHAPTER 3

The politics of employment inequality in Canada: gender and the public sector

ANNIS MAY TIMPSON

In the period since the Second World War government bureaucracies and state-regulated agencies have become key sites for women's employment. As female labour force participation rates have intensified in industrial societies, more and more women have been absorbed into state employment (Morgan 1988, Watson 1990). In many countries the initial growth of women's employment at both national and local government levels was linked to the rise of welfare states and the accompanying expansion of job opportunities in the public sector (Jenson *et al*. 1988: 8). However in the more recent era of public sector contraction the continuing feminisation of state agencies reflects the efforts that many governments have made to redress gender imbalances in the staff of their own bureaucracies (Buckley and Anderson 1988, Mahon 1991, United Kingdom, Cabinet Office 1991).

The equal opportunity and anti-discrimination policies that have been developed in many western democracies in recent years may have increased the rate of female employment in the public sector. But have they enhanced the careers of those women who work in government bureaucracies and state-regulated agencies? The experience of most women who are employed by the federal government in Canada suggests that they have not.

Although women now constitute just under half of the staff of federal government organisations they work primarily in the lower echelons of these agencies and are under-represented at senior management levels. Recent research on the Canadian public service revealed that although women made up 43 per cent of its permanent staff, they accounted for 83 per cent of those employed in the administrative support category and only held 13 per cent of the senior management posts (Morgan 1988: 1). Similar discrepancies are found in Crown corporations and agencies that are regulated by the federal government. In these organisations women currently make up 44 per cent of the staff but still account for 74 per cent of those in the administrative support category and only 8 per cent of those employed in senior management positions (Canada, Employment and Immigration 1991: 22).

This evidence provides cause for concern, particularly as the federal government is the single largest employer of women in Canada and therefore offers an arena in which many women may seek to develop their careers. Moreover the Canadian government has long declared its commitment to the principle of equal employment opportunity for men and women. This became apparent when it ratified the 111th Convention of the International Labour Organisation (ILO) and agreed that it would 'declare and pursue a national policy designed to promote equality of opportunity and treatment in respect of employment and occupation with a view to eliminating any discrimination in respect thereof' (Canada 1970: 67). And it has been reinforced not only by the Canadian human rights and employment equity legislation of the past two decades but also by the constitutional entrenchment of gender equality in the Canadian Charter of Rights and Freedoms.

This chapter examines the development of Canadian anti-discrimination and equal opportunity programmes during the 1970s and 1980s and considers why these policies have not had a greater influence on improving career opportunities for women who work in federal agencies. It suggests that this is because questions about women's careers have been overshadowed in the course of policy development, firstly by the government's concern to demonstrate its general commitment to human rights, and secondly by the need to develop policies that would expand the pool of female labour on which, as an employer, it could draw. This is apparent not only in the way that the policy agenda was shaped in the late 1960s and early 1970s but also in the subsequent development and implementation of policies to combat sex discrimination in the workplace and promote equal employment opportunities for men and women.

If we consider how questions about gender discrimination in employment emerged in the Canadian political arena during the 1950s and 1960s we can see how concern about extending human rights into the field of employment came to shape anti-discrimination and equal opportunity policies in the 1970s. Moreover we can identify how issues that were pertinent to the development of women's careers were deflected away from the political agenda in the early stages of policy development.

Gender on the agenda: early debates about women's rights at work

There is little doubt that a discourse on human rights dominated early debates about the development of equal employment strategies throughout the industrial world. This was manifest in the declarations of both the United Nations (UN) and the ILO in the 1950s which advanced the concept of the worker-citizen and called not only for the extension of equality rights into the field of employment but also for an end to discrimination on the grounds of an individual's race, religion or sex.

The Canadian human rights lobby, backed by the active support of both the UN and the ILO, played a crucial role in raising the issue of fair employment on both federal and provincial policy agendas (Kaplansky 1967: 7). Its political influence was reinforced not only by this international backing but also by the fact that many of its members were prominent in the Canadian labour movement and therefore doubly concerned to make sure that both federal and provincial governments upheld each of the international labour codes which they had ratified (Canadian Labour Congress 1970: 11).

It was in this political environment – with two major social movements espousing a discourse on human rights – that the feminist movement took root in the 1960s. It is hardly surprising therefore that many women took up the cause of human rights and argued that its emphasis on outlawing racial discrimination should be broadened to address the issue of sexual discrimination in Canada. Their impact within the labour movement can be seen both in the increasing level of union debate about women's rights at work (Eady 1979, Briskin and Yantz 1984) and in the 1968 decision of the Canadian Labour Congress to include the objective of eradicating sexual discrimination within its constitution (Canadian Labour Congress 1968: 9). Moreover women's success in bringing questions about sexual discrimination to the forefront of the human rights debate in Canada is evident in the federal government's decision to establish a Royal Commission on the Status of Women (RCSW) in 1967 and consider what measures it should take to ensure equal opportunities for women in all aspects of Canadian society.

In some respects, therefore, the resurgent feminist movement reinforced the way in which the dominant discourse on human rights shaped early debates about gender equality in the workplace. Indeed the common ground shared by the human rights, labour and feminist movements was that sexual discrimination should be eradicated in the workplace first through the introduction of adequate human rights legislation and secondly through the development of new policies to equalise men's and women's opportunities for employment. However, if we look more closely at the concerns that were voiced in the women's movement we can see how they contained a complex conception of employment opportunity, that sought not only to eradicate sexual discrimination and extend women's equality rights in the field of employment, but also to recognise the particular nature of the obstacles that most women faced in starting and sustaining their careers.

The double edged nature of these concerns was reflected in the Report of the RCSW. On the one hand the Report called for an extension of human rights legislation in order to outlaw discrimination and ensure the equal treatment of men and women within the federal workplace. On the other hand it argued that equality could only be realised if three more specific problems were addressed in the design of new policies. First, the particular skills that women brought to the labour force as a result of their experience of household management should be recognised in hiring criteria and supplemented where necessary with appropriate occupational training. Secondly, the ways in which maternity affected so many women's working lives should be acknowledged both through the provision of adequate maternity leave and through the development of greater institutional support with childcare. And thirdly, the procedural blocks that restricted women's opportunities for in-service training and promotion should be identified and removed (Canada 1970). At the core of these recommendations was a view that equal employment opportunities would only come about if the varying skills that men and women brought to their work were fully recognised.

Looking back over these debates it can be seen how two different perspectives shaped the early demands for policies to eradicate sex discrimination at work and promote women's opportunities for employment. The first was that the federal government should recognise the citizenship of all workers by developing adequate human rights legislation to ensure that any individual who worked within its jurisdiction was not discriminated against on the grounds of their innate or culturally constructed characteristics. And the second was that the particular obstacles that faced women both in starting and developing their careers should be recognised in the design and implementation of a range of employment opportunity policies. If we turn now and examine the initial stages of policy development, we can see how the first of these concerns was addressed more fully than the second.

The 1970s: equal opportunity and overt discrimination

The publication of the Report of the RCSW in 1970 placed the concept of equal employment opportunity for men and women firmly on the Canadian political agenda and emphasised both the symbolic and practical importance of the federal government developing employment practices that respected and pursued this goal. The federal government's response to these recommendations was gradual and evolved throughout the 1970s, combining equal opportunity initiatives with the development of a more coherent policy on human rights.

Equal opportunity initiatives

The federal government's response to the call for an equal opportunities policy took two forms. The first was institutional and demonstrated by the 1971 creation of an Office of Equal Opportunity within the Public Service Commission, which was set up with a general mandate to promote employment opportunities for women within the public service. The second was procedural and emerged in 1972 in the form of a cabinet directive to all deputy ministers and directors of Crown corporations encouraging them to 'take steps to assign and advance more women into middle and upper echelon positions within their own organisations' (Morgan 1988: 24). Although both these initiatives indicate that there was some recognition of the need to develop career opportunities for women who worked within federal organisations, neither the Office of Equal Opportunity nor the cabinet directive were backed by legislation that required mandatory action. Indeed because the cabinet directive carried no instructions for compliance it was implemented inconsistently across departments (Morgan 1988: 24).

It was not until 1975 when the federal government introduced its Equal Opportunities for Women (EOW) programme that a more systematic approach to the question of equal opportunities was developed. This programme was introduced in International Women's Year which is itself a reflection of the way that the international human rights agenda has shaped the development of equal opportunities policy in Canada. It was designed to ensure that 'women were accorded equal access to employment and career opportunities in the Public Service of Canada' and also that 'within a reasonable period of time the representation of male and female employees within the public service should approximate the proportion of qualified and interested persons of both sexes, available by department, occupational group and level' (Canada, Treasury Board 1979). The strategy that EOW embraced, through procedural and goals oriented in design, emphasised the importance of setting hiring targets that would not undermine the merit system on which public service employment was based. Indeed it aimed to recruit, promote and accelerate *qualified* women throughout the public service and to achieve this end it implemented a review of departmental regulations and practices together with a five year plan of action 'based on measurable objectives and annual numerical targets' (Canada, Treasury Board 1979: 1).

This programme clearly did encourage female recruitment to the public service as 21,443 new women were hired over the next four years (Canada, Treasury Board 1980: 1). However this increased feminisation of the public service did not manage to undermine the concentration of women in traditional female-dominated occupations or to counteract their under-representation in senior management posts (Canada, Treasury Board 1980: 1). What this suggests therefore is that the EOW programme encouraged the feminisation of the public service but failed to restructure the promotional criteria in a way that would facilitate women's progress up through the ranks of

the public service. In this respect it could be argued that the programme failed to meet its objective of rooting out those practices that
'militated against the participation of women in all levels of any occupational group' (Canada, Treasury Board 1979: 39).

Although the federal government did not manage to restructure its
promotion criteria in a way that would enhance women's career
opportunities within the public service, it did recognise that equal
opportunity measures would fail if there was an inadequate supply of
skilled female labour to fuel the hiring process. Training programmes
were therefore introduced to improve the skills of potential female
employees in the belief that if retraining was coupled with equal
opportunity initiatives, there would be no reason for women to fail to
gain access to employment within the public sector. However as these
programmes involved 'repeated periods of low-level training' (Weinfield 1981: 24) and were not fine-tuned to ensure that women could
fill gaps in the labour market, they did little to enhance the long-term
career opportunities of women who entered the public service. However, as this lack of correlation between training and demand was not
recognised at the time (Canada, Employment and Immigration 1981:
91), explanations for the difficulties that women encountered in pursuing their careers were traced back to the sexism of employers
(Morgan 1988: 23). The solution to this aspect of gendered employment inequality was therefore thought to lie in the development of
more stringent legislation to outlaw sexual discrimination in the federal sphere.

Human rights policy

The second major strand in the federal government's emerging
employment equality strategy was lodged within its decision to follow
provincial governments and develop a coherent human rights policy
(Cook 1976: 187). The issue of removing discrimination in the federal
workplace was central to this policy, which was developed with a
view to outlawing overt discrimination against any individual on the
grounds of their race, nationality, sex, language or religion.

Between 1970 and 1972 amendments outlawing discrimination on
the grounds of sex and marital status were added to the Unemployment Insurance Act, the Fair Wages and Hours of Labour Act and
the Public Service Employment Act. However it was only with the
introduction of the Canadian Human Rights Act in 1977 that a comprehensive policy, designed to outlaw acts of overt discrimination in
any area of federal jurisdiction, was introduced and a more coherent
approach to the eradication of discrimination in the federal workplace was set in place.

Although the immediate objectives of the Act were to outlaw overt
acts of discrimination it contained the seeds of a more systemic

approach to the problem of institutionalised discrimination. This is evident in the way that the Canadian Human Rights Commission (CHRC), which was established to oversee the Act's implementation, was empowered to use 'special programmes to prevent future disadvantage' (Section 15) and 'contract compliance' (Section 19) as methods for eradicating systemic employment discrimination in government agencies and in companies under contract to the federal government.

If we look back at the 1970s we can see that the issue of equal employment opportunity for men and women clearly emerged on the federal government's policy agenda. Their response took two forms: a goals oriented equal opportunity programme in the public service accompanied by mandatory human rights legislation to outlaw overt acts of discrimination in any area of federal employment. As has been pointed out, there was an implicit recognition in both the EOW programme and the Canadian Human Rights Act that employment inequalities could result from institutional procedures rather than overt acts of discrimination. However, the emphasis at this stage in the policy process was on addressing discrimination as and when it occurred rather than on adopting a pro-active, procedural approach to employment inequality that would seek to identify systemic discrimination and thus make the institutional framework in which women were employed more conducive to the development of their careers.

The 1980s: employment equity and systemic discrimination

The federal government's approach to women's employment inequality began to change in the late 1970s as understanding about the causes of employment discrimination began to shift. A growing recognition of the institutionalised nature of discrimination moved the federal policy focus away from the actions and inactions of employers towards an analysis of the way that employment inequality was rooted in institutional practices.

In the same period awareness about the economic benefits of promoting women's employment within key sectors of the workforce increased. This became patently clear in 1980 when the Treasury Board declared that although 'it was for reasons of equity that the cabinet set out its EOW policy in 1975, today it is for efficiency and the smooth operation of the national economic system that the government must ensure that women take part in all fields of economic activity, particularly those where there are few women employed' (Canada, Treasury Board 1980: 2).

In this section we shall consider how the human rights objectives of eradicating systemic discrimination against women became conflated with the economic goals of encouraging Canadian women to learn critical skills and enter relevant sections of the federal labour force.

The emergence of awareness about systemic discrimination and the under-employment of women

The shift towards a systemic analysis of employment discrimination was rooted in the 1971 decision by the Supreme Court of the United States on the case of *Griggs v. Duke*. It demonstrated how apparently neutral hiring policies could reinforce systemic discrimination, in this particular case against blacks, but by implication against other groups of citizens. This sentiment was echoed in the first annual report of the CHRC which claimed that 'we cannot define discrimination purely in terms of behaviour motivated by evil intentions; the definition has to include the impact of whole systems on the lives of individuals – what is called structural or systemic discrimination' (Canada, Employment and Immigration 1981: 92).

Awareness of the systemic nature of employment inequality was reinforced by the publication of a substantial number of studies on women's work at the end of the 1970s (Gunderson 1976, Armstrong and Armstrong 1978, Connelly 1978, Canadian Advisory Council on the Status of Women 1980). These studies highlighted the persistent nature of the discrimination that women experienced in employment and exposed the minimal impact that federal anti-discrimination and equal opportunity policies had made on the career structures of women who worked in the federal jurisdiction.

Recognition about the under-utilisation of the female labour pool came from two different sources. The first was a growing awareness that if women were properly trained they could help to resolve the problem of critical skills shortages in certain areas of the federal labour force (Canada 1981). The second source arose from the tightening of Canadian immigration policy in the mid-1970s which meant that the traditional pool of immigrant labour would have to be filled by drawing new groups of Canadians into productive employment (Canada, Employment and Immigration 1981: 16).

The shift to a systemically oriented approach to the problem of employment inequality was marked by the throne speech of the new Liberal government which declared that 'its part in responding to the economic challenges of the 1980s without accepting injustice' (Canada 1980) would be to implement affirmative action within its own bureaucracy and investigate the adoption of employment opportunity programmes as part of a broader strategy to enhance labour market development. This process was realised in three stages. First, an affirmative action programme was introduced into the public service in 1980. Secondly, a series of task forces and commissions was set up to explore the introduction of affirmative action measures in the wider federal sphere. And finally employment equity measures

were introduced in 1986 which not only affected the hiring and promotion policies of Crown corporations and federally regulated agencies but also brought employment accountability into those companies under contract to the federal government. Each of these
developments will now be discussed in turn.

Affirmative action within the public service

The adoption of affirmative action within the public service began in
August 1980 and put the first pound of flesh on the bones of the
parliamentary throne speech. It was introduced cautiously with pilot
schemes in three ministries and extended to cover the entire public
service by 1983. Its emphasis was once again on the establishment of
goals and timetables to improve the representation of women at all
levels of the federal bureaucracy (Morgan 1988: 49). Each deputy
minister had to produce an analysis of the status of women (native
peoples, the disabled and, after 1985, visible minorities) and set
annual targets for the hiring and promotion of *qualified* employees in
each of these target groups (Canada, Public Service Commission
1984: 16).

Although the affirmative action programme was aimed at four
different target groups it was in many respects little more than an
incremental extension of the EOW programme. Like its predecessor
this affirmative action initiative emphasised the setting of goals and
timetables and was designed in a way that would not undermine the
merit system that had traditionally lain at the heart of the public
service appointment and promotions system. Indeed the Public Service Commission claimed that 'it cannot be overemphasised that the
affirmative action programme implemented in 1983 does not conflict
with merit, which requires only that qualified persons be appointed'
(Canada, Public Service Commission 1983: 16).

In view of this emphasis on qualifications it is not surprising to find
that the affirmative action programme has had a greater impact at the
lower and middle levels of the public service than in the ranks of
senior management. Men leaving the lowest ranks of the public service have often been replaced by women and therefore the feminisation of the federal bureaucracy has continued, with women now
accounting for just under half of its staff. However the effects of the
programme have been mixed in terms of the promotion of female
public servants, because although the number of women in senior
executive positions has definitely increased, the proportion of men in
these positions is still far greater than that for women. In the
National Capital Region alone, where the number of women
employed at this level increased from 81 to 345 between 1976 and
1985, the number of men employed in the senior executive category
went up from 2,850 to 3,620 over the same period (Morgan 1988: 54).

The affirmative action initiative was different from the EOW programme in one significant respect. It was designed from the outset as a model to be adapted for use in Crown corporations, federally regulated agencies and also in companies under contract to the federal government. And it is to the consensus building that was necessary to begin that process of adaptation that we now turn.

Building consensus: the Royal Commission on Equality in Employment

While affirmative action had been identified as the policy that would realise both the human rights concerns and the labour force objectives that confronted the federal government in the early 1980s, opinions differed about the way it should be developed beyond the confines of the public service. While the Task Force on Labour Market Development which reported in 1981 called for voluntary affirmative action measures, feminist organisations argued that mandatory measures were the only way to ensure that women eventually shared equal employment opportunities with men. Their case was a strong one given the limited impact that voluntary measures had made on the asymmetry in men's and women's career opportunities in the public service. Moreover it had added poignancy given that both the Canadian Human Rights Act and the Charter of Rights and Freedoms had legitimised the use of mandatory programmes to redress historical discrimination and prevent future disadvantage.

The absence of consensus, both within and outside the cabinet, led to the establishment of the Royal Commission on Equality in Employment (RCEE) in 1983. Designed to test the acceptability of affirmative action in the federally regulated sphere, it was set up to 'inquire into the opportunities for the employment of women, native peoples, disabled persons and visible minorities in Crown corporations' and to report on 'the most efficient, effective and equitable means of promoting employment opportunities, eliminating systemic discrimination and assisting all individuals to compete for employment opportunities on an equal basis' (Canada 1984: ii).

Perhaps the most distinctive contribution of the RCEE's report was its introduction of the term 'employment equity' into the arena of employment politics. This has now become the Canadian term for affirmative action, designed to disassociate the goal setting and reporting that it advocates from the policies of imposed hiring quotas that had been implemented in the United States during the 1970s. What is interesting about the Report in the context of a discussion on women's careers is that it emphasised the importance of addressing not only the *employment* conditions 'that militate against equal participation' but also those *pre-employment* handicaps 'that affect access to employment' and stem, in the case of women, from inappropriate training and inadequate support with childcare (Canada 1984: 6). Moreover it dismissed the idea of voluntary affirmative action, arguing that employment equity would only come about if federally regulated employers and companies under contract to the government were required to set goals and timetables for developing equitable employment practices and then report their progress in achieving these objectives to a designated enforcement agency (Canada 1984: 204).

Implementing employment equity throughout the federal sphere

When the Report of the RCEE was tabled in 1984 a Conservative government committed to deregulation had replaced the Liberal government which had established the Commission. In view of this it is perhaps surprising that a regulatory instrument appeared on the statute books at all. The legislation that was passed focused narrowly on questions of employment inequality and did not take up the problems of pre-employment access that the Report had identified. The Employment Equity Act that was implemented in June 1986 adopted both the goals oriented approach and the mandatory reporting that had been recommended by the RCEE. It required the 375 federally regulated employers with a hundred or more employees to set goals and timetables for the employment and promotion of women (in addition to aboriginals, the disabled and visible minorities) and to report annually to the Minister for Employment and Immigration on their success in achieving these targets. The regulations laid down that the goals, though flexible, should be set in relation to regional labour market data generated by Statistics Canada. The fine for non-compliance ran to $50,000.

The politicians who designed the legislation assumed that, in the process of trying to attain their targets, employers would identify the systemic blocks in their organisations that restricted the hiring and promotion of members of the target groups. They also assumed that employers would be encouraged to do this by the knowledge that if they failed to identify these blocks and continued to uphold discriminatory employment procedures, they could be subject to investigation by the CHRC for systemic discrimination.

An accompanying document formed the basis of the Federal Contractors Programme, which required companies with over one hundred employees that were engaged in a federal contract worth $200,000 or more to implement employment equity programmes that would be monitored by Employment and Immigration Canada. The programme affects over 700 companies who face a sanction for non-compliance of 'eventual exclusion from further government business' (Canada, Employment and Immigration 1986: 9).

What is interesting about the Employment Equity Act is the way that it addresses both the human rights and labour market objectives of this second phase in policy development. On the one hand, the Act emphasised the importance of identifying and eradicating the causes of systemic discrimination in any organisation. On the other

hand, however, the quantitative goal setting and mandatory reporting of the level of success in achieving these targets emphasises the
objective of drawing on and expanding an under-utilised pool of
labour.

Conclusion

As the data at the beginning of this chapter indicated, the Employment Equity Act has not led to a dramatic change in the patterns of
women's career opportunities within federally regulated organisations. Since the Act came into force in 1986 there has been a small
increase of 2.8 per cent in the proportion of women who work in
these organisations. However even though women now account for
44 per cent of the labour force covered by the Act, they are still over-
represented in the administrative support sector (where they hold 74
per cent of the posts) and under-represented at the level of senior
management (where they hold 8 per cent of the posts) (Canada,
Employment and Immigration 1991: 22).

The introduction of the Employment Equity Act has certainly
increased awareness about systemic discrimination. The reporting
process has gone on apace with federal employers and Employment
and Immigration Canada annually processing screeds of data tabulat-
ing the hiring, promotion and termination of target group employees.
More significant perhaps is the fact that the CHRC have not only
finally gained the data they need to identify the systemic roots of
employment discrimination in the federal domain but are empowered
to make employers take remedial action to redress systemic employment inequalities. And although no major systemic recommendations
have been made to date, the 1987 Supreme Court decision which
required the Canadian National Railway to implement a temporary
affirmative action programme to increase the representation of
women in non-traditional occupations provides an important
precedent for such an action (Cormack and Osborne 1989: 223).

However, despite this landmark decision the general patterns
emerging from the annual employment equity reports indicate that
the Act has not made a dramatic impact on the career opportunities
of those women who work within these organisations. And this
suggests, once again, that the concern with quantitative goal setting
and accountability may have detracted from the qualitative changes
in employment procedures that must come about if the career patterns of women who work within these agencies are to be enhanced
in a way that ensures their employment equity with men.

The politics of employment inequality in Canada over the past few
decades have been characterised by debate about both the objectives
and the appropriate design of policies to equalise men's and women's
employment opportunities. The dominant view has been driven by a

desire to enhance the equality rights of women as citizens and has therefore sought not only to outlaw sexual discrimination in federal employment but to encourage women's proportionate representation at each level of government employment. This perspective has tended to overlook demands for equal opportunity policies that not only recognise the equality of men and women but in so doing acknowledge the different cultural, educational, biological and institutional blocks that members of each gender face in developing their careers. The evidence and arguments in this chapter suggest that the career opportunities of women working in the federal domain in Canada will not be fully enhanced until the current emphasis on targets and non-discrimination in Canadian employment equality policies is supplemented by a clear understanding of both the procedures and prejudices that inhibit the full realisation of these goals.

References

Armstrong, P. and Armstrong, H. (1978) *The Double Ghetto: Canadian Women and their Segregated Work*, Toronto: McClelland and Stewart.

Briskin, L. and Yantz, L. (eds) (1984) *Union Sisters: Women in the Labour Movement*, Toronto: Women's Press.

Buckley, M. and Anderson, M. (eds) (1988) *Women, Equality and Europe*, London: Macmillan.

Canada (1970) *Report of the Royal Commission on the Status of Women*, Ottawa: Information Canada.

Canada (1980) *Hansard House of Commons Debates*, 14 April.

Canada (1981) *Work for Tomorrow: Report of the Parliamentary Committee on Employment Opportunities for the 1980s*, Ottawa: Ministry of Supplies and Services.

Canada (1984) *Report of the Royal Commission on Equality in Employment*, Ottawa: Ministry of Supplies and Services.

Canada, Employment and Immigration (1981) *Labour Market Development in the 1980s*, Ottawa: Ministry of Supplies and Services.

Canada, Employment and Immigration (1986) *Employment Equity Act and Reporting Requirements*, Ottawa: Ministry of Supplies and Services.

Canada, Employment and Immigration (1991) *Employment Equity Act: Annual Report*, Ottawa: Ministry of Supplies and Services.

Canada, Public Service Commission (1983) *Annual Report*, Ottawa: Ministry of Supplies and Services.

Canada, Public Service Commission (1984) *Annual Report*, Ottawa: Ministry of Supplies and Services.

Canada, Treasury Board (1979) *Equal Opportunities for Women in the Public Service of Canada*, Ottawa: Ministry of Supplies and Services.

Canada, Treasury Board (1980) *Equal Opportunities for Women in the Public Service of Canada*, Ottawa: Ministry of Supplies and Services.

Canadian Advisory Council on the Status of Women (1980) *Women in the Public Service: Overlooked and Undervalued*, Ottawa: Canadian Advisory Council on the Status of Women.

Canadian Labour Congress (1968) 'CLC adopts change in structure', *Canadian Labour*, **13**(4): 9.

Canadian Labour Congress (1970) 'Macdonald receives human rights award', *Canadian Labour*, **15**(2): 11.

Connelly, P. (1978) *Last Hired, First Fired*, Toronto: Women's Press.

Cook, G. (ed) (1976) *Opportunity for Choice: A Goal for Women in Canada*, Ottawa: Information Canada.

Cormack, R. and Osborne, R. (1989) 'Employment equity in Canada and fair employment in Northern Ireland', *British Journal of Canadian Studies*, **4**(2): 219–32.

Eady, M. (1979) *Address to the Ontario Federation of Labour Women's Conference*, Toronto: Ontario Federation of Labour.

Gunderson, M. (1976) 'Work patterns', in Cook, G. (ed.) *Opportunity for Choice*, Ottawa: Information Canada: 93–142.

Jenson, J., Hagen, E. and Reddy, C. (eds) (1988) *Feminization of the Labour Force: Paradoxes and Promises*, Cambridge: Polity Press.

Kaplansky, K. (1967) 'Human rights and the International Labour Organisation', *Canadian Labour*, **12**(12): 7–27.

Mahon, E. (1991) 'Women and equality in the Irish civil service', in E. Meehan and S. Sevenhuijsen (eds) *Equality politics and gender*, London: Sage.

Morgan, N. (1988) *The Equality Game: Women in the Federal Public Service*, Ottawa: Canadian Advisory Council on the Status of Women.

United Kingdom, Cabinet Office (1991) *Programme of Action on Women: Progress Report*, London: HMSO.

Watson, S. (ed.) (1990) *Playing the State: Australian Feminist Interventions*, London: Verso.

Weinfield, M. (1981) 'The development of affirmative action in Canada', *Canadian Ethnic Studies*, **13**(2): 23–39.

CHAPTER 4

Career prospects for mature women students: aspirations and achievements

ALICE BROWN AND JANETTE WEBB

Introduction

The belief that demographic changes were causing labour shortages in the late 1980s focused the attention of policy-makers in Britain on measures to encourage more women to return to the labour market. For example, it was estimated that there would be a fall of 28 per cent in the number of young people aged between 16 and 19 in the period 1983–93, and that even by the turn of the century there would be 14 per cent fewer school-leavers than there were in 1990 (Lennon 1990). As a smaller cohort of young people entered the labour market during the 1990s, it was anticipated that women returners would provide the greatest element in the growth of the workforce.

One feature of the increased interest in women returners is the Conservative government's plan to widen access to institutions of higher education to adults with non-traditional entry qualifications (HMSO 1987). It is contended that the lack of formal qualifications act as a barrier to women in pursuing employment opportunities in the labour market. With the acquisition of the appropriate skills and qualifications, women would be able to pursue a career. The result would be a gain, both for the individuals concerned and for the economy as a whole.

The logic inherent in the above argument will be familiar to students of human capital theory, which identifies the lack of qualifications as a significant barrier for women returning to work and gaining entry to career-type jobs. With the opening up of access to higher education for mature students, it is assumed that their labour market prospects will be enhanced. Evidence from a previous study of returners to the labour market conducted by the authors (Brown and Webb 1990), would indicate that the relationship between the provision of equal opportunity of access to higher education and equal opportunity of access to the labour market is not so straightforward. Not only has the access model of equal opportunity proved to be unable in itself to guarantee equality of outcome for men and women, but such an approach ignores the potential differences between the aspirations of male and female mature students, their experience of university life and their success in gaining professional employment on leaving university.

In the Introduction to this volume, Julia Evetts says: 'The question that now needs to be addressed is what happens to women who do embark on careers in professions and in occupations with promotion ladders.' But, as evidence from our survey of mature graduates indicates, for mature women wishing to return to the labour market and to begin a career somewhat later than is accepted by traditional career norms, the problem of entry to professions and careered occupations can also be acute.

This chapter seeks to trace the experience of mature students in returning to study and pursuing careers in the labour market in Scotland. Our observations are based on a postal questionnaire survey of all contactable university graduates who entered a first degree course at a Scottish university at the age of 25 or over and graduated in the period 1985 to 1990. The objectives of the project were to study the career aspirations and achievements of women returners in the over-25 age group, graduating with a first degree, compared with men in the same age group. Unlike men, women returners are more likely to have taken time out of the labour market to look after their children before deciding to re-enter.

Second, we wished to evaluate the effectiveness for women returners of a higher education qualification in overcoming the pattern of downward occupational mobility commonly experienced by this group when they return to the labour market. As Hardhill and Green (1991) have argued, women returners, in contrast to other workers, are more likely to return to part-time work and to enter occupations that require fewer qualifications than their previous employment. In our conclusions we question whether a university degree in itself is sufficient to overcome the barriers to professional careers experienced by mature women graduates returning to the labour market; and challenge the access model of equal opportunity implicit in government policy.

The survey

The postal questionnaire was developed from a variety of sources. A literature review encompassed other surveys of mature students and graduates (Brennan and McGeever 1987, Brown and Webb 1990, Graham 1991, Tarsh 1989). Interviews were held with those working in the field of career advice and informal meetings were held with mature students and graduates known to the project team. A draft of the questionnaire was piloted among mature graduates at the University of Edinburgh both individually and with a panel of students. It became obvious from this preliminary work that mature graduates

are by no means a homogeneous group. We modified the questionnaire to allow the graduates to express their views and experiences
through a more biographical approach in their own words. It was
considered that this qualitative dimension would add to the value of
the survey.

Our sample was drawn from lists of graduates supplied by the
university registrars in Scotland. The quality and accuracy of the
information provided was dependent on the records held by individual universities, and had some impact on the response rates. In spite
of the problems associated with contacting people some years after
they have graduated the response to the questionnaire was good. The
overall response rate for the survey was 51.2 per cent, although this
varied between institutions from 43.7 per cent to 62.2 per cent. Once
we had excluded students whose names had been given to us in error,
because they had been doing a second degree, a total of 541 questionnaires were left to be analysed.

The questionnaire was divided into three sections in order to
identify the different stages undertaken by our mature returners. The
first section was designed to provide information on the pre-university profile of our entrants, and included questions relating to sex,
age, number of children, entry qualifications, labour market experience and reasons for going to university. Section Two explored the
experience of the mature students at university. They were asked
questions relating to their subject choice, difficulties they encountered at university and their class of degree on graduation. The final
section was concerned to provide information on the post-university
outcomes for the mature graduates and to analyse whether they had
been successful in achieving occupational mobility and pursuing professional careers.

The findings

Pre-university profile

More than half the respondents to the questionnaire were women –
306 women (56.6 per cent) compared to 235 men (43.4 per cent).
Although the majority of entrants were aged between 25 and 39, a
higher percentage of men were in the younger age group (25–29),
whereas women formed a higher percentage in the 30–39 and 40–49
age groups (see Table 4.1).

On entering university the majority of mature students, 300 (55.5
per cent), were married or living as married, although women formed
a larger percentage of this group (60.5 per cent of the total female
cohort compared with 48.9 per cent of men from the total male
cohort). Women were more likely to have partners who have degrees
and also more likely to have children.

Table 4.1 **Age profile of mature entrants (sample survey)**

Age group	Female		Male		Total	
	No.	*%*	*No.*	*%*	*No.*	*%*
25–29	77	25.4	106	46.3	183	34.4
30–39	170	56.1	94	41.0	264	49.6
40–49	47	15.5	20	8.7	67	12.6
50–59	8	2.6	6	2.6	14	2.6
60 +	1	0.3	3	1.3	4	0.8

(Missing Values = 9)

The majority of students entered university with Scottish Highers obtained from a further education college (45.4 per cent women and 31.9 per cent men). In support of our previous findings (Brown and Webb 1990), men were more likely to enter with other, more labour market oriented qualifications, such as an HNC or HND (11.4 per cent women and 21.7 per cent men). Some 5.2 per cent of women entered with an Access course qualification and only 1.3 per cent men. These findings are in line with the evidence from the survey conducted by Barbara Graham (1991).

Immediately before entering university, 34.4 per cent of students were in full-time employment, 24.2 per cent of women and 47.7 per cent of men. A smaller percentage had part-time work (12.6 per cent), although women were much more likely to be found in this category (20.6 per cent of women and 2.1 per cent of men). Similarly, women were more likely to be engaged in voluntary work (14.1 per cent of women and 2.6 per cent of men), although more men than women stated they were unemployed (5.2 per cent of women and 17.4 per cent of men). Over 40 per cent of women (40.2 per cent) described themselves as 'housewives', compared to less than 1 per cent of men (0.9 per cent). Women were also more likely to be responsible for looking after children, with 43.8 per cent of women and only 1.7 per cent of men answering this question.

Although 23.1 per cent of students were undertaking full-time pre-university education (21.9 per cent women and 24.7 per cent men), and 26.4 per cent part-time education (34.3 per cent women and 16.2 per cent men), the majority of students, 55.5 per cent, left their last job specifically to enter full-time study. However, more men than women, 60.9 per cent compared to 50.7 per cent, left their last job with this aim in mind. Not surprisingly, women were much more likely to have had a break in their employment to have and look after their children, a substantial 63.4 per cent of women compared to only 3.0 per cent of men.

The reasons behind the decision of these students to return to university is of interest in tracing their future career patterns. The majority of students, 56.4 per cent, stated that a career was their main objective, although significantly more men than women (65.0

per cent of men compared to 47.9 per cent of women). More women than men were interested in the educational experience of being at university and in their own personal development. However, age was also a factor in determining peoples' response to this question, with the younger graduates more likely to cite a career or job as their prime objective (see Table 4.2).

Table 4.2　**Reasons for returning to university (sample survey)**

Reason	All		Female	Male	By Age		
					20s	30s	40s
	No.	%	%	%	%	%	%
Career/job	303	56.4	47.9	65.0	68.5	55.3	38.8
Subject interest	65	12.1	10.4	14.0	14.9	9.5	16.5
Educational experience	151	28.1	30.9	24.6	39.3	23.7	32.8
Personal development	115	21.5	23.0	19.4	17.7	21.8	26.9
College experience/ encouragement	166	30.9	37.4	22.5	24.3	35.5	35.8
Family grown/crisis in marriage	41	7.6	11.9	2.2	2.8	9.9	14.9
Fits in with domestic life	39	7.3	12.2	0.8	6.7	7.6	7.5
Fresh start/redundancy	67	12.5	9.2	16.9	14.9	11.8	9.0
Social – family/friends gone	20	3.7	4.6	2.5	2.8	3.5	6.0
Missing	1	0.2	–	–	0.6	–	–

Asked to elaborate on their decision to return to higher education, women expressed their interest in pursuing a career. Samples of the responses to this question are:

To learn professional skills and enhance career prospects.

To improve prospects of securing interesting, well rewarded, mutually beneficial employment.

Views concerning occupational mobility were also expressed, very directly by one respondent:

Wanted occupational mobility.

and graphically by another:

I always wanted to do medicine, therefore decided to do it while working in hospital as a physiotherapist. Doctors kept telling me *my* job, so I decided I would do *their* job.

Finally, the desire to escape from low-paid, unrewarding work was expressed most directly by the woman who asked:

Would you be happy washing dishes part-time?

The experience of university

Given the emphasis on a future career in the decision to return to study, we asked our graduates whether this was an important factor in making their subject choice. Just over one-third of the respondents, 36.8 per cent, and fewer women than men (32.1 per cent of women and 44.1 per cent of men), considered that this had influenced their choice of subject. The majority, 67.4 per cent, indicated that it was interest in the subject which had most influenced their choice. Again, there were differences in the response to this question depending on the age of the graduates. In general, younger returners were more interested in career prospects than the older entrants, who listed subject interest as their main incentive. Future job prospects were, however, 'very important' in making the choice of subject for 32.5 per cent (30.1 per cent of women and 35.7 per cent of men); 'quite important' for 30.7 per cent (34.0 per cent of women and 26.4 per cent of men); and 'not important' for 35.7 per cent (34.3 per cent of women and 37.4 per cent of men).

The most popular subjects chosen by both women and men were Arts and Social Sciences, with 28.8 per cent of women and 23.5 per cent of men choosing Arts, and 23.5 per cent of women and 14.9 per cent of men choosing Social Sciences. In general, women and older graduates were more likely to have made the decision to study Arts, Social Sciences or Education and men were more likely to have studied Engineering, Science and Law.

We were interested to know the extent to which women and men experienced university differently and whether or not this may have affected their ability to fulfil their objectives and career potential. Clear gender differences were identified in relation to the additional commitments on top of their studies for which students were responsible, and subsequently the difficulties they experienced in managing both the demands of their personal commitments and academic study. While almost half of the respondents noted that they had childcare responsibilities at university (46.4 per cent), 65.7 per cent of them were women and only 21.3 per cent were men. Indeed 50.2 per cent of men stated they had no other commitments whilst at university as opposed to only 17.3 per cent of women. It is not surprising, therefore, that more women than men encountered difficulties in balancing domestic responsibilities (38.9 per cent women and 17.4 per cent men) and childcare commitments (31.7 per cent women and 7.2 per cent men) with their studies. As a result more women than men considered leaving university and not completing their studies (32.7 per cent women and 20.0 per cent men).

Our next enquiry concerned the class of degree obtained by our respondents. In our previous study based on a survey of the statistical records available from the University Statistical Records Office, we found that women returners performed better than men returners in terms of degree outcome. The evidence from the sample responses to the questionnaire survey does not entirely reflect this picture. Almost one-third of the students completed Ordinary degrees (32.7 per cent of women and 31.9 per cent of men). In terms of Honours classification of degree, men performed slightly better than women with 5.9 per cent of women obtaining a first-class degree, compared with 7.7 per cent of men; 27.5 per cent of women obtaining a 2.i classification, compared with 31.5 per cent of men; and 27.1 per cent of women obtaining a 2.ii classification, compared with 22.6 per cent of men. The use to which the graduates put their degrees is explored below.

Post-university

On leaving university, 59.3 per cent of the graduates entered full-time employment, but significantly more men than women (52.6 per cent women and 68.1 per cent men). These findings support evidence from our previous survey (Brown and Webb 1990). Our survey also supports evidence from surveys conducted by Graham (1991) and Tarsh (1989), which indicate that older graduates are more likely to experience difficulty in obtaining employment post-university. Of the 6.1 per cent of graduates who entered part-time employment, there were more women than men (8.8 per cent women and 2.6 per cent men). A further 16.8 per cent of graduates entered an educational course, with more women than men making this decision (19.9 per cent women and 12.8 per cent men). There is evidence to suggest that graduates often made the choice to pursue post-graduate study because they were unable to find suitable employment. Some 8.5 per cent of the graduates were unable to find employment (4.9 per cent women and 13.2 per cent men).

In order to obtain more information on the type of career pursued by the graduates, we asked them to categorise their employment. We used the Registrar General's classification of occupational categories for this exercise. It would appear from the evidence (see Table 4.3) that most graduates who entered the labour market were successful in achieving occupational mobility. Before entering university only 2 per cent of the sample held jobs in Category 1, and this increased to 18.5 per cent on graduation, although almost three times more men than women were successful in obtaining jobs in this classification of employment (11.4 per cent women and 27.7 per cent men). Therefore our result would support Brennan and McGeever's (1987) conclusions that:

Women are less likely than men to obtain those types of employment which offer the best prospects for professional training and status, high salaries, a working environment with a number of graduate colleagues, etc.

The number of graduates successful in achieving Category II type employment also increased from 28.3 per cent to 40.7 per cent. In this category, women exceeded men. In all other job classifications the representation of the graduates decreased. There was also variation between the age groups with graduates in the 20s age group

Table 4.3 **Job status before and after university – by sex (sample survey)**

Job classification	Last job before university				Job after graduation			
	All		Female	Male	All		Female	Male
	No.	%	%	%	No.	%	%	%
I	11	2.0	1.0	3.4	100	18.5	11.4	27.7
II	153	28.3	29.4	26.8	220	40.7	47.1	32.3
III NM	202	37.3	47.1	24.7	39	7.2	6.9	7.7
III M	61	11.3	4.9	19.6	2	0.4	–	0.9
IV	44	8.1	6.5	10.2	2	0.4	–	0.9
V	15	2.8	1.3	4.7	–	–	–	–
Armed forces	6	1.1	–	2.6	–	–	–	–
Indeterminate	37	6.8	6.9	6.8	25	4.6	4.6	4.7
Missing	12	2.2	2.9	1.3	153	28.3	30.1	26.0

(NM = Non-Manual
M = Manual)

Table 4.4 **Job status before and after university – by age (sample survey)**

Job classification	Last job before university			Job after graduation		
	20s	30s	40s	20s	30s	40s
	%	%	%	%	%	%
I	1.6	1.1	1.5	20.2	18.2	14.9
II	31.1	26.9	23.9	34.4	47.3	41.8
III NM	31.1	41.7	40.3	9.3	6.1	7.5
II M	14.2	9.5	14.9	0.5	0.4	–
IV	10.9	8.0	4.5	–	0.8	–
V	3.8	3.0	–	–	–	–
Armed forces	0.5	0.8	3.0	–	–	–
Indeterminate	5.5	7.6	4.5	7.7	3.0	1.5
Missing	1.1	1.5	7.5	27.9	24.2	34.3

(NM = Non-Manual
M = Manual)

being more successful in obtaining Category I employment than those in their 30s and 40s (see Table 4.4).

Supporting evidence from our previous study, mature graduates were more successful in finding employment in the public sector, with 51.5 per cent of women being employed in the public sector and 38.7 per cent men; and 12.1 per cent of women being employed in the private sector and 24.7 per cent men. Before entering university 38.1 per cent of the entrants held jobs in the public sector, and 47.0 per cent in the private sector. After graduation, employment in the public sector increased to 46.0 per cent, while employment in the private sector decreased substantially to 17.6 per cent. Further, as Tables 4.5 and 4.6 show, the private sector was more likely to discriminate in favour of younger graduates and men.

Table 4.5   **Employment sector before and after university – by sex (sample survey)**

Sector	Before university					After graduation			
	All		Female	Male		All		Female	Male
	No.	%	%	%		No.	%	%	%
Public	206	38.1	30.2	44.1		249	46.0	51.6	38.7
Private	254	47.0	52.8	42.5		95	17.6	12.1	24.7
Self-employed	35	6.5	8.1	5.2		10	1.8	1.6	2.1
Unknown	33	6.1	7.2	5.2		22	4.1	3.3	5.1
Church	–	–	–	–		14	2.6	1.0	4.7
Missing	13	2.4	1.7	2.9		151	27.9	30.4	24.7

Table 4.6   **Employment sector before and after university – by age (sample survey)**

Sector	Before university			After graduation		
	20s %	30s %	40s %	20s %	30s %	40s %
Public	35.5	40.5	32.8	39.9	51.9	49.3
Private	52.5	45.1	43.3	24.0	15.9	10.4
Self-employed	4.9	8.3	3.0	1.6	2.7	–
Unknown	6.0	4.9	10.4	4.9	3.8	3.0
Church	–	–	–	1.6	2.3	3.0
Missing	1.1	1.1	10.4	27.8	23.5	34.3

Given the importance which age also plays in the likelihood of returning to the labour market, the respondents were asked an open-ended question about age discrimination. Almost half, 49.2 per cent, said they had not experienced age discrimination, but 36.5 per cent said they had experienced it in seeking employment (35.9 per cent of women and 37.0 per cent of men). Only 1.5 per cent of graduates felt they had been discriminated against on the grounds of age during their return to education. Therefore, it is at the point of returning to the labour market where discrimination is perceived as a problem.

Some of the graduates felt bitter about their experience in attempting to return to the labour market or postgraduate study. Views were also expressed about the restriction of choice for older graduates to 'caring' professions including social work and teaching. The lack of interest on behalf of private sector employers was also noted. The following samples of responses from women graduates illustrate their experience. On postgraduate courses and careers, a respondent stated:

My researches revealed that 'care type' courses and careers were in abundance for 30+ females. More challenging courses and jobs such as journalism, archive and fine art work were age-restricted.

Another echoed this view:

Many employers seem to feel that mature people are too old to begin new careers. As a mature female graduate, it tended to be assumed that I wished to either go into teaching or social work. ... There were times when I despaired at the attitudes which seemed to prevent me getting a job. Basically, I was caught in the situation of either being considered too old for some jobs/careers or too highly qualified for others.

A graduate, who wished to enter industry, stated:

I would like to have had the opportunity to work in industry, but my age appeared to be unacceptable to employers.

Another, who distinguished between different job opportunities, said:

I believe if I had applied for a position in the private sector, i.e., industry/commerce, I would definitely have been at a disadvantage because of my age. Also, unlike a young student, I am not mobile in the sense that I cannot uproot my home and children who are at critical stages in their school careers.

Even graduates with more vocationally orientated qualifications experienced difficulty. A Science graduate noted the lack of response to her applications:

When applying for laboratory positions prior to taking up my postgraduate teaching course, I never received any replies.

While an Economics graduate, aged only 27, felt disadvantaged as a woman with children trying to enter the labour market:

Women with child responsibilities seem to be considered a bad risk by employers.

As a result she also pursued a postgraduate course in an attempt to enhance her career prospects.

In the light of their experience, we asked the respondents to consider whether obtaining a degree had 'changed their lives'. The majority of graduates spoke positively about their experience of higher education and cited their increase in confidence as an important benefit. However, those who responded in relation to their subsequent labour market positions were more divided in their reactions. For example, those who obtained the type of work they desired felt their degree had been instrumental in achieving their objectives:

I got exactly the job and job satisfaction I wanted [in Careers service].

Gave me the opportunity to do what I wanted to do, teaching. Without it, I would have returned to shop work.

Gave me more confidence which allowed me to apply for the lecturing post I now have.

Others were less satisfied, noting sex, age, and parenthood as perceived disadvantages.

Not an advantage to have maturity and to be female when you are looking for employment.

I think being a woman with childcare responsibilities has more effect on what I can do, where, and for what hours, than the fact that I went to university.

On graduating 4–6 years ago, both my daughters started work on salaries higher than my present salary. How is it that employers can value a 22-year-old with little life experience so much higher than the parent who has helped encourage and sustain that individual?

Conclusions

For women returners, starting a career late is not simply a matter of arming themselves with the graduate credential and stepping on to the bottom rung of a professional or managerial ladder alongside younger counterparts, with at least the expectation of steady movement onwards and upwards. Nevertheless, evidence from our survey shows that a degree was beneficial in enabling some occupational mobility for mature graduates, both men and women: just over 30 per cent held professional or related occupations prior to university, increasing to almost 60 per cent after graduation. On closer examination, however, the general picture of upward mobility, which is greater for men than women, obscures the variations in experience and the limited opportunities which many respondents perceived themselves as having. This reveals evidence of age discrimination operating as a significant constraint for both men and women seeking a conventional career on graduation, and differential experiences for men and women. For the younger career-oriented men, the degree credential may be an extra bonus if they already had one foot on the ladder in their previous jobs. Their age and marital status may mean less mobility, if they have a family, but employers are not noted for their reluctance to employ fathers. The situation of the older men seems to have more in common with that of would-be women returners: employers continue to prefer young graduates and to see them as future 'high flyers'. Relevant occupational experience may counter some of the disadvantage of age for the men but their female counterparts are less likely to have work experience which employers of graduates regard as valuable. Women, on the contrary, are more likely to have spent time out of the labour market with children, or to have taken part-time, low-status jobs to fit in with their domestic responsibilities. They are more likely to be trying to start a career late and, it seems, employers continue to regard motherhood as a problem, rather than an asset, when selecting new graduates. As demonstrated above, women are less likely than men to find employment on graduation, and when they do they are less likely to enter professions or career-type occupations. From qualitative data, it would appear that women are more likely to be segregated into the caring professions, including social work and teaching. All mature graduates were more likely to find employment in the public sector, with women faring even worse than men in the private sector.

Clearly the routes into graduate occupations are more restricted for older entrants. Neither men nor women appear to have the same range of opportunities as their younger counterparts, but age and gender combine to ensure that older women experience the greatest degree of constraint and exclusion:

Being female and over 40 when I graduated closed many doors.

Thus although a degree does enhance the career prospects of women returners on average, it is not sufficient in itself to overcome the barriers which women experience in returning to the labour market. Many of our respondents were sceptical about the value of a degree in pursuing a career, whatever the personal benefits of higher education. If the attainment of a professional or managerial career in the private sector is a goal for women returners, then the evidence from this survey is not encouraging. One woman expressed this succinctly when she stated:

Basically I feel as if I've wasted four years of my life. I'm in the same type of job that I had fifteen years ago – unskilled, labour-intensive, low-paid work. I feel bitter and I get quite angry. I really enjoyed my time at university and couldn't wait to get a degree-based job.

There is some evidence that the gendered character of jobs and career paths experienced by younger men and women is even more rigidly applied to older graduates. It could, for example, be argued that employers are deliberately creating gendered occupational niches for mature women graduates while equally excluding them from jobs open to younger women and men. Employers may recognise the value of 'maternal qualities' for certain occupational roles and deliberately seek older women graduates, making them highly acceptable within a narrow band of credentialed caring work, whilst they remain unacceptable, and are deemed inherently unsuitable by virtue of the same attributed maternal qualities, for the prestigious, high-flyer careers which are identified with youth. Hence women graduates may be paid better than before, as a qualified social worker, for example, than as a low-paid care assistant. If older women have, however, sought to escape the 'maternal role' through the degree credential, they may find themselves with very limited prospects in the labour market. Where higher education has raised expectations of increased choice, the reality is considerable constraint and circumscribed opportunity.

Overall, older graduates appear to fare best in those occupations where there is a national, public sector career structure, making access to the competition for jobs formally open and not subject to explicit age constraints, as in much of the private sector. The current dismantling of such formal structures could paradoxically disadvantage women returners to an even greater extent. In both public and private sectors, however, it seems that employers continue to perceive women who 'start late' as a problem rather than a valuable asset. Consequently, they are not seeking to change their employment practices to incorporate older women graduates. The result is a severe mismatch between the expectations of those women over the age of 30 who imagined themselves embarking on a conventional, upwardly aspiring career and the expectations of employers of significant numbers of graduates, who identify 'career' with youth, a record of continuous employment and an espoused commitment to the employer over and above domestic ties. The consequence is frustration and disappointment for the women.

Government policy, based on the access model of equal opportunity, does not alone guarantee equal outcomes for older women graduates. For such women in particular there is still a 'closed door', where their daughters may be gaining entry if not access to the top jobs. The lessons for policy-makers are that providing better access to higher education for mature students is insufficient in itself if the recruitment practices of employers do not respond to the changing make-up of the graduate labour supply. These findings have implications for those encouraging women to return to full-time study. Unless employers change their attitudes to women returners then both the women themselves and society as a whole will be denied their potential contribution. In the context of recession and high unemployment, employers are unlikely to change. As younger graduates struggle to find jobs, whither demographic change and the new career openings for the woman returner?

Acknowledgements

The authors wish to acknowledge the valuable research assistance of Cathlin Macaulay in analysing the questionnaire survey.

References

Brennan, J. and McGeever, P. (1987) *CNAA Graduates: Their Employment and Their Experience After Leaving College*, London: CNAA.

Brown, A. and Webb, J. (1990) 'The higher education route to the labour market for mature students', *British Journal of Education and Work*, **4**(1): 5–21.

Graham, B. (1991) 'Messages from mature graduates: a report by the sub-committee on the employment and training of older graduates', *Association of Graduate Careers Advisory Service*.

Hardhill, I. and Green, A. (1991) 'Women returners: the view from Newcastle upon Tyne', *Employment Gazette*, March **99**(3): 147–52.

HMSO (1987) *Meeting the Challenge: White Paper on Higher Education*, Cmnd 114.

Lennon, P. (1990) 'Facing the demographic challenge', *Employment Gazette*, January **98**(1): 41–4.

Tarsh, J. (1989) 'New graduate destinations by age on graduation', *Employment Gazette*, November **97**(1): 581–98.

CHAPTER 5

The language of the professions: discourse and career

JENNIFER COATES

Introduction

In this chapter, I want to argue that gender-differentiated language use may play a significant role in the career differences between men and women in professional occupations. It is now widely accepted that women and men talk differently, that is, that women and men make differential use of the linguistic resources available to them (Thorne and Henley 1975, Thorne, Kramarae and Henley 1983, Coates 1986, Graddol and Swann 1989). There is a great deal of evidence to suggest that male speakers are socialised into a competitive style of discourse, while women are socialised into a more co-operative style of speech (Kalcik 1975, Aries 1976, Coates 1989, 1991, forthcoming). Maltz and Borker (1982), using an ethnographic approach, argue that same-sex play in childhood leads to girls and boys internalising different conversational rules, with boys developing adversarial speech, and girls developing a style characterised by collaboration and affiliation. Support for such a distinction comes from more psychologically-oriented research on gender identity and moral development (Gilligan 1982, Gilligan *et al.* 1988) and on gender differences in epistemological development (Belenky *et al.* 1986), which characterise the feminine orientation as focusing on the relationship, on connection, and the masculine orientation as focusing on the self, on separateness.

In public life, it is the discourse patterns of male speakers, the dominant group in public life, which have become the established norm. The isomorphism of male discourse patterns and public discourse patterns is the result of the split between public and private spheres; it was at the beginning of the last century that the division between public and private became highly demarcated in Britain. This demarcation involved the exclusion of women from the public world. In other words, in the early nineteenth century, patterns of gender division changed: men were firmly placed in the newly defined public world of business, commerce and politics; women were placed in the private world of home and family (Hall 1985: 12).

One significant consequence of the gendered nature of the public–private divide is that the discourse styles typical of, and considered appropriate for, activities in the public domain have been established by men. Thus women are linguistically at a double disadvantage when entering the public domain: first, they are (normally) less skilful at using the adversarial, information-focused style expected in such contexts; second, the (more co-operative) discourse styles which they *are* fluent in are negatively valued in such contexts.

As women start to enter the professions in greater numbers, there are calls for women to adapt to the linguistic norms of the public domain. Daley (1990) in the *Independent* criticised women for not 'fighting back' in public debate; she argued: 'If women genuinely want to succeed in these [public] spheres, they can learn to hold their own. And learn they must if they wish to have a voice.' The possibility that adversarial talk might not always be the most appropriate or effective does not cross this writer's mind; if women want to succeed in the public domain, then women will have to change. This view is endorsed by women who have themselves been successful in the public domain. In a forceful article in the *Daily Telegraph*, Mary Warnock (Mistress of Girton College and ex-chair of the Warnock Committee) is highly critical of women's behaviour on committees. 'I wonder whether women themselves realise quite how bad they can be as members of boards' (Warnock 1987). She lists what she sees as women's shortcomings, such as their proneness 'to think they are entitled to make fey, irrelevant, "concerned" interventions' and 'to disregard economic considerations for "human" ones'. She urges women 'to adapt to what is required', implicitly accepting the male-dominated discourse patterns of conventional committee meetings.

Women who succeed in adopting a more competitive discourse style in public meet other problems. Jeanne Kirkpatrick, former US ambassador to the UN, describes the dilemma faced by women in high positions, where there is a clash between gender and work identities.

There is a certain level of office the very occupancy of which constitutes a confrontation with conventional expectations. ... Terms like 'tough' and 'confrontational' express a certain general surprise and disapproval at the presence of a woman in arenas in which it is necessary to be – what for males would be considered – normally assertive.

(Kirkpatrick, quoted in Campbell and Jerry 1988)

In other words, women are in a double-bind: they are urged to adopt more assertive, more masculine styles of discourse in the public sphere, but when they do so, they are perceived as aggressive and confrontational.

In contrast with this, a different point of view is now starting to be heard, a point of view which emphasises the *positive* aspects of women's communicative style. There is space here for only three examples. A female environmental engineer working for the Bonneville Power Administration of Portland, Oregon, claims: 'As a woman, you can communicate in a different way which is helpful in a sphere usually analytical' (quoted in Barker 1988). Carol Tongue, talking about her work as MEP for London East, contrasts 'the friendly and supportive meetings of the women's committee' of the European Parliament with 'the all-male environment of industrial affairs', another committee she serves on (quoted in Lovenduski 1989). The writer Jill Hyems, interviewed for Channel 4 (*Ordinary People*, 6.2.90) expressed a preference for working with female producers and directors 'because there are a lot of short cuts, one's speaking the same language'.

These conflicting views are indicative of the lack of consensus and social confusion about women's role in the public arena. The long struggle to give women equal access to professions and to careers is now giving way to the struggle over whether women have to adapt to androcentric working practices. Victory in terms of equal opportunities may turn out to be Pyrrhic if the price demanded by the dominant group is acceptance of dominant group norms.

The language of the professions

The talk which takes place between professionals and clients, such as doctor–patient talk or teacher–pupil talk, can be seen as prototypical professional discourse. The distinguishing feature of such encounters is that they are *asymmetrical*: the professional uses language not only to carry out particular professional tasks but also to construct and maintain power relations.

So what is this discourse like? What are the linguistic features which characterise professional talk? In this paper, I shall focus on three features – questions, directives, and interruptions – in order to illustrate the language used by professionals in their work. Examples will be drawn from the domains of law, medicine and education.

Questions

In the discourse of the public sphere, questions function as *information-seeking* devices. This is illustrated in example 1. This is an extract from an asymmetrical encounter between magistrate and defendant. (Questions in these examples are underlined.)

(1) [Magistrates' court dealing with arrears and maintenance]
    Magistrate: Are you paying anything at all?
    Defendant: No I haven't been able to at all sir

(Harris 1984: 15)

In this example, one of the participants asks a question in order to gain information. But questions don't just seek information; they are also used to establish power and status. Discourse analysts have identified questions as potentially powerful forms, as they oblige the addressee to produce an answer, and to produce an answer which is conversationally relevant (see Grice 1975). The following extract, taken from doctor–patient interaction, shows how the doctor's questions constrain what the patient can say.

(2) Doctor: What brings you here today?
    Patient: My head is killing me
    Doctor: Have you had headaches before?
    Patient: No

                                    (Beckman and Frankel 1984: 693)

The doctor's second question here is close-ended, and effectively narrows the focus of the consultation from the outset.

Not surprisingly, questions are asymmetrically distributed in asymmetrical discourse: powerful participants typically ask many more questions than less powerful participants, as Table 5.1 below demonstrates.

Table 5.1   Distribution of questions in professional discourse

Field	Research	% of questions asked Professionals	Laypeople
Medicine	Todd 1983	85	15
Medicine	West 1984	91	9
Medicine	Frankel, in press	99	1
Law	Harris 1984	97	3
Education	Barnes 1971	97	3

In some contexts, such as the law court, the asking of questions by less powerful participants is explicitly disallowed:

(3) Magistrate: I'm putting it to you again – are you going to make an offer – wh – wh – to discharge this debt?
    Defendant: Would you in my position?
    Magistrate: I – I'm not here to answer questions – you answer *my* question

                                              (Harris 1984: 5)

Through the use of questions, powerful participants are able to control the topic of discourse. Recent analysis of doctor–patient interviews (Mishler 1984; Fisher 1991) shows how the structure of such interviews constrains patients' ability to tell their stories coherently. Doctors' choice of questions does ideological work, promoting the values of medicine and the status quo, and silencing the alternative values of the patients' life experience.

Directives

A directive can be defined as a speech act which tries to get someone to do something. Directives can range from the bluntness of impera-tive forms (e.g. <u>Shut the door</u>) to more mitigated forms (such as <u>Could you possibly shut the door</u>?). Typically, powerful participants will demonstrate their power (i.e. their ability to ignore the face-needs of their addressees) by using direct commands. Those given in example (4) are from the classroom; those in example (5) are from the doctor's surgery (imperatives underlined).

(4) (a) <u>Raise</u> your hand, any children whose name begins with this letter

(Mehan 1979: 163)

   (b) Now <u>don't start</u> now, just <u>listen</u>

(Stubbs 1983: 51)

(5) (a) <u>Lie down</u>
   (b) <u>Take off</u> your shoes and socks
   (c) <u>Pull off</u> a shirt (taps patient on knee) for me
   (d) <u>Sit</u> for me right there

(West 1990: 92)

To show how these are embedded in discourse, here is a more extended example from the medical domain:

(6) Doctor: ... if you don't flow, <u>call</u> me, then I will give you an injection, <u>don't take</u> any more tablets then
   Patient: Uh huh
   Doctor: I'll give you an injection and I'll, uh, get you started with your menstruation and I'll give you a different type of pill
   Patient: Okay
   Doctor: Okay?
   Patient: All right
   Doctor: But meanwhile <u>stay</u> on the pills. <u>Don't you get</u> into trouble.
   Patient: Right

(Todd 1983: 169)

The doctor's use of unmitigated forms here emphasises the power asymmetry of the situation. He clearly feels that since what he is saying to the patient is 'for her own good', there is no need for him to protect her face-needs.

Sometimes less aggravated forms are chosen, as the following examples from classroom discourse illustrate:

(7) Teacher: I could do with a bit of silence

(Stubbs 1983: 51)

(8) Teacher: Can you come up and find San Diego on the map?
    Pupil: (goes to board and points)

$$\text{(Mehan 1979: 54)}$$

Covert imperatives like (7) and (8) constitute a more subtle exercise of power; but like bare imperatives, they assume a universe where the speaker ('I') is all-powerful, and the addressee ('you') has no power. The use of more aggravated directives helps maintain a universe where professionals are constructed as repositories of wisdom, and clients are viewed as objects to be helped, rather than as subjects in their own right.

Turn-taking and interruptions

The Sacks, Schegloff and Jefferson (1974) model of turn-taking in conversation views simultaneous speech by two or more participants as an aberration. Their rules for turn-taking are designed to ensure that (i) one speaker speaks at a time and (ii) speaker change recurs. In terms of this model, interruptions are seen as 'a violation of a current speaker's right to complete a turn' (Zimmerman and West 1975: 123), while overlaps are merely cases of slight mis-timing or over-eagerness on the part of the next speaker. So example (9) below would be viewed as an overlap:

(9) J: because they've only got to win two seats =
    R: two = yes I know

$$\text{(Coates 1991: 299)}$$

However, if speaker R had begun to speak any earlier, this would have constituted an illegitimate bid for the floor, that is, an interruption.

The Sacks Schegloff Jefferson model of turn-taking works well for language in the public domain. Normally, one speaker speaks at a time and speaker change recurs. Simultaneous speech represents a breakdown in the system, and is nearly always the result of the more powerful participant in asymmetrical discourse interrupting the less powerful, as the following examples illustrate. (A double slash // indicates the start of an interruption.) The first comes from doctor–patient interaction:

(10) Doctor: Swelling or anything like that that you've noticed?
     Patient: No, not th//at I've noti
     Doctor: //tender to the touch? pressing any?
     Patient: no, just when it's – sitting
     Doctor: OK=
     Patient: = er lying on it
     Doctor: Even lying. Standing up? walking around? (singsong)

Patient: No //just
Doctor: //not so much, just – lying on it . . . . .

(West 1984: 61–2)

The second example comes from a legal context, and demonstrates what happens when a defendant attempts to provide more than a brief response to the magistrate's questions:

(11) Defendant: – I realise entirely that it's up to me to
      Magistrate: //are you paying any-
      thing
      Defendant: counterbalance that by paying//you know I know (xx)
      Magistrate: at all   //are
      Defendant: no I haven't been able to – at all sir – //no I
      Magistrate: you supporting anyone else
      Defendant: get (xx)   not at all, no – I live on
      Magistrate: and how much do you receive then
      Defendant: my own sir   fourteen
      Magistrate: well can't you spare something of
      Defendant: pounds thirty five
      Magistrate: that for your children – um //when did you last
      Defendant: yes – I would do (xx)
      Magistrate: pay anything

(Harris 1984: 15–16)

Interruption is used as a strategy by powerful participants in discourse to gain the floor and to control the topic of conversation. Research on doctor–patient interaction (Frankel 1983, Beckman and Frankel 1984, West 1984) has revealed how physicians regularly intrude into patients' turns at talk. At first sight, such intrusions may seem warranted by the external constraints of medical examination and treatment. 'But when these inquiries cut off the patient's utterance-in-progress, particularly when that utterance-in-progress is the presumed necessary response to a prior necessary question, then the physician is not only violating the patient's right to speak, but is also systematically cutting off potentially valuable information that is necessary to achieve a diagnosis' (West and Frankel 1991: 186). This comment is presumably equally applicable to other professional contexts where the professional's interruptions cut off the client's response. Example (11) is a case in point. Professionals need to learn to listen, otherwise they, as well as their clients, have much to lose.

Women's discourse patterns in the professional sphere

As we saw in the previous section, the language of the professions, like all-male discourse, tends to be information-focused and adversarial in style, favouring linguistic strategies which foreground status differences between participants. Women's talk in the private sphere, by contrast, is interaction-focused, favouring linguistic strategies which emphasise solidarity rather than status. This dichotomy is in part functional: the chief goal of discourse in the public domain is the efficient exchange of information; that of discourse in the private domain is the creation and maintenance of good social relations. However, those working in the professions need to be sensitive to the interpersonal function of language: interaction in any context involves more than the exchange of information.

Analysis of all-female discourse patterns is beginning to establish which linguistic features have a significant role in the construction of co-operative discourse (see Coates 1989, 1991, forthcoming). For example, women typically use questions and directives in different ways from men, in ways that differ from how they are normally used in formal public discourse. Moreover, turn-taking strategies in all-female discourse do not always correspond to those assumed by current models of turn-taking (e.g. Sacks, Schegloff, Jefferson 1974). Simultaneous speech (that is, two or more people speaking at the same time) is common in all-female discourse, yet it is rarely a sign of conversational malfunction. One the contrary, it seems to function as a way of symbolising joint activity.

In the public sphere, there is evidence to suggest that some women have resisted adapting to the androcentric discourse norms which prevail there. Instead, they are employing their own more co-operative speech style. In this section I shall examine some examples of this phenomenon: Fisher's (1991) work on the questions used by nurse practitioners; West's (1990) analysis of directive-response sequences in doctor–patient talk; Atkinson's (in press) exploration of simultaneous speech in the talk of home helps with elderly clients; and Nelson's (1988) description of the collaborative interactive patterns adopted by teams working in a university writing centre.

Nurse practitioners and the use of questions (Fisher 1991)

Sue Fisher compares how nurse practitioners and doctors communicate with women patients during medical encounters. The nurse practitioner is a relatively new health care professional in the United States, who claims to provide care differently from doctors, by adding caring to curing. Fisher describes two cases, comparable in all respects except that one patient is seen by a doctor, while the other is seen by a nurse practitioner. The patients were both young women in their 20s who had vague, non-specific complaints. Fisher focuses on the role of questions in structuring the discourse. The (male) doctor uses questions 'which pay little linguistic attention to the life context of patients' symptoms, with an emphasis on technical information and a technical fix even when the medical complaint is marked as social' (Fisher 1991: 161). The (female) nurse practitioner, on the other hand, 'probes for the life context of the patient's symptoms and emphasises the social rather than the technical' (*ibid.*). The doctor's questions are narrowly focused in such a way as to constrain the range of answers possible and to keep control of the discourse (see above). The nurse practitioner, on the other hand, uses questions to open up the discourse, to get the patient to explore her feelings and to give a full picture of the situation. When the patient describes how she got a job to get her out of the home, the nurse practitioner comments:

(12)   You know that's a real growth step for you, to realise those needs and then to go take some action, to do something about them. Do you see that as a growth step?

(Fisher 1991: 169)

Notice how the question allows the patient to accept or reject the professional's assessment. The nurse practitioner constantly encourages the patient to talk about her symptoms in the context of her emotional and social life, through the use of sensitive questions. The professional is inevitably the dominant interactional partner, and questions are used as a way of controlling topics. But professionals can use this control in very different ways. Throughout the encounter, the nurse practitioner accepts the patient's definition of the situation and validates her opinion. The doctor is committed to a traditional discourse, in which motherhood is seen as a full-time job, while the nurse practitioner supports an alternative discourse in which women take control of their lives. The nurse practitioner's use of questions arises directly from her different conception of her role.

Women doctors' use of directives (West 1990)

Candace West analysed directive-response speech sequences between doctor and patient, drawing on Marjorie Goodwin's (1980, 1988, 1992) work on gender differences in children's use of directives. West discovered that women and men doctors issued directives in very different ways. Moreover, women doctors are more likely than men to use directive forms which elicit a compliant response from the patient. While male doctors preferred to use imperative forms, or statements in which they told patients what they 'needed' to do, or what they 'had to' do, female doctors preferred to use more mitigated forms. For example, women doctors often made directives in the form of proposals for joint action, using the form <u>let's</u>:

(13)   Okay! well let's make that our plan

(14)   So let's stay on uh what we're doing right now, OK?

They also used the pronoun <u>we</u> rather than <u>you</u> in their directives:

(15) Maybe what <u>we</u> ought to do is, is stay with the dose of di(ava-meez) you're on

Where a woman doctor did use <u>you</u>, she typically mitigated the directive by the use of modal forms such as <u>can</u> or <u>could</u>, as well as <u>maybe</u>:

(16) one thing you <u>could</u> do is to eat the meat first

(17) and then <u>maybe</u> you <u>can</u> stay away from the desserts and stay away from the food in between meals

West measured the compliance rates for different types of directives for male and female doctors. Male doctors' bare imperatives (e.g. <u>lie down</u>!) elicited compliant responses in 47 per cent of cases in which they were used, while their statements of patients' needs elicited only 38 per cent compliant responses. As West puts it 'the more aggravated the directive, the less likely it was to elicit a compliant response' (West 1990: 108). Female doctors' proposals for joint action (using <u>let's</u>) elicited compliant responses in 67 per cent of the cases in which they were used. Suggestions for action (you <u>could try</u> taking two every four hours) had a 75 per cent success rate. Overall, the women doctors used far fewer aggravated directives than the male doctors, and their overall rate of compliant responses was 67 per cent, compared with the male doctors' 50 per cent.

This study shows women using more collaborative interactive strategies in the medical profession. The women doctors used more mitigated directive forms, thus minimising status distinctions between themselves and their patients. The evidence from this study is that such an approach has better outcomes for patients than more traditional approaches which emphasise asymmetry in doctor–patient relationships.

Simultaneous speech in talk between home helps and elderly clients (Atkinson, forthcoming)

Karen Atkinson has carried out long-term participant observation of the interaction between young home helps and elderly clients. The majority of carers who look after the elderly are female, as are most of the elderly population. Thus, the inter-generational talk occurring in home help–elderly person dyads tends to be all-female. Despite the asymmetry of both age and status, Atkinson has observed a significant amount of simultaneous speech in such dyads, similar in kind to that found in the talk of female friends. The following is an example from her data (words in double brackets are indistinct; / = end of unit type):

(18) [elderly client (EC) talks to home help (HH) about new gadget for arthritis]
    1   (EC: now if my knee [b], got bad again/

```
2  (HH:                          yeah yeah now that'd
3  (EC: that might be worth it/. ((your)) knee
4  (HH: be lovely ((there)/      yes    yeah where
5  (EC:        you would use it on yourself/    yes/
6  (HH: you can use it           yourself/that's it, yeah/
```

This short extract from one of Atkinson's 60 audio-recorded conversations between young female home helps and their elderly female clients illustrates the way overlapping speech is used in these interactions. Speakers perform as a single voice, saying the same thing in different words ('now that'd be lovely'/'that might be worth it', lines 3–4) and even saying the same thing at the same time ('yourself', lines 5–6). Speakers use minimal responses (<u>yes, yeah, that's it</u>) to confirm that what one has said has the support of the other. In terms of the conventional norms of turn-taking, virtually all the simultaneous speech occurring here should be labelled 'interruption', since the overlapping segment involves more than the last syllable of a speaker's turn. But in all-female conversation such categories are inappropriate: participants do not view conversation as a battle to hold the floor; the floor can be (and often is) jointly held. When EC says <u>you would use it on yourself</u> in line 5, she is not trying to seize the floor from HH, but is agreeing with HH and saying the same thing in her own words. These 'conversational duets' (Falk 1980, Coates 1991) are a central feature of all-female discourse.

It seems that young female home helps are bringing to their job as carers the collaborative speech styles typical of symmetrical all-female talk. This suggests that gender may be over-riding age and status differentials. While this may be good professional práctice, we should note that professions which are female-dominated (such as nursing, certain kinds of social work, nursery and infant teaching, caring for the elderly), and which are therefore capable of supporting more co-operative speech styles, have lower status and prestige than those which are male dominated (such as medicine, law, university teaching).

Interactive patterns in teacher-research teams (Nelson 1988)

Nelson observed and recorded the interactive patterns of five successive teacher-research teams working in a university writing centre in Washington, DC. These teams were made up of graduate Teaching Assistants (TAs), who were mostly female. Nelson's research shows how the women successfully used the interactive patterns familiar to them, while the occasional male TAs adapted to these interactive patterns and were positive about the experience. The members of the team enjoyed the trust and closeness engendered by close collaborative work. Transcripts of team discussion sessions confirm the claim that women's interactions are rooted in emotional openness and reciprocity, and are co-operative rather than competitive. They show what Miller (1976) calls 'productive conflict', that is, conflict which is beneficial to all participants, as opposed to conflict which results in one winner and many losers.

The success of this collaborative venture is borne out both in the achievement of the teams in helping students to write better, and in the comments of participants on how much they had gained from the experience. One graduate TA, who subsequently worked for a large corporation, described the contrast between the competitive ethos of the large corporation, and the collaborative ethos of the university research teams:

The corporation emphasises only negative aspects of performance, but we female teachers have been used to stressing the positive first. Our emphasis has always been on what students do right – to help students build on what they do well instead of discouraging them. In addition, we've all been used to using collaborative methods.

(Nelson 1988: 220)

Nelson discusses the problems women face in trying to maintain their collaborative style in more competitive environments, but argues that we must try to overcome these problems since the interactive patterns into which women are socialised 'offer substantial benefits to academic and professional teams' (Nelson 1988: 203).

Conclusion: women, language and career

The studies described in the previous section are only a few of a growing number of research projects which demonstrate the positive aspects of incorporating co-operative discourse styles typical of women into the public domain. Troemel-Ploetz (1985) compares male and female TV interviewers and shows how female interviewers encourage more open and more equal discussion through their interactive strategies. Graddol and Swann (1989: 178–81) describe how some firms are trying to encourage the promotion of women and to introduce more 'feminine' styles into management. Campbell (1988) argues that women's presence on high-powered committees has had beneficial effects. She quotes Tessa Blackstone, Master (sic) of Birkbeck College, who said of her experience as a member of the Central Policy Review Staff: 'Women are less competitive for a start and there's less confrontation in a group that's got women in it. ... I just think that organisations that have women are more in touch with the society in which they work' (Campbell 1988).

On the other hand, women attempting to pursue careers in the public domain will continue to encounter problems. If they adopt a more adversarial, more 'male', interactive style, they are in danger of being labelled 'unfeminine'. If they attempt to retain a more co-operative style of interaction, they risk being viewed as ineffectual. This cultural contradiction for women poses a real dilemma for women's careers and for their prospects of promotion.

As women enter the professions and careered occupations in greater numbers and with higher expectations, it remains to be seen whether the more co-operative discourse style which women are skilful in will be welcomed in the public sphere as a new resource, or whether it will be challenged. More overt forms of discrimination against women are slowly being eradicated. But the fact that women are still having difficulty progressing in their chosen careers suggests that other, covert means of discrimination are still at work. The androcentric norms of public discourse are alien to most women. This discourse is extremely powerful in promoting and maintaining the competitive ethos of the world of work. If the dominant elite insists that women must acquire a public 'voice' in order to take their place in the public sphere, then society as a whole will be the loser. Some (female) professions already benefit from the use of more collaborative discourse styles. It is time the value of such discourse patterns was acknowledged.

References

Aries, E. (1976) 'Interaction patterns and themes of male, female and mixed groups', *Small Group Behaviour*, **7** (1): 7–18.

Atkinson, K. (forthcoming) *Elderly Talk*, London: Longman.

Barker, D. (1988) 'Saving money and the world', *Guardian*, 11 Nov.

Barnes, D. (1971) 'Language and learning in the classroom', *Journal of Curriculum Studies*, **3** (1).

Beckman, H. B. and Frankel, R. M. (1984) 'The effects of physician behaviour on the collection of data', *Annals of Internal Medicine*, **101**: 692–6.

Belenky, M., Clinchy, B., Goldberger, N. and Tarule, J. (1986) *Women's Ways of Knowing*, New York: Basic Books.

Campbell, B. (1988) 'Master class', *Guardian*, 5 Oct., p. 16.

Campbell, K. and Jerry, C. (1988) 'Woman and speaker: a conflict in roles', in S. S. Brehm (ed.) *Seeing Female: Social Roles and Personal Lives*, New York: Greenwood Press.

Coates, J. (1986) *Women, Men and Language*, London: Longman.

Coates, J. (1989) 'Gossip revisited: language in all-female groups', in J. Coates and D. Cameron (eds) *Women in their Speech Communities*, London: Longman, pp. 94–121.

Coates, J. (1991) 'Women's co-operative talk: a new kind of conversational duet?' in C. Uhlig and R. Zimmerman (eds) *Proceedings of the Anglistentag 1990 Marburg*, Tubingen: Max Niemeyer Verlag, pp. 296–311.

Coates, J. (forthcoming) *Women Talking to Women*, Oxford: Blackwell.

Daley, J. (1990) 'Some women confine themselves to the nursery pool of life', *Independent*, 20 Dec., p. 16.

Falk, J. (1980) 'The conversational duet', *Proceedings of the 6th Annual Meeting of the Berkeley Linguistics Society*, **6**: 507–14.

Fisher, S. (1991) 'A discourse of the social: medical talk/power talk/oppositional talk?', *Discourse and Society*, **2** (2): 157–82.

Frankel, R. (1983) 'The laying on of hands: aspects of the organisation of gaze, touch and talk in a medical encounter', in S. Fisher and A. D. Todd (eds) *The Social Organisation of Doctor–Patient Communication*, Washington, DC: Center for Applied Linguistics, pp. 19–54.

Frankel, R. (in press) 'Talking in interviews: a dispreference for patient-initiated questions', in G. Psathas (ed.) *Interactional Competence*, New York: Irvington.

Gilligan, C. (1982) *In a Different Voice*, Cambridge, Mass.: Harvard University Press.

Gilligan, C., Ward, J. V. and T. and McLean, J. (eds) (1988) *Mapping the Moral Domain*, Cambridge, Mass.: Harvard University Press.

Goodwin, M. H. (1980) 'Directive-response speech sequences in girls' and boys' task activities', in S. MacConnell-Ginet *et al.* (eds) *Women and Language in Literature and Society*, New York: Praeger, pp. 157–73.

Goodwin, M. H. (1988) 'Cooperation and competition across girls' play activities', in A. D. Todd and S. Fisher (eds) *Gender and Discourse: The Power of Talk*, New Jersey: Ablex, pp. 55–94.

Goodwin, M. H. (1992) *He-said, She-said*, Bloomington: Indiana University Press.

Graddol, D. and Swann, J. (1989) *Gender Voices*, Oxford: Basil Blackwell.

Grice, H. P. (1975) 'Logic and conversation', in P. Cole and J. L. Morgan (eds) *Syntax and Semantics, vol. 3: Speech Acts*, New York: Academic Press.

Hall, C. (1985) 'Private persons versus public someones: class, gender and politics in England, 1780–1850', in C. Steedman, C. Urwin and V. Walkerdine (eds) *Language, Gender and Childhood*, London: Routledge & Kegan Paul, pp. 10–33.

Harris, S. (1984) 'Questions as a mode of control in magistrates' courts', *International Journal of the Sociology of Language*, **49**: 5–27.

Kalcik, S. (1975) '. . . like Ann's gynaecologist or the time I was almost raped – personal narratives in women's rape groups', *Journal of American Folklore*, **88**: 3–11.

Lovenduski, J. (1989) 'Euro resolve', *Guardian*, 6 June, p. 17.

Maltz, D. and Borker, R. (1982) 'A cultural approach to male–female miscommunication', in J. Gumperz (ed.) *Language and Social Identity*, Cambridge: Cambridge University Press, pp. 195–216.

Mehan, H. (1979) *Learning Lessons: Social Organisation in the Classroom*, Cambridge, Mass.: Harvard University Press.

Miller, J. B. (1976) *Toward a new Psychology of Women*, Boston: Beacon Press.

Mishler, E. G. (1984) *The Discourse of Medicine: Dialectics of Medical Interviews*, New Jersey: Ablex.

Nelson, M. W. (1988) 'Women's ways: interactive patterns in predominantly female research teams', in B. Bate and A. Taylor (eds) *Women Communicating: Studies of Women's Talk*, New Jersey: Ablex, pp. 199–232.

Sacks, H., Schegloff, E. and Jefferson, G. (1974) 'A simplest systematics for the organisation of turn-taking in conversation', *Language*, **50**: 696–735.

Stubbs, M. (1983) *Discourse Analysis*, Oxford: Blackwell.

Thorne, B. and Henley, N. (eds) (1975) *Language and Sex: Difference and Dominance*, Rowley, Mass.: Newbury House.

Thorne, B., Kramarae, C. and Henley, N. (eds) (1983) *Language, Gender and Society*, Rowley, Mass.: Newbury House.

Todd, A. D. (1983) 'A diagnosis of doctor–patient discourse in the prescription of contraception', in S. Fisher and A. D. Todd (eds) *The Social Organisation of Doctor–Patient Communication*, Washington, DC: Center for Applied Linguistics, pp. 159–87.

Troemel-Ploetz, S. (1985) 'Women's conversational culture: rupturing patriarchal discourse', ROLIG-papir 36, Roskilde Universitetscenter, Denmark.

Warnock, M. (1987) 'Why women are their own worst enemies', *Daily Telegraph*, 19 Jan., p. 10.

West, C. (1984) *Routine Complications: Troubles with Talk Between Doctors and Patients*, Bloomington: Indiana University Press.

West, C. (1990) 'Not just "doctors' orders": directive-response sequences in patients' visits to women and men physicians', *Discourse and Society*, 1 (1): 85–112.

West, C. and Frankel, R. (1991) 'Miscommunication in medicine', in N. Coupland, H. Giles and J. Wiemann (eds) *'Miscommunication' and Problematic Talk*, London: Sage Publications.

Zimmerman, D. and West, C. (1975) 'Sex roles, interruptions and silences in conversation', in B. Thorne and N. Henley (eds) *Language and Sex: Difference and Dominance*, Rowley, Mass.: Newbury House, pp. 105–29.

CHAPTER 6

Paid and unpaid work: women who care for adult dependents

OLIVE STEVENSON

Just to outline my situation: My mother is 89 and is very compos mentis, but has a lot of things wrong physically, so that she is unable to do much. She can walk to the toilet with her Zimmer in the daytime, with difficulty, but cannot get in and out of bed, so needs help to get on the commode at night. She washes her face and front sitting down, but needs help with the rest of her washing. She eats well, within her diabetic diet, but it is a struggle, because she hasn't many teeth and her mouth has been very sore. She has been having frequent visits by ambulance to the dental department at a hospital about 11 miles away. It tires her out, but as she can only get out if carried down-stairs (there is no lift and since breaking her hip in 1989 she has not been able to manage the stairs) it is quite a sociable outing. Some of the ambulance people recognise her, as do the staff at the hospital.

We are very well blessed with 'back-up' help. There is a local voluntary organisation. They come for 3 hours 5 days a week to cover the bulk of the time that I am at work. There is also a very small convent, the Little Sisters of Mary, whose main work, apart from prayer and worship, is to nurse people at night. On rare occasions when I am really tired, I have asked them for some help and they have come 4 nights out of 8, so that I can recharge my batteries. They come at 9 p.m. and leave at 6.45 a.m. I would feel less happy having agency people, as I have had experience dealing with people who work some nights each week and whose health (and families) have suffered.

We also have a very helpful neighbour, who will give the key to people who need to get in when I am at work and someone else who does a couple of hours' housework each week. Mother has a Piper Lifeline, so in an emergency she can summon help.

(Lucy, a part-time social worker who cares at home for her mother.)

This chapter is about women who combine paid employment with caring for adult dependents. I have found it difficult and, at times, painful to write. Later, I shall explore the limitations of our knowledge about the choices and decisions, large and small, which face women who seek to combine paid work and care of dependent adults. At the heart of such choices and decisions, however, lie deep feelings about what is 'right' for the persons involved. They raise questions of identity, on which there is unresolved feminist debate, about profoundly internalised concepts of social norms and roles. Small wonder, then, that although I am not currently obliged to face the problem head-on, as are so many women of my age, the work on this chapter gave rise to uncomfortable tensions, to a series of 'what if' questions about my own position: a woman whose career has effectively taken precedence throughout my life over the needs of adults as they have grown old. Indeed, it may not be fanciful to suggest that my academic interest, over the past 15 or 20 years, in the social care needs of frail elderly people has been powerfully fuelled by guilt at the choices which I have made.

The purpose of this 'confession' is not, I hope, self-indulgent. Rather it is to draw attention yet again to the inextricable connections of the 'personal' and the 'political', which have direct and dramatic force in this sphere, as much (or perhaps even more) in the field of adult care as in child care. It is to acknowledge that I do not write as an outsider, an academic 'looking on' but as a woman who has been deeply troubled by these matters, albeit never put to the test of giving up work.

For the chapter I interviewed and corresponded with a handful of women who were combining work and adult care. They do not constitute a research sample in any formal sense. What they have done – and for this I am extremely grateful – is to sensitise me, to raise my awareness of what is actually involved in these daily activities. I am not alone in finding such conversations extremely moving but also very impressive in the qualities which they reveal. They were in and out of my head all the time the chapter was in preparation, as the vivid symbols of an issue which needs to be on the agenda of this book.

The literature on this theme of caring for adult dependents has burgeoned in the last ten years. There is also a substantial literature on women who work and care for children. What has been missing are discussions of women who are in paid work *and* care for adult dependents.

Research on caregivers' employment status carries a danger of emphasising excessively the notion of the 'burden of care', which can be criticised on two grounds. First, it may overstate the dependence of the other party. Some disabled people argue strongly that their need is for a reduction of dependence on others and a recognition of their rights to a 'normal' life. Reference to old people as 'burdens' is unhelpful because it does not acknowledge that many old people are themselves carers. Furthermore, there is no set pattern of ageing, determining the degree of dependence in later years. Indeed, since most of the dependence centres on illness, of mind or body, there is no certainty about whether the 'compressed morbidity' of later years will, in time, be reduced, new disease arise, or life be still further extended.

The second danger of this analysis is that it ignores the quality of interaction between the people involved. This chapter will not illuminate adequately the gratification and satisfaction which many carers obtain from their role, and will not explicitly consider the feelings and views of those cared for.

The social and demographic background to this issue is well known. An increasing number of people, especially women, are living to a very old age, with associated health problems, which show a sharp increase about age 70 (OPCS: 20 Table 3.4, Martin *et al.* 1988). Some indication, though not entirely satisfactory, of the scale and importance of this issue is given by the report prepared for the Carnegie Inquiry into the 'Third Age' (Tinker *et al.* 1992), which re-analysed data from the General Household Survey of 1985. The 'Third Age' is defined as people between 50–75. Thus, the data on younger people relevant to this discussion about employment is not readily available. The data shows that 47 per cent of all women between 50–59 were carers; of these 12 per cent were co-resident and 12 per cent were providing more than 20 hours of care each week; 20 per cent of these carers were women who worked full-time and 22 per cent part-time: 22 per cent did not work (p. 23, Table 10). The GHS differentiated between those who cared for an adult dependent who lived in the same household and those who lived apart. In 1980, 48 per cent of all old women lived alone. Amongst women over 75, 53 per cent lived alone (GHS Survey 1980, Table 10:2); the figures are higher now. A very significant number of these very old women require considerable support. Thus it would be misleading to suggest that co-resident carers take most of the strain. Indeed, working women with other family responsibilities face particular difficulties when the person cared for is living separately.

The feminist literature of the 1980s (see for example: Finch and Groves 1983, Nissel and Bonnerjea 1982, Lewis and Meredith 1988, Qureshi and Walker 1989), opened up a debate on the significance of women's role in care of adult dependents. Finch (1991) has pointed out that 'caring' and 'carers' may be viewed in two ways. On the one hand, there is the literature of 'moral virtue' in which caring is extolled as 'natural', an emphasis seen at its strongest in some government pronouncements. On the other hand feminists see the issue as problematic. The use of the terms, it is argued, obscures the fact that it is unpaid work and hence, conveniently, sets aside for policy-makers the issue of payment. It also obscures the fact that it is mainly women who do it. The assumption of 'virtue' in informal care is challenged by those who see it as a manifestation of a society oppressive to women.

Arber and Ginn (1992) have shown that some feminist writing underestimated the numbers of men providing care. However, these are heavily concentrated in the group of elderly, usually retired, spouses living with each other. They conclude: 'in terms of time spent, spouse care by elderly people breaks "normal" gender boundaries of caring. ... Overall, women provide 63 per cent of all informal care to elderly people, with middle-aged women making the greatest contribution' (p. 136). For the purposes of this chapter, the focus on women is justified for two reasons. First, there are indeed more women caring (though this should not lead us to ignore the implications of male caregiving). But also, women's employment status has been and continues to be more problematic than that of men.

Whatever the controversy about women's roles, the family remains by far and away the most important element in support. It far exceeds 'neighbouring', which as Abrams *et al.* (Bulmer 1986) have shown, is restricted in scope, variable in availability and less likely to flourish in more prosperous societies. In quantitative terms, care of older people (typically of parents) is the most significant and is given most emphasis in this chapter. Indeed, Brody (1985) in the USA, argues that long-term parent care is becoming a 'normative experience':

Between 1900–1976, the number of people who experienced the death of a parent before the age of 15 dropped from 1 in 4 to 1 in 20, while the number of middle aged couples with 2 or more living parents increased from 10 per cent to 47 per cent (Uhlenberg 1980). [In 1963], about 25 per cent of people over the age of 45 had a surviving parent (Murray 1973). By 1980, 40 per cent of people in their late 50s had a surviving parent.

(p. 20)

Brody also discusses 'caregiving carers' and the position of 'women in the middle'. She shows that:

For many women, parent care is not a single time limited episode in the life course. . . . Not only can it begin at widely differing ages . . . but dependence/ independence issues can be replayed many times. It can be multiple and multi layered as one's parents and parents in law and even grandparents and other elderly relatives require help sequentially or simultaneously.

(p. 25)

This response to care needs is played out against a background of considerable ambivalence and uncertainty about these roles in western societies, in which norms of filial piety are not consensual across the generations, nor between different cultural groups within it. In eastern societies, social norms, reflected in law, may *require* parent care; in western countries there is a kind of pseudo-voluntarism when it comes to personal care and an assumption that parents should not depend financially on their children. (An assumption which is often shared both by children and by parents.) Thus, women who have the opportunity to get, or stay in, paid employment make individual decisions in a social context which gives them no clear lead. There are also variations within western countries as to the expected ways of expressing 'filial piety'. For instance, in Denmark, there is a much lower expectation that carers will help with the domestic and personal care of their parents. A much higher proportion than in the UK receive 'home helps' (Holstein 1991).

The 1970s and 1980s in the UK saw a sharp rise in women's participation in the labour market. The numbers of women between 50 and

59 who are employed has risen over the past 20 years. For women aged 50–54, it has risen between 1973 and 1991 from 64 per cent to 73 per cent; for women aged between 55 and 59, from 51 per cent to 54 per cent. However, as the Social Security Advisory Committee points out, 'this is cancelled out by a recent steepening of the declining participation by age' (SSAC 1992). We do not know the extent to which caring for adult dependents plays a part in decisions to leave paid work.

Research on women who care for adult dependents

In the past decade, there have been a considerable number of studies in the UK, and elsewhere, of women who care for dependent adults. This literature is relatively recent and feminists have been slow to address this 'later age' issue, perhaps reflecting their own preoccupations through the life cycle.

The studies tend to be small-scale and qualitative, since their purpose was to explore women's position, views and feelings in some depth. They add up to a substantial body of evidence that conflict, ambivalence and stress are all present in great measure in these family situations. In bringing these hidden 'personal' matters into public view, feminists have contributed greatly to the quality of debate concerning women's role in caring for adult dependents.

A number of issues have been assessed by researchers and these include:

1. Difficulties in sustaining employment.
2. Strain and isolation.
3. Financial problems.
4. Health.
5. Employment: the world of work.

These items will be reviewed in turn.

1. Difficulties in sustaining employment

The focus of the studies so far has been mainly on the domestic domain, with passing reference only to employment. Even from those references, however, one thing is clear. It is extremely difficult to sustain employment in the face of heavy caring responsibilities, to the point that many give up the unequal struggle and leave work.

This issue is also examined by Brody (1985). She asks 'Do work and parent care compete?' She found that '28 per cent of non-working women had quit their jobs because of the ... need for care. ... A similar proportion of working women were conflicted: they were considering giving up their jobs for the same reason and some had already reduced the number of hours they worked' (1985: 25). Thus in her sample about 60 per cent found the difficulties of balancing home care and paid work to an extent irreconcilable.

The evidence of the characteristics and situation of carers most likely to give up work paints a vivid and compelling picture. Brody found that the decision to give up work accorded with a higher degree of perceived caring strain on a whole range of factors. For example, both carers who had left their jobs, and those who were considering doing so, reported the most difficult parent care situation and the most functionally dependent mothers. 'They had been helping their mothers for a longer time and they tended to be the only ones providing that help. And they more often felt that parent care made them feel tied down and as though they had missed out on something in life.' Furthermore, the women who *had* quit their jobs 'had an additional set of problems'. They more often shared their household with their mothers (a living arrangement which is a strong indicator of strain). They reported deterioration in health.

2. Strain and isolation

Carers who do not go out to work frequently comment on their social isolation; indeed, the social stimulation of work is often valued as much as the money. Withdrawal from paid work is often much regretted for this reason. The degree of social isolation is often painful to behold and has a profound effect on self-esteem. A vicious circle may set in when, 'with nothing to look forward to', self-care becomes less important. 'I don't get my hair done/buy new clothes any more.' In a significant number of cases, in which the dependent is mentally infirm, the lack of meaningful conversation becomes desperate. Cries of boredom are familiar from isolated mothers of very young children. However, when adults are cared for, similar cries have an added poignancy for two reasons. First, there is often a chronic sense of loss when the adult has been formerly of sound mind. Secondly, there is no predictable course which has to be run, unlike the care of children. Although intellectually, the carer knows 'it can't go on indefinitely', the time scale is unknown, often lasting many years, with no expectation of improvement, only decline. One can see, in theory, every good reason for staying in employment as long as possible. Yet many do not. The strain is just too great.

To analyse the nature of this 'strain' is to go deep into the nature of the activity and the role of the carer and the feelings which it arouses. Research has shown (Braithwaite 1990) that women, more than men, feel that in this role they cannot do enough; that they never fully match up to what is needed and to what is required of them to do. Women who work know all too well the conflicts which persist in this dual role and, as feminists have shown, how oppressive this can be. For those with disabled children, we know that feelings of guilt, however irrational, are often present. For those who care for their parents, earlier relationships affect current interaction. Sometimes as a consequence of earlier experiences with the parent, there may be suppressed hostility or anxiety at not caring as well as parents did, which in turn causes guilt.

Thus many different elements are involved in decisions about employment, from the pragmatic and practical to the deepest emotions. Social roles and expectations lie in between, powerfully affecting and affected by the experiences and feelings of individuals.

3. Financial problems

A study by Glendinning (1992) provides the fullest and most recent UK evidence on the financial problems which women who care for adult dependents face. (Glendinning's study included some men but the large majority were women respondents.) She concluded (1992: 104) that earnings were reduced, even for those who remained in employment, and disposable incomes were lowered by the purchase of substitute care.

Glendinning also shows the inadequacy of the present benefit structure; for example, the low earnings limit on those women who claim the Invalid Care Allowance (until recently married women had no claim on it) may lower motivation to get or stay in work.

In addition to current financial responsibilities, which include the additional costs to the household of the disabled person, such women may also be financially disadvantaged in the longer run. As Glendinning writes:

Carers who had withdrawn from or been unable to re-enter the labour market anticipated considerable difficulty in returning once the period of caring was over. These difficulties were expected to increase as the period of time out of work lengthened and were viewed with particular anxiety by carers in their late 40s and 50s. ... A lengthy period out of the labour market meant that the chances of being able to replenish those depleted resources before retirement were not high.

(Glendinning 1992: 105)

This in turn affects pension levels.

4. Health

The issue of health is considered by Neil *et al.* (1990). They compared the positions of employed women who care for children with those who care for elderly and disabled adults. They found differences between the two. Childcare responsibilities led to more absence from work than adult care, but carers of adults experience more stress in relation to their personal health.

There is no evidence of a causal relationship between the combination of paid employment and caring and poor health. Indeed, the data on caring and health is not easy to interpret. As the Carnegie Study (Tinker *et al.* 1992) points out, 'any perceived association between caring and physical health depends on the nature of the sample studied' (1992: 33). However, a high proportion of those who care for adults, whether they work or not, report health problems, physical and emotional. Since conflict of priorities and loyalties is a striking feature of what many carers report, it is also reasonable to assume that the demands of employment add to these. So whilst the benefits of employment, financially, socially and emotionally, may be highly valued, there may come a time when, in terms of daily living, 'the game is simply not worth the candle'.

There is evidence (EOC 1982) that women who 'care' in the same household as dependents have been less likely than men in comparable situations, and less likely than old people living alone, to receive statutory help from social services. In the past decade there has been a growing appreciation amongst professionals of the needs and problems of carers, but it is clear that the practical support given still falls far short of what is required. Much of this is attributable to acute resource constraints but it may still reflect ambivalent attitudes amongst professionals to women's relative priorities in the domestic and employment spheres.

The new Community Care legislation and associated publications (Community Care 1989) accept the need for an interweaving of formal and informal care, with the primary aim of complementing (not replacing) the part played by carers. There is understandable mistrust of political motives which combine financial expediency with an assertion of 'family values' based on dubious, if not false, generalisations about the past behaviour of families. However, workers within social services (influenced in training by feminist writers such as those referred to above) are much more understanding than heretofore of the position of carers and are interested in this process of 'interweaving', even though they operate within increasingly tight budgetary controls.

Women who care, especially those who work, often need a range of support services. Whilst domestic and personal care is often at the core of such provision, the needs of the dependent and carer may go well beyond that. The complexity of the arrangements required has led to the notion of 'packages of care', a rather unfortunate term since it is too neat and tidy for the changing realities. In the new legislation, social services are required to appoint care managers who will work with carers and users to create and sustain appropriate systems of support. Ideally (and formally enshrined in government guidance) the needs and wishes of the user and carer are of paramount significance, although in practice there will be limitations dictated by resource shortages.

Currently few of the community services required are yet available in the private sector. Whether this market will develop, as government hopes, remains to be seen. In any case, the cost of intensive home care on the private market is far too high for most earners. Thus statutory and voluntary sector provision are often crucial in supporting carers, whether it be in the home or in day and respite care. It is not uncommon to find as many as 10 or 12 individuals paying visits to such people, in the course of a week. Where there is a serious element of risk if the dependent is left alone, this may assume the proportions of a minor military exercise. Indeed the high level of daily organisation required to move from home to work was a marked feature in the lives of those carers to whom I spoke.

The practical difficulties which working carers face include the availability of *what* they need *when* they want it and the way the services knit together in relation at least in part to the requirements of their particular job.

5. Employment: the world of work

What do women say about work itself? In general, much less; the emotional focus of their lives is more often home-centred, which may be in itself significant. There are, however, a number of recurring themes in the literature surveyed. Whilst much of the conflict may be intrinsic to the situation, the evidence suggests the nature of the work and the attitudes of employers are important. Some of the women to whom I spoke were able to work from home, either altogether or for some purposes. This was practically speaking more convenient but the combination of both duties within the home was not unproblematic.

'A degree of flexibility or autonomy over working arrangements' (Glendinning 1992) is also important. Whilst in part this relates to the nature of the work, much may also depend on the sympathy and understanding of employers, often at an informal level of first-line management. For example, one woman to whom I spoke, who worked in a supermarket, complained of the inflexibility of shift arrangements.

Lewis and Meredith (1988) found that this was a key factor. 'Where employers were flexible it was usually beneficial for respondents to keep their jobs: I had a very accommodating Head who let me have time off when I wanted it.' The contrast with women who were allowed no leeway at all is acute. 'Our leave year ends in March which is unfortunate because it meant that I couldn't take any holiday in the summer in case I had to use it in the winter', when her mother was particularly susceptible to bronchitis, requiring nursing (1988: 75). As one woman put it:

'They wanted people to arrange illnesses to happen in the holidays. . . . I used to run home in the lunch times ... and that was hard. ... You were a nuisance because you interfered with *work*. ... Most of them were men so they've never had to look after anyone.'

(Lewis and Meredith 1988: 75)

Conclusion

In general we have a long way to go before achieving even the level of understanding (variable enough) of childcare responsibilities. Indeed, it was characteristic of the women to whom I spoke that they did not share their concerns about caring duties with those at work, even their peers. Some, but not all, said they would have a sympathetic ear if needed but I sensed a reluctance to share domestic anxiety ('will I be a bore?'). It may be that women feel the anxieties and conflicts of adult care are less socially acceptable than those of child care. Much may depend on the age of those with whom they work.

More fundamentally, the position of carers of adults in the context of Equal Opportunities is in need of clarification. Many large employers now have such policies which usually refer to particular groups as of special importance. Typically these are black people and other ethnic minorities, disabled people and women. Policies on women have, of course, implications for carers of children and of adult dependents but the former have received the lion's share of attention. One employee of a County Council to whom I spoke recognised the value of a council policy which allowed five years' unpaid leave (with pension rights protected) to *all* carers. This can be of particular value to women as they move towards retirement.

Such policies may also lead to the question of provision in the workplace – typically, the day nursery in the case of children. Parallel provision in the field of adult care is clearly very difficult; it could be demeaning, the range of adult dependents may be too wide, their needs too diverse. This, however, means that all too often the needs of that group are invisible to employers. Nonetheless, in any serious consideration of Equal Opportunities policies, those employees who care for adults must be 'in the frame', not least because these policies should (but often do not) have regard to the needs of older people, as well as women. Whilst such consideration may readily lead to discussion of better financial arrangements and more flexible employment practices, the role employers might play in the provision of services is rarely taken into account. Much here would depend on the pragmatic and flexible response of employers. Take, for example, the case of a Tesco's supermarket in the north of England which employed older people. Given the likelihood that a number will have elderly dependents, why should consideration not be given to suitable day-care provision?

Once the question is asked, its difficulties will be identified. Those who have done battle for childcare facilities will be familiar with the opposition which presents as rational but which is part of deeply entrenched attitudes which find the intrusion of the domestic domain to the public area deeply threatening. This is not, however, to say that in such matters it would be easy to develop practical strategies. Moreover, the idea raises crucial questions concerning the role of employers in such a sphere. In the UK employers and trade unions (until very recently) have paid scant attention to the welfare of dependents. In the Welfare State, support systems have traditionally been the responsibility of the state, with varying degrees of assistance from the voluntary sector (usually funded by local or central government).

The present UK government has challenged fundamental assumptions on this. The concept of welfare pluralism is at the heart of their community care proposals. This concept in practice means greater use of the 'independent' sector in welfare provision. By 'independent' is meant voluntary and 'for-profit' organisations; the latter, as currently discussed, involves private agencies developing to sell services to dependent people or their carers. There has been little or no discussion of the role of employers in overall provision for adult dependents and the issue is not raised in any of the (burgeoning) literature of guidance to local authorities on the development of community care. There is therefore an important question for the political agenda. What is the role of employers in the concept of welfare pluralism? What is the nature of the employer's responsibility to the community in this sphere? Employers have been seen as central to certain political initiatives, in education and in the rehabitation of inner cities. What about older workers and their dependents? Of course, there are many involved in community care today who resist the whole concept of welfare pluralism: we cannot here debate the role of the state in such provision. The point here raised is that the role of employers in a vitally important aspect of community care merits further consideration if welfare pluralism is accepted as a framework for policy.

For many women doing the day-to-day caring, this debate seems remote. If progress is made on these matters it is likely to be in the public sector or large private enterprises. Many of the women here considered, a large number of whom are in part-time work, are entirely pragmatic about their choice of employment. Convenience in terms of location and hours may well be more important than anything else, including even financial rewards, and this may lead them towards small businesses. It requires a huge leap of imagination, perhaps into fantasy, to envisage any cooperative behaviour between them, centred upon provision for adult dependents! Furthermore, unlike childcare, the need may be as often for care at home as for care outside it. We cannot therefore envisage a situation in which employers took a major share of responsibility for provision. What can be legitimately expected is that employers place the general issue of older employees and their adult dependents firmly on the agenda of concern, alongside that of parents who care for children, which is (very slowly) becoming accepted. Such concern will include consideration of working practices and provision of support. Whilst it is understood that the costs to employers will be a central part of the argument, ultimately these decisions reflect moral and social values. Nor is the possibility of state support to employers for these purposes to be ruled out. Older women save the state vast sums by their unpaid care. Their support is now widely accepted, in theory at least, as an essential component of community care. The extent to which such support will be mediated through their place of employment is a matter for discussion but it is surely essential that their role as carers should be better understood and respected by those who employ them.

The social and political climate in Britain today offers little encouragement to those who would wish to see a radical transformation of the traditional underlying assumptions about women's roles in informal care. Very many women continue to struggle on, their interest in, and need for, employment in conflict with their powerful commitment to the care of adult dependents. To such women conventional notions of 'career' are often irrelevant. These are put aside; expedient considerations usually rule. In a book such as this which focuses upon the world of work, their position in contemporary British society deserves recognition. Without it a vital element of the picture is missing.

References

Arber, S. and Gilbert, G. N. (1986) 'Men: The forgotten carers', *Sociology*, **23**(i): 111–18.

Arber, S. and Ginn, J. (1992) *Gender and Later Life*, London and California: Sage.

Braithwaite, A. (1990) *Bound to Care*, London: Allen & Unwin.

Brody, E.(1985) 'Parent care as a normative family stress', *Gerontologist*, **25** (1): 19–29.

Bulmer, M. (ed.) (1986) *Neighbours: The Work of Philip Abrams*, Cambridge University Press: Cambridge.

Community Care (1989) *Caring for People*, Cmnd 849, HMSO.

Equal Opportunities Commission (1982) *Who Cares for the Carers?* Manchester: Equal Opportunities Commission.

Finch, J. (1991) 'The concept of caring: feminist and other perspectives', Paper to European Conference on Informal Care, York.

Finch, J. and Groves, D. (1983) *A Labour of Love*, London: Routledge & Kegan Paul.

Glendinning, C. (1992) *The Costs of Informal Care: Looking Inside the Household*, SPRU, HMSO.

Holstein, B. (1991) 'Formal and informal care for the elderly: lessons from

Denmark', Paper to International Conference on 'Better care for dependent people living at home'.

Lewis, J. and Meredith, B. (1988) *Daughters who Care*, London: Routledge & Kegan Paul.

Martin, J., Meltzer, H. and Eliot, D. (1988) 'The prevalence of disability amongst adults', Office of Population Censuses and Surveys. OPCS Surveys of Disability in Great Britain 1. HMSO.

Murray, J. (1973) 'Family structure in the Preretirement Years', *Social Security Bulletin*, Oct., **36**: 25–45.

Neil, M. B., Chapman, N. J., Ingersoll-Dayton, B., Emlen, A. C. and Boise, L. (1990) 'Absenteeism and stress among employed caregivers of the elderly, disabled and children', in D. Biegel and A. Blum (eds) *Aging and Care*, London and California, Sage.

Nissel, M. and Bonnejea, L. (1982) *Family Care of the Handicapped Elderly: Who Pays?* London: Policy Studies Institute.

Qureshi, H. and Walker, A. (1989) *The Caring Relationship. Elderly People and their Families*, London: Macmillan.

Social Security Advisory Committee (1992) 'Report on Options for Equality in State Pension Age: a case for equalising at 65', London: HMSO.

Tinker, A., Askham, J. and Grundy, E. (1992) 'Carnegie Inquiry into the Third Age: study of carers', Age Concern Institute of Gerontology, Kings College, London, Cornwall House Annex, Waterloo Road, SE1 8TX.

Uhlenberg, P. (1980) 'Death and the family', *Journal of Family History*, **5**: 513–20.

CHAPTER 7

Swedish women and employment: the absence of careers

GUDRÚN KRISTINSDÓTTIR

I remember a particular women's magazine in the late 1960s. It had an illustrated advertisement, covering the whole back page, which pictured a bride in a full length wedding gown. The text said: 'It ends with a Lilly model.' As young Scandinavian women, born in the 1950s or the 1940s, most of us had mothers who had left their jobs to become housewives when they married. As we saw it, it had 'ended' for them in a sense when they married.

Now, however, this is not typical for Swedish mothers with children; they usually combine parenthood and employment before and after childbirth. It is widely known that relatively extensive welfare policy facilitates this to a much greater extent in Sweden than in other countries.

This chapter examines women's employment in Sweden. Swedish research on the question of women's careers is limited; only a few Swedish women have careers in the sense of achieving promotions to higher positions.

Changes in the labour market

Since the 1950s there have been considerable changes in women's employment and particularly in the employment of married women in Sweden. From 1963 to 1988 the percentage of women who worked increased from 54 to 80 per cent and is now around 85 per cent (Ds 1989: 44). The numbers of married women in employment increased four-fold (Qvist 1973).

There have also been changes in the nature of employment. From the mid-1960s public services, such as teaching, health and social services, have expanded (Ds 1989: 44, Furåker 1989). The greatest increase in women's employment occurred within the public sector. Indeed, apart from defence forces, women *are* the public sector. In 1988 the public sector employed 1.6 million workers (i.e. 36 per cent of the whole labour force) and 69 per cent of public employees were women (Hirdman and Åström 1992: 149). In a sense, caring was transferred from the family to the public sector. Large numbers of housewives took jobs in the public sector which absorbed virtually all the increase, since the proportion of married women employed in the private sector remained the same between 1968 and 1981 (Axelsson 1992).

Social policy reforms for equal opportunities

The reshaping of the Swedish labour market was facilitated through various governmental measures, by general social policy reforms, such as the expansion of day-care for children, family allowances and parental leaves, which expanded into contemporary family insurance in 1980 and has been in existence ever since. Labour market policy aimed at introducing equal opportunities for men and women, and enhancing possibilities for shared parenthood was another part of these governmental reforms. An Equal Opportunities Act came into force in 1980.

The intentions of official equality and labour market policy changed as the Swedish labour market was reshaped (Ds 1989: 44). In the 1950s the conflict between the dual roles of women, both as mother and as employee, was at the forefront of the debate. It was argued that women should be allowed to choose freely and enabled to take waged work without serious consequences for the family. The woman's life cycle should consist of two periods of employment, one before and one after the years of caring for children. Policy should stimulate young women's educational opportunities and access to employment, increase part-time employment and provide economic support to mothers with children. The right to six months of unpaid childbirth leave was introduced in 1945; in 1954 limited economic support was provided during a three-months period. From 1962 onwards benefits were extended to six months.

In the early 1960s a reaction arose against this 'conditioned liberation' of women as it was called. Critics said that women were allowed to work only on condition that they fully cared for the family and they were supposed to adjust their work in accordance with this. In 1962 Dahlström *et al.* pointed out forcefully that the conflict between work and family was not only a women's issue, it was also men's concern and was a matter of unequal sex roles. Efforts towards equality were required and this demanded that the man's role changed as well as the woman's.

Gradually this standpoint influenced Swedish policy. In a report to the United Nations in 1968, the goals of Swedish equality policy were put forward and they are still valid: 'The aim of a long-term program for women must be that every individual, irrespective of sex, shall have the same practical opportunities, not only in education and employment, but also, in principle, the same responsibilities for the upbringing of the children and the housekeeping' (in Ds 1989: 44, translations my own).

The official goals of the 1960s centred on equal opportunities for entry to all kinds of jobs and to education and equal wages. In the 1970s the main emphasis shifted to women's opportunities to combine employed work and unpaid work. The National Labour Union Federation (LO) saw equality policy as consisting of general social reforms, such as the expansion of the public sector, day-care for all children, increased labour market training, equal wages and union struggle for better working conditions as the most efficient measures to achieve labour market equality (Waldemarsson 1992: 114). When women with small children entered the labour market, the importance of day-care was increasingly accentuated.

In 1973 the demand for a six-hour working day for all was presented by LO as a 'long-term goal' (Waldemarsson 1992: 116). This demand was modified later to include only the parents of small children as a way of increasing equal care by parents. A six-hour working day was expected to create time for the father to spend on house and childcare and for the mother to increase her union and political activity. Also children's needs for contact with both parents were underlined. During the 1980s, when the majority of women were linked to the labour market, conditions in the workplace and career possibilities were emphasised in support of the six-hour day. Women in the labour union movement have actively supported the six-hour day without support from their male colleagues.

The 1970s became the decade of equal opportunity reforms. To supply the market with labour was the prime driving force behind the various goals of labour market policy and women's employment was stimulated (Ds 1989: 44). Thus, individual taxation (instead of shared taxation for married couples), the provision of subsidised day-care for children and the elderly, childbirth leave and health services shaped the essential conditions for women's employment (Axelsson 1992, Dahlberg *et al*. 1989).

The policies to increase equality between men and women had three characteristics: supply, consumption orientation, and gender neutrality (Widerberg 1986, Ds 1989: 44, Axelsson 1992, Åström 1992). A ready supply of workers to meet the demands of the labour market was the first characteristic. Secondly, according to Axelsson (1992), Swedish social policy was aimed at providing families with increased choice for consumption, for instance by providing all parents with several non-income related subsidies, such as child allowance. In addition, when housing allowance and social welfare support are income-related, and the core social policy measures, i.e. the social insurances (health insurance, supplementary pension, parental insurance) correlate positively with wage income then women are encouraged to enter paid work.

The family and equality policy reforms have been criticised for being presented as gender-neutral while their construction is typically gender-stereotyped, assuming the mother to be the prime care-taker and placing the father in a secondary caring position (Widerberg 1986). Åström (1992: 183) sees this paradox as resulting from rhetorical claims. On an ideological level the argument is far removed from real circumstances. For example, parental insurance is ideologically aimed to encourage the sharing of childcare. In reality, however, parental insurance compensates for loss of wage income in such a way that it pays in most cases for mothers to stay at home rather than fathers. Although 'father' is now 'formally' a parent, he has not yet come home. Only around 7 per cent of fathers use the right to paid leave from employment after childbirth. A certain group of fathers was from the beginning ready to use the right but others have not yet responded. At the same time as the right gave fathers free choice, it put a strong pressure on mothers to change their behaviour. Family insurance is a good example of how these reforms have linked women more to the labour market than earlier, as it gives more benefits to employed women than unemployed. It has, however, increased women's dependency on the market–state relation. This seems to be a much more substantial change than its effects on shared parenthood and the achievement of other equality intentions.

Three characteristics of women's employment

Labour market equality between men and women is far from achieved. There are three characteristics of Swedish women's paid employment which demonstrate the differences: the high degree of gender segregation in the labour market; the preponderance of part-time employment among women; and the documented wage discrimination against women.

Gender segregation

The Swedish labour market is strongly divided by sex (SOU 1990: 44). In 1985, 42 per cent of all employed women worked in jobs consisting of not less than 90 per cent women (Scb 1990); 45 per cent of all men had jobs consisting of not less than 90 per cent men. Women work mostly as assistants in business firms, in shops, hotels and restaurants. In public service, teaching and caring are the largest female dominated areas. To achieve an equal distribution of men and women in all jobs, the Ministry of Labour estimated what percentage of employed women would have to change jobs. In 1960, 74 per cent of women would have had to change jobs; in 1970 the percentage had fallen to 71 per cent and in 1980 to 68 per cent (SOU 1990: 44). According to this, the rate of gender segregation is falling marginally but is still high in the Swedish labour market.

The gender segregation of employment seems hard to break. A Nordic project to 'break the gender segregated labour market' (Wikander 1992: 63) has been on-going for several years. The Swedish part of this project was aimed at motivating girls and young women to take on typically male jobs, i.e. technical work. The results were positive as far as education was concerned – it was possible to interest and motivate girls in technical subjects in pre-school, elementary school and high school. But in fitting into the rigid and masculine labour market – with its norms and marginalising mechanisms – difficulties arose for the trained young women. Women simply do not get jobs according to their qualifications and knowledge but on the basis of their gender. One of the conclusions of this particular project was that as long as labour market conditions persist, what is done in education will have only a marginal impact.

The reproduction of gender segregation in employment has not changed radically despite equality policy, research, special projects and other efforts. Studies of this during the last decades have shown how new segregations and marginalisation of women are produced (Wikander 1988, Lindgren 1985).

Part-time employment

The ideals of Swedish equality policies of the 1960s were that both men and women would work part-time in the 1970s and be able to share housework and parenthood. Changes in the sharing of housework have been only marginal, however. Studies of housework show that men participate a little more than before, but it is only a slight change. Women still take the initiative, have the main responsibility and work much more than men in the household (Gisselberg 1986, Nyberg 1989).

The switch to part-time work has been made only by women. Women's part-time work is an important characteristic of the Swedish labour market. During the 1960s and 1970s the expansion of women's employment was mainly in part-time employment (defined as less then 35 hours a week). During 1979–80, 75 per cent of the employment expansion among women was part-time. The numbers of women who worked part-time expanded from 38 per cent in 1970 to 47 per cent in 1982 when it reached a peak (Ds 1989: 44, 104). Now around 45 per cent of Swedish women work part-time. During the 1980s the rate of women working full-time increased, a change which was especially notable among mothers of young children.

Part-time employees experience several difficulties in the labour market while they work and also when they retire. For example, pension benefit is related to length of employment, with the result that women often get much less pension than men. Also in terms of career, length and extent of experience are required for promotion, thus limiting the promotions of part-time workers. Although part-time employment is extremely common, legal regulations and agreements on working hours still use full-time work as the norm.

Problems also arise in respect of part-time employment and parental leave. Women are sometimes placed in a worse position after childbirth leave (Calleman *et al.* 1984, Dahlberg *et al.* 1989). The law clearly entitles women to keep their jobs, and to return to the same positions with the same salaries. Replacement is allowed, however, but only if working hours for part-timers are hard to arrange. Nonetheless, there are replacements and changes of jobs which occur that do not meet this criterion. Women who return to low-pay caring work in hospitals are quite often placed in a reserve pool, a practice which is legally doubtful. Dahlberg *et al.* (1989) recommend that women find ways to get fathers to share more of the leaves because long breaks obviously make a return to the old job more and more difficult. Research confirms that men's promotion chances are not negatively affected after childbirth leaves (Schönnesson 1987: 7). This demonstrates discrimination against women who are responding positively to the encouragement to take part in the so-called equality reforms.

This demonstrates also that the intention to meet the demand for labour (i.e. the supply orientation of policy), prevails over the equality intentions. Women meet the demand for labour and are promised full subsidies *and* equality but lose distinctively in status in the labour market compared with men when they use their rights. Why this gap exists between the ideology and reality of the reforms is, therefore, an important issue.

Wage discrimination

Women's part-time employment is not the only reason why they only 'take home' around 40 per cent of total wage income in Sweden. Another reason is the wage discrimination against women which means that women are generally paid less and are also paid less than men for the same work (Åström 1986). Women get around 90 per cent of men's wages as industry workers and 75 per cent of men's wages in public health and caring (Scb 1990a). Until the 1960s the tariffs for the same kind of jobs were divided by sex. Then a labour market agreement introduced the principle of equal pay for the same kind of work. This was intended as a transitional arrangement while wage discrimination was to be eliminated through gender-neutral equality efforts. This was an optimistic ambition, however, which resulted in increased gender segregation of tasks (Wikander 1992: 62).

Wage differences between full-time employed men and women were in fact reduced during the 1960s and the 1970s (Scb 1990b). However, recent investigations show a widening wage gap between men and women since the mid-1980s and this has caused considerable debate. So far the only response to this depressing news is to try to develop new tools to evaluate the equivalency of jobs. What this technical approach will lead to is still not known, but wage discrimination, together with occupational segregation and part-time work, continue to be factors influencing women's employment situation.

Women and promotion

Swedish women's relatively high degree of participation in employment is not reflected in their promotions and careers. Few Swedish women hold managerial posts and this is true both in private and public sectors of employment. A few examples will illustrate the general position.

Gender segregation of labour is seen in top positions in industry. Complete statistics on the numbers of female and male directors and top managers within different organisations and industries does not exist. However, only a minority of women reach such positions. This is shown in the statistics of the National Swedish Employers Confederation (SAF). The numbers of men and women in three of the best paid director positions are shown in Table 7.1. Salary categories range from 00 to 08, category 00 being the highest paid. Categories 00 and 01 contained only one post held by a woman in 1988. In category 02 are the directors of large firms. In categories 03 and 04 are the director posts of medium-sized firms. In total there were around 380,000 posts included in these categories for the year 1988 and around 25 per cent were held by women.

Table 7.1   *Numbers of directors of firms 1978 and 1988*

Category	1978		1988	
	Men	Women	Men	Women
02	3,381	9	2,901	39
03	15,873	201	7,762	652
04	44,958	1,811	58,497	4,575

Source: SOU 1990: 41,113.

In the public sector only a few women hold high positions. In March 1986 only 5 out of 20 ministers in the Swedish government were women. In March 1990, 8 out of 21 ministers were women. In 1989 women held around 15 per cent of top positions in government administration (secretary to the minister, vice-secretary etc.). Of 82 central authorities in Sweden 3 had women as directors and 79 had men in 1989.

Also, in large public service occupations women are not promoted to the same extent as men. This can be illustrated by the case of Swedish social workers, although only studies of small samples can be referred to since national statistics of occupational distributions in social work by gender are not available. Björkdahl Ordell (1990) interviewed 72 social workers ten years after they qualified; 52 had social work related jobs. Of the 44 women in this group none had a managerial position whereas 2 of the 8 men had managerial positions at the top level. Larsson and Swärd (1992) studied a group of 79 social workers twenty-five years after they got their social work degrees; 52 had social work related jobs, 40 women and 12 men. Their promotion positions showed the familiar gender differences. Thus, 24 women and only 1 man had a practitioner social work position. The middle range managerial group consisted of 14 women and 6 men. At the top level there were 2 women and 5 men. Larsson and Swärd also asked about salaries and numbers of hours worked and concluded that women, part-time work and low salaries were closely related. When the salaries of the female and male social workers were converted to full-time equivalents and compared, the women earned 75 per cent of the salaries of their male colleagues.

These figures indicate clearly that equal access to career promotion is far from being reached in Swedish society. Men usually hold the top posts in the Swedish labour market and female directors and managers are unusual (SOU 1990: 41,112). In respect of this, it is not surprising to note a lack of knowledge of official equality policy. In May 1992, the Central Equality Board (Jämo) reported that leading persons in many of the largest Swedish private firms did not even know of the Equal Opportunities Act which has existed since 1980.

Studies of women's careers

For a long time labour market research was male-focused. This changed considerably during the 1980s as women's studies expanded in Sweden and as changes in women's employment led to research into their working conditions (Baude *et al.* 1987). These studies have so far focused mainly on women in low or middle-range occupations and on unemployment (i.e. Davies and Esseveld 1988, Lindgren 1985, Gunnarsson and Ressner 1983). In addition, historical studies have increased understanding of how gender segregation has been reproduced and occupational closures have been established (Florin 1987, Sommestad 1992, Wikander 1988). Few Swedish studies have yet focused directly on women's careers, however. In fact few Swedish women have careers, in the sense of achieving promotions to the highest positions. There has been some research, however, into career attitudes and aspirations and in these respects gender differences are apparent.

Asplund (in Wahl 1992: 63) compared men's and women's career patterns and career-related attitudes in a Swedish organisation. Of the men, 82 per cent thought that promotion happened regardless of sex, but only 30 per cent of the women shared this opinion. The explanations given for the fact that women were not promoted to the same extent as men were also different. The men explained that this was because women got too little support from their families, they dared not take risks and did not want to develop a career. The women in this study answered that women did not have the correct education, they did not get positions leading to career progression, and they were not encouraged by their bosses to the same degree as men. In other words the men explained the lack of women's career progress as due to women's own problems; the absence of promotion resulted from the women themselves or their family situations. In contrast the women's explanations were linked instead to conditions in working life and processes in work organisations.

The two types of reasons given in this study are common in debate as well as in research findings. Either explanations are related to women themselves or they are related to features, processes and the organisation of the labour market, i.e. structural conditions. The structural category also sub-divides into two: either explanations are based on gender differences in working lives or they refer to organisational patterns in the work place itself, for instance the lack of encouragement women get from their superiors in the organisation.

These ways of explaining why women do not have careers to the same extent as men are not specifically Swedish. But in Sweden women have entered the labour force in larger numbers and social policy measures have enabled Swedish women to combine aspects of their paid and unpaid work more easily than for women in other industrialised countries. Why then, have Swedish women not been able to build careers to a greater extent? Where should we look for explanations of the Swedish situation?

Wahl's (1992) thesis offers some interesting general points. It is a study of female Swedish civil engineers and civil economists, covering 261 women who finished their studies over a long period, from 1936 to 1981. As students these women had positive and high expectations in respect of career opportunities. They did not engage in feminist struggles nor did they believe that they would face gender-discrimination problems. Their experiences, however, did not confirm their expectations.

The most common career position among these women was a middle-rank post; only 4 to 7 per cent held top posts. Most worked in a male-dominated environment; 90 per cent had no other women on higher levels and 85 per cent had male bosses; 80 per cent of the women had their own children. Their husbands usually had academic qualifications also, but more often held top management positions. The careers of the husbands generally had higher priority in the marriage than the wives'. This asymmetry was visible in the household, domestic work and childcare. A majority of the women, 75 per cent, said that they did more, or much more, of the domestic work compared with their husbands.

The higher the position, the more discriminated against the women felt, as regards wages, promotion and acknowledgement. No less than 40 per cent of them felt that they faced discrimination by male managers, and 30 per cent of the women believed that they had invested more in their careers than they had achieved.

These women used different strategies to handle the dilemmas posed by being in a male-dominated environment and maintaining a positive identity as a woman. First, the positive effects of being a woman in the organisation were stressed by underlining women's special advantages in being different. Secondly, the women explained career position as due to external conditions, they looked upon discrimination as structural and unrelated to themselves. A third gender-neutral strategy involved denying the meaning of gender. In the fourth type of strategy the women did not see gender as significant, since they saw themselves as being in a 'relatively less male-dominated' environment than was usual.

The first two strategies, which involved underlining women's special qualities or emphasising structural factors uncoupled from the employment situation, were prominent. Wahl sees it as typical for women in male-dominated occupations to use a positive strategy. To stress the individual advantages for women in a male-dominated environment was much more common. The lack of power in the organisation was obvious in the descriptions given by these women. They did not, however, look upon themselves as victims. On the contrary, Wahl finds that they expressed resistance through their alternative definitions of goals in life.

The schism between expected and experienced career was reflected in contradictory attitudes and actions towards career-making. It was common for these women to define career by descriptions of general life goals. The majority looked upon promotion in the career as only a part of career. To get all the pieces together in the life situation was seen as a prime goal. Promotion was rejected if it was impossible to combine with family life; for instance the women often underlined the importance of adapting career to caring for children, not vice versa. Other conflicts were based on the combination of marriage and career. To accept traditional career conceptions of promotion often created conflicts in the marriage, which in its turn affected the women's careers.

Wahl refers to Haavind's (1982) concept of 'relative subordination' which she finds to prevail in many of the marriages. 'Relative subordination' is the special way couples organise their relationship to give the impression and experience of equal partnership. The equality ideal requires an atmosphere in marriage partnerships where equality seems to prevail. This demands the relative subordination of the wife, who is in fact second to her husband in respect of paid work. Nevertheless, while traditional roles remained intact, the partners behaved and experienced their own behaviour as if equality *was* achieved, for instance in respect of career, shared parenthood or housework.

The issue of the importance of combining family life with employment is addressed in several Swedish studies of women in other occupations. Wahl's findings are confirmed in Björkdahl Ordell's study (1990) of social workers. The female social workers enjoyed their paid work but adapted it to a large extent to family life. At the same time as they expressed satisfaction at having become 'something' through their training and position as social workers, they emphasised the importance of combining employment and family life. They had often adapted their occupational roles to this requirement by, for instance, negotiating suitable working hours or finding a job near the home.

In Wahl's study the importance of childcare and responsibilities for family and household do not only affect career perceptions but also the women's attitudes and actions. Women are subjected to discrimination in employed life and subordination in their private relations. But, as we have seen, strategies are labelled by Wahl as being positive rather than negative. Should the relatively low level of frustration expressed by women be interpreted as a high degree of tolerance towards structural gender discrimination? Or does it reflect a genuine preference for being able to combine other goals in life, such as childcare, with something which at least sometimes resembles a career? This seems in Wahl's study to diminish the dissatisfaction through the use of strategies of distancing oneself from the reasons behind the difficulties.

Wahl's female engineers and economists anticipated career progress when they were studying. They achieved less than they expected from their investment in working life, but were relatively complacent about their situation, especially as they had succeeded in combining family and employed life. Maybe this is as far as Swedish women in careered occupations want 'equality' in employed life?

Conclusion

The future for Swedish women's career progress is pessimistic. Future policy intentions have their limitations. The government plan now, in the name of free choice, is to introduce payments to parents (mothers) to care for children in the home or to pay for day-care if they prefer. Efforts to privatise and reorganise various forms of care, such as day and elderly care, primary health services and hospitals are proceeding apace. This development means that the care of children, old and the sick, which have been transferred to the public arena will probably now be moved back home. A gender polarisation again occurred in Swedish society during the 1980s, which is demonstrated by the increasing wage gap reappearing between men and women.

This situation is not entirely met with apathy by women, however. A recent wave of resistance is occurring among Swedish women. The crises and frustrations caused by slow progress towards equality have led, for instance, to the idea of establishing a Women's party before the next parliamentary election. Throughout the country, pressure groups of women are demanding equality action and anti-discriminatory measures from the existing political parties. By this, women are demanding more space in political life and a general improvement of women's situation. This development has a short history, however, and its impact cannot yet be assessed.

While the question of career among Swedish women is not yet widely studied, more attention has been given to the possibilities of increasing the quality of family life and how this can be achieved and combined with employment. Considering the various research findings referred to here, this question has so far centred more around the behaviour of women than of men.

The Swedish model of combining family care with part-time employment among women seems in many ways successful. As seen above, women especially have responded positively to family policy measures. Swedish family planning is viewed as extremely rational in a comparative perspective. (*DN* Oct. 1992). The high degree of women's employment combined with childbirth and the stability of the two-parent family is explained in demographic studies as stable and representative of the ideals both of the general public and of the political will. Two-parent family patterns continue to be preserved despite the building of mixed families through remarriage (Scb 1990). To this can be added notable beneficial changes among Swedish parents. Fathers have become objects of attention through public propaganda for shared parenthood and through specific research on their caring roles (Schönnesson 1987). Although nothing much has in fact changed, the introduction of formal rights and the ideology of 'new fatherhood' has changed the image of fathers. Moreover mothers who work part-time often report feelings of well-being compared to periods when fully employed (Axelsson 1992, Moen 1989). Altogether this supports stability in traditional patterns of family building. If nothing radical has happened this probably points to the perseverance of the gender-based family system regarding the combination of employment and family care.

This has also been preserved by relative subordination in the marriage partnership, which serves to keep women in their traditional place. We have seen that even women in careered occupations put their family and their husbands' careers first and their own careers second. The traditional gender-based family situation still has a powerful impact on women's lives. It seems, therefore, that the preservation of family ideology has been a code underlying the various public measures used to regulate women's employment opportunities.

Women have responded actively to the demand for their labour, which is as much as the labour market has asked of them so far. Opportunities for careers among Swedish women seem rather far away. In terms of having a career, it will be interesting to see if the Swedish case of a stable combination of rather traditional family-building and widespread women's employment gives rise to new ways of organising everyday life, in the workplace and at home. The holistic re-definition of career as described by the female engineers and economists may be a significant sign. They demand to be able to enjoy both family and working life, which underlines their preference for life quality. Undoubtedly the generally high living standard together with the strong norms of protective and planned parenthood are Swedish characteristics which place far-reaching demands on the well-being of families. This will probably influence future patterns for the combination of family caring and employment and also the demands of Swedish women when they start increasingly to claim their rights also to achieve careers.

References

Åström, Å. (1986) *Diskriminering på Svensk Arbetsmarknad*, Umeå Economic Studies No. 196, University of Umeå.

Åström G. (1992) 'Fasta förbindelser', in Y. Hirdman and G. Åström, *Kontrakt i Kris*, Stockholm: Carlssons.

Axelsson, C. (1992) *Hemmafrun som Försvann*, Stockholm: Institutet för social forskning 21 Stockholms Universitet.

Baude, A. *et al.* (1987) *Kvinnoarbetsliv*, Stockholm: Arbetslivscentrum.

Björkdahl Ordell, S. (1990) *Socialarbetare*, University of Gothenburg: Acta Universitatis Gothoburgensis.

Calleman, C., Lagercrantz, L., Petersen, A. and Widerberg, K. (1984) *Kvinnoreformer på Männens Villkor*, Lund: Studentlitteratur.

Dahlberg, A., Nordborg, G. and Wicklund, E. (1989) *Kvinnors rätt*, Stockholm: Tiden/Folksam.

Dahlström, E. *et al.* (1962) *Kvinnors Liv och Arbete*, Studieförbundet näringsliv och samhälle, Stockholm: Prisma.

Davies, K. and Esseveld, J. (1988) *Att Hoppa Hage i den Svenska Arbetsmarknaden*, Stockholm: Rabén & Sjögren.

DN (1992) *Dagens Nyheter* 12.17.27, Oct. 1992.

Ds (1989: 44) *Arbetsmarknad och arbetsmarknadspolitik. Allmänna förlaget.*

Florin, C. (1987) *Kampen om katedern*, Stockholm: Almqvist & Wiksell.

Furåker, B. (1989) (ed.) *Välfärdsstat och Lönearbete*, Lund: Studentlitteratur.

Furåker, B. (1991) (ed.) *Arbetets Villkor*, Lund: Studentlitteratur.

Gisselberg, M. (1986) *Att stå vid Spisen och Föda Barn*, University of Umeå: Research Reports of Department of Sociology.

Gunnarsson, E. and Ressner, U. (1983) *Från Hierarki till Kvinnokollektiv*, Stockholm: Arbetslivscentrum.

Haavind, H. (1982) 'Makt og kjaerlighet i ekteskapet', in *Kvinneforskning, Bidrag till Samfunnsteori*, Bergen: Universitetsforlaget.

Hirdman, Y. and Åström, G. (1992) *Kontrakt i Kris*, Stockholm: Carlssons.

Larsson, S. and Swärd, H. (1992) *Att bli Välfärdens Tjänare*, University of Lund: School of Social Work (forthcoming).

Lindgren, G. (1985) *Kamrater, Kolleger och Kvinnor*, University of Umeå: Sociologiska institutionen.

Moen, P. (1989) *Working Parents*, London: Adamantine Press.

Nyberg, A. (1989) *Tekniken – Kvinnornas Befrielse?* Linköping University: Department of Theme Research.

Prop, (1990/91:113) *Förslag till ny jämställdhetslag*, Regeringsproposition Band B 17 Riksdagen.

Qvist, G. (1973) *Statistik och Politik*, Stockholm: Prisma.

Scb (1990a) *På Tal om Kvinnor och Man*, Stockholm: Statistiska centralbyrån.

Scb (1990b) *Om Familj och Barn*, Stockholm: Statistiska centralbyrån.

Schönnesson, L. (1987) *Föräldraskap – Föräldraledighet – Jämställdhet*, Jämfo rapport nr 9.

Sommestad, L. (1992) *Från Mejerska till Mejerist*, Lund: Arkiv.

SOU (1990: 41) *Tio år med Jämställdhetslagen*, Betänkande av jämställdhetsutredningen, Stockholm: Allmänna förlaget.

SOU (1990: 44) *Makt och Demokrati i Sverige*, Stockholm: Allmänna förlaget.

Wahl, A. (1992) *Könsstrukturer i Organisationer*, Stockholm: Ekonomiska Forskningsinstitutet Handelshögskolan.

Waldemarsson, Y. (1992) 'Kontrakt under förhandling', in Y. Hirdman and G. Åström, *Kontrakt i Kris*, Stockholm: Carlssons.

Widerberg, K. (1986) 'Från marxism till feminism, till könskamp till ... ett könskampsperspektiv på arbetsdelningen och rätten', in H. Ganetz, E. Gunnarsson and A. Göransson, *Feminism och Marxism*, Stockholm: Arbetarkultur.

Wikander, U. (1988) *Kvinnors och Mäns Arbeten*, Lund: Arkiv.

Wikander, U. (1992) 'Delad arbete, delad makt', in Y. Hirdman and G. Åström, *Kontrakt i Kris*, Lund: Carlssons.

Concepts and Explanations in Particular Careers

PART TWO

Concepts and Explanations in Particular Careers

The papers in this section consider various concepts and explanations which have been developed to account for the career differences between men and women in particular occupations and professions. The concepts of reputation-building, service, discrimination and management are examined in specific careers. King examines the position of women in science in Chapter 8 in an attempt to get a more exact sense of the nature of women's career marginalisation. In considering the processes by which women are marginalised in careers in science, he examines to what extent the procedures involved in 'building a reputation' in science involve cultural, as well as structural, limitations for women.

Chapter 9 discusses women's position in the Church of England. Aldridge explains how women have been admitted to the clerical profession since 1987 but, until 1992, only to its lowest rung, the diaconate. This clearly represented a severe limitation to their career opportunities. However, Aldridge examines the appropriateness of the concept of 'career' in the clerical profession where the sacred terminology of 'vocation' or 'calling' supposedly substitute for the secular concerns of career and promotion.

Women surveyors form the career context in Chapter 10 where Greed explains how the male majority in surveying still perceive the women surveyors' role as that of assistant or as a stop-gap to fill the present labour market shortage. In career terms in surveying, 'vertically' women encounter a 'glass ceiling' in their quest for seniority and 'horizontally' they are relegated into secondary supporting roles and lower status 'female' specialisms. Greed examines the mechanisms and processes which marginalise women in surveying and how the association of surveying with building sites leads to additional gender/work identity dilemmas for women.

The next three chapters focus on the difficulties which management poses for women's careers. In Chapter 11 I consider secondary headship and the problems experienced by the minority of women who achieve secondary headship positions in their careers in teaching. The chapter demonstrates gender differences in the experience of headship, both in the process of *becoming* a headteacher and in the everyday experiences of *being* a head. Such difficulties seem to stem from women's minority position in management in schools. In Chapter 12 Dunlap considers how perceptions of gender interact with women's career development in university administration. She demonstrates how the different perceptions we have of male and female administrators stem from gender differences in our imbedded concepts of power and authority and she discusses the implications of such perceptions for women's careers in management and administration. In Chapter 13 Ashburner also considers the management theme, in this case in respect of women's careers in building societies. She examines the promotion policies and processes within building societies where career ladders into management remain rife with indirect discrimination. She examines the particular problems faced by women who aim for management careers and suggests a redefinition of the concept of career as a way of increasing opportunities for both women and men as well as expanding the productive potential of organisations.

In Chapter 14, Allison and Pascall consider midwifery as still predominantly *the* women's profession. Their chapter examines to what extent career *is* the issue for women midwives and to what extent professional autonomy and competition (and the significance of gender in that competition) have overwhelmed the issue of career. Allison and Pascall consider recent recommendations for change in respect of the professional autonomy of midwives but they warn that improved status may have other consequences. The evidence of other women's professions is that increased autonomy and improved status will draw men into the hierarchy, particularly at the higher levels.

CHAPTER 8

Women's careers in academic science: achievement and recognition

MICHAEL KING

The evidence enabling comparisons to be made between men's and women's careers in academic science is patchy, but what systematic data there are point to a consistent pattern that appears to run through different scientific fields and across national boundaries. Women who become academic scientists tend to achieve less than the men who work alongside them, win less recognition, earn less, and find their way less often into positions of prestige, authority and influence at the top of the profession. Why is this? Why are women under-represented in the scientific elite, and why, at all levels in the scientific community, do their careers tend to lag behind those of men?

An obvious way of approaching this issue is to start from an under-standing of the ways in which scientific careers are made – how scientific achievement is turned into career success. The main purpose of this chapter is to discuss one highly influential and productive charac-terisation of these processes of career building in academic science, and to show how this approach sets about mapping careers and explaining why women tend to have less success than men.

The approach I have chosen to examine is that of the 'Columbia School' of sociologists whose empirical surveys of scientific careers have been inspired by the now classic account of how the scientific community works, developed originally by Robert Merton – the long-time professor of sociology at Columbia University. These studies gather information on career patterns and then, with the help of Merton's sociology, develop a model of the career building process in the scientific community which explains how these patterns are gener-ated.

I have concentrated on a central aspect of career building: the ways in which individuals make a reputation for themselves as scientists. In the second part of the chapter, I discuss the biography of a dis-tinguished woman scientist which suggests that models of the kind put forward by the Columbia School sociologists fail to capture some of the complexities of the process by which scientific reputations are made. In academic science, of all fields of work, one might expect reputation to be a faithful reflection of actual achievement. But it appears that even highly productive women scientists face special difficulties in winning recognition in their own right as creative research workers and in gaining an authoritative voice in their disciplines. Given that an individual reputation is a crucial resource in making a career, this helps to explain why they tend to enjoy less success than do men with no better research records.

Reputation and career building in academic science

The data collected by the Columbia School sociologists on scientific careers is presented in a form associated with the 'status attainment' approach to the study of career mobility. Studies of this kind, undertaken in the main by American sociologists, set out to identify the social and personal characteristics that tend to take an individual down one career path rather than another. The aim is to estimate the relative causal weights of the different characteristics that shape individual careers, and in particular to establish whether achieved statuses (such as education and occupational history) outweigh ascribed statuses (family background, race, sex, age) as initial or continuing influences on their development, and thus reach a judgment as to how open a given occupational structure is to talent.

The Columbia School sociologists have collected information of this kind for samples of American scientists working in a variety of disciplines who began their careers in American universities between the mid-1950s and the early 1970s – for example, chemists who obtained PhDs between 1955 and 1961 (Reskin 1978); biologists, chemists, psychologists and sociologists awarded PhDs in 1957–8 (Cole 1987); and astronomers, chemists, biochemists, geologists, mathematicians and physicists obtaining PhDs in 1969–70 (Cole and Zuckerman 1984). The fullest analysis of the results of these studies is given in Jonathan Cole's *Fair Science* (1987). This book presents a general model of career building in academic science which represents the process as being governed by the following principles:

1. The main driving force behind a scientific career is research performance. The chosen indicators of career progression – the academic rank scientists hold, the prestige of the departments in which they work and the number of honorific awards (meritorious fellowships, medals, prizes, and other marks of professional esteem) they have received – are all strongly associated with scientists' publication records. However, because promotion up the academic hierarchy is affected by such ascriptive considerations as age, seniority and length of service, it is less tightly tied to research productivity than are the other two dimensions of career progression.

2. The momentum of an individual's career is sustained by building up a personal reputation. Reputation is also closely linked to research performance. It acts as a kind of flywheel, storing the

recognition accorded the individual's work and transforming it into upward career momentum.

3. The processes of reputation and career building are affected by feedback mechanisms which ensure that reputations, promotions and awards won in recognition of past research performance bring fresh research opportunities that promote further activity and achievement (Cole 1987: 125). Thus all the different forms of formal recognition of research achievement – honours, promotion, affiliation to a prestigious department – are mutually reinforcing and, both collectively and severally, work back to promote individual productivity and to enhance personal reputation.

4. The effect of this feedback process is to fan out of careers in academic science, progressively widening the gap between success and mere survival. Scientific careers are thus governed by what Merton has called the principle of cumulating advantage – or cumulating disadvantage (Merton 1988: 606). Initial advantages in personal capability, training and academic location promote early productivity and so trigger off a flow of rewards which add to the advantages enjoyed by successful scientists and increase their chances of more success.

At the centre of this simple model of career building in science is the proposition that the linkages between research achievement and career progression are generated by acts of recognition. But it needs to be stressed that this interpretation of the way opportunities and rewards are allocated in academic science is not dictated by the career data itself. Path or causal chain analysis (Pawson 1978) of the data does nothing more than establish statistical connections between indicators of career progression and the personal characteristics and previous histories of individuals who enjoy more or less success. It tells us nothing about the social processes that are responsible for producing these statistical relationships. Thus the notion that in the case of scientific careers they are produced by a *recognition system* that turns research achievements into the symbolic and material rewards which constitute success comes from elsewhere. As has already been indicated, it is derived from Robert Merton's account of the functioning of the scientific community, to which we must now turn.

Recognition in the scientific community

Merton (1957) sees science as a circumscribable intellectual and social enterprise which is set apart from other human activities and pursued under a unique set of procedural rules enforced within a uniquely constituted social formation, the scientific community. It is as members of this community that men and women participate in science, contribute to the advance of scientific knowledge, and make their reputations as scientists. According to Merton, the operation of the scientific community's recognition system is dependent on a crucial component of its normative structure, namely its rules of intellectual property: the complex of norms that define the rights that scientists have in the results of their own work. The scientific community practices a form of intellectual 'communism' – the knowledge its members produce is not individually owned but is held in common. Scientists who make original contributions establish property rights in their discoveries only by publishing them and thus adding them to the common stock of certified knowledge on which other scientists are free to draw. Thus, paradoxically, the discoverer's individual right to a discovery only comes into being when it is made the common property of the scientific community (O'Neill 1990). The right that is instituted in this way takes the form of an entitlement to recognition (through citation in the first instance) by those who make use of a scientist's ideas. Recognition here means something more than a straightforward acknowledgement of the fact that a particular scientist was responsible for a particular discovery. In a community that is constituted by ethical as well as technical imperatives, it has a moral or social dimension. It involves a collective acknowledgement that, in making the discovery, the scientist has lived up to the demands of the scientific role: 'To have recognition in this sense is to be the object of moral respect on the part of others whose opinion is valued' (Parsons 1954: 58). Thus, although property rights in scientific discoveries are not, as Merton describes them, a direct source of power or profit they bring the social esteem (the 'reputational capital') that legitimates claims to positions of influence and authority in the scientific community.

Two further features of Merton's account of the scientific community need to be noted. First is his presupposition that it measures the cognitive value of scientific work objectively against '*pre-established impersonal criteria*: consonance with observation and with previously confirmed knowledge' (Merton 1957: 553). The recognition system Merton describes converts this hard coin of cognitive worth into the softer currency of social prestige: into what Merton calls 'pellets of peer recognition' which 'aggregate into reputational wealth' (Merton 1988). The scientific community is thus on a reputational gold standard: scientific reputations are not conjured out of the air simply by the acclaim of others but reflect real achievement, measured by objective standards. Secondly, the scientific community only rewards originality: recognition for objectively validated discoveries is reserved exclusively for the scientists who are first to publish them. This makes science intensely competitive. It gives great urgency to scientific work and encourages an active concern with priority, with getting discoveries published and claims of authorship fully acknowledged. This preoccupation with gaining recognition is,

Merton argues, entirely normal in science. Indeed, it testifies to the strength of the community's institutional imperatives. At the same time, the preoccupation with originality creates pressure to out-distance one's competitors by making premature, poorly grounded or fraudulent claims. However, given that knowledge claims come under the scrutiny not, as in other professions, of a lay audience or clientele, but of a scientist's immediate colleagues and that their worth is measured against objective standards, deviant careers built on spurious claims are likely to be short-lived. The whole scientific community is geared to recording, recognising and rewarding real achievement and discounting insecure claims. This being the case, there is only a narrow and clearly marked path for all scientists to follow. The only legitimate way to advance in science is by building a personal reputation for doing original work whose worth is recognised by a circle of peers who are uniquely competent to evaluate it.

In the view of the Columbia School sociologists, the close linkage between research performance and individual reputation can be explained by assuming that the scientific community works in the way Merton describes. Further, to the extent that the academic system – the complex of institutions that allocate research opportunities and career rewards – takes its cue from the scientific community, the careers of academic scientists will be propelled forward by converting accumulated reputational wealth into institutional position.

Women in academic science

One of the principal findings of the Columbia School surveys is that good scientific careers are built on foundations that are laid at the point of entry into professional life: scientists who start well by taking their professional 'entry qualification', the PhD, at one of the small number of high prestige graduate schools (which tend to recruit the students with the greatest natural aptitude, at least as measured by IQ) have a greater chance of being given a post-doctoral fellowship in a strong research department, and this in turn increases their chance of being offered, comparatively early in their working lives, a position from which a successful career can be launched – namely, a tenured post at a premier research university. The surveys also show that men and women have the same chance of gaining PhDs from the leading graduate schools. In this sense they start their careers on level terms. But thereafter all women, including those who start well, tend to progress less fast and go less far than their male counterparts. They tend to be employed for significant periods in a succession of unestablished posts, to take longer than men to get a tenured position and, once on the academic ladder, to be promoted more slowly. Those women who do secure tenured positions at the same sort of age as the more successful of their male contemporaries, and who have subsequently been promoted at the same rate and to the same levels in the academic hierarchy, tend either to have taken up positions in lower prestige institutions or to be working in less prestigious fields. Thus it appears that most women have to make a trade-off between the different dimensions of success measured in the status attainment studies: working in high prestige fields and at high prestige institutions reduces their chances of academic promotion; starting in lower prestige disciplines or moving to lower prestige institutions increases their chance of progression up the academic ladder, but at the cost of sacrificing the research opportunities and status rewards that come from being in an elite department and working in the most highly regarded disciplines.

If we accept the Columbia School account of the workings of the recognition system in science there are three alternative ways in which these differences between men's and women's careers in science can be explained. First, it may be that women do not match the achievements of men, they are (for whatever reason) simply less productive than their male colleagues and this lower productivity comes to be reflected in lower levels of recognition and external reward. Alternatively, academic institutions may discriminate, whether knowingly or unknowingly, against women and be slower to reward their achievements with jobs, promotions, honours, and research grants. Or, thirdly, it may be that women find it more difficult to build personal reputations, to accumulate the 'reputational capital' which, as we have seen, is needed to propel their careers along an upward trajectory.

To begin with the questions of productivity and discrimination, Cole cites evidence to show that from the outset of their careers women scientists are on average significantly less productive than men with the same educational background (Cole and Zukerman 1984). He further contends that the career surveys demonstrate that men and women with the same publication records have virtually the same chance of being appointed to posts in high quality departments and of receiving scientific awards and honours. Thus, according to Cole, if differences in productivity are allowed for, the only significant career difference that remains relates to promotion: once in post women tend to climb the academic ladder more slowly than do men with similar publication records. He argues that this last remaining difference occurs largely because academic promotion is, as we have noted before, less closely related to productivity than are the other dimensions of career progression. The fact that advancement up the academic hierarchy is governed as much by length of service and seniority as by performance works to the disadvantage of women. They experience voluntary and involuntary career breaks more often and for longer periods than do men and so take longer to accumulate the years of service that are needed to be considered for tenure or for promotion to higher grades. Thus in Cole's view the resort to these non-performance criteria for career advancement is the only major way in which the academic system departs from the principle of universality: in all other respects it faithfully institutionalises the governing principles of Merton's ideal scientific community, and operates a recognition system that relates advancement directly to performance. He concludes that academic science is in this sense 'fair': if women are less successful than men it is mainly because they are less productive as research workers (Cole 1987).

If these claims regarding the lower productivity of women are accepted there remains the issue of reputation building: is there a gender bias in the scientific community's recognition system making it more difficult for women to transmute achievement into the personal prestige that fuels career advancement? According to Cole's findings (Cole 1987: 92–142) male scientists in general do have bigger reputations than female scientists: on average their work is known to larger numbers of other scientists and is more highly regarded. But much of this difference, according to Cole's findings, again appears to be attributable to the 'publication gap' between the sexes. The more work scientists publish the more likely it is that they will be both widely known amongst their peers and highly regarded. This being so, women are in the main less well known and less esteemed for their work than men mainly because, on average, they are less productive.

There is however one qualification in the data Cole presents which is particularly significant because it relates to the most productive 25 per cent of scientists. The relatively small proportion of women who are amongst this highly productive elite, and thus match the research records of the top male scientists, tend to be both less widely known and less highly regarded than their male counterparts (1987: 129). It seems, on Cole's own findings, that the recognition system works in a more loose-linked way for women than for men. Women find it more difficult to build personal reputations on the basis of their research achievements, especially, as it happens, when these are of a high order. This relative invisibility of even highly creative women scientists may help to explain why they so rarely find places in the 'inner circle' of the academic community (Zuckerman *et al.* 1991).

Reputation making in science: the case of Rosalind Franklin

At the heart of the Cole-Merton model of reputation building is an economic analogy. According to the model the 'pellets of peer recognition' scientists receive for original work 'aggregate' into 'reputational wealth' (Merton 1988: 620). It is this store of reputational wealth that underwrites their self-identities, confirms their professional authority and fuels their academic careers. In the final part of this chapter I want to use a case study to cast doubt on this notion that reputations are 'system-built'. Rather they are constructed through complex interactions and negotiations among active human beings who are fired by different interests and ambitions and have different material and rhetorical resources at their disposal.

The case I have chosen to examine is that of the British crystallographer Rosalind Franklin who played a key role alongside the Nobel Prize winners James Watson, Francis Crick and Maurice Wilkins in the discovery of the structure of DNA but who was, at least according to her principal biographer Anne Sayre (1975), denied the recognition that her work merited. The bare facts of the story can be briefly told. In April 1953, after two years of collaboration at Cambridge's Cavendish Laboratory, the American biologist James Watson and the English physicist-turned-biologist Francis Crick published a paper in *Nature* proposing a structure for DNA which showed how it could store and transmit genetic information. The same issue of *Nature* included two further papers reporting experimental evidence in support of the Watson-Crick double helix model, gathered by two research groups working at King's College, London, under Maurice Wilkins, another physicist-turned-biologist who had pioneered the British work on DNA, and Rosalind Franklin, who had been brought to King's two years earlier to use her expertise in X-ray diffraction techniques to refine and intensify the experimental work Wilkins had initiated.

As Crick later put it, 'the structure made Crick and Watson' (Stent 1981: 144). They both became famous overnight, and subsequently made highly successful academic careers. In 1962 they shared a Nobel Prize with Wilkins for the discovery. In contrast Rosalind Franklin remained relatively obscure. In the same month as the *Nature* papers were published she moved from King's to Birkbeck College to do X-ray work on viruses, and stayed there as a research fellow until her death from cancer in 1958, at the age of thirty-seven. She received little recognition in her lifetime for her part in solving the DNA structure – and some years after her death, when the extent of her achievement had become clearer, it was still thought apposite to call a BBC Radio 3 programme on her life and work *The Dark Lady of DNA*.

In deciding whether Franklin was justly treated there are a number of different points at issue. First, there are matters of fact to be established relating to the nature of the discovery, how it was made and Franklin's role in it. Secondly, the question of whether she received the recognition that was her due (in terms, say, of the property laws that Merton sought to codify) has to be answered. Beyond this, if it is shown that her work was not properly recognised, it has to be decided why this was so, and whether the 'case' provides evidence that the recognition system in science operates in a way that tends to disadvantage women and diminish their professional reputations.

It is instructive to compare the way these issues are addressed in two rival accounts of the discovery: Watson's own attempt in *The Double Helix* (1968) to recall, as he puts it, 'the way I saw things then, in 1951–1953: the ideas, the people, and myself' (Stent 1981: 3 – all quotations below are from this edition), and Anne Sayre's subsequent effort to set the record straight, to show that Watson had in his book systematically distorted both events and personalities in an attempt, as she sees it, to conceal the fact that he and Crick had 'robbed' Rosalind Franklin – had come by her results improperly, made use of them without her knowledge, and failed to ensure that she was given the recognition that was her due. *The Double Helix*, she contends, inadvertently tells how the robbery was done and shows why it escaped detection.

First, the two books give very different accounts of the discovery and of Franklin's contribution to it. In a review of *The Double Helix*, Sir Peter Medawar emphasised the totality of Watson and Crick's achievement:

The great thing about their discovery was its completeness, its air of finality. If Watson and Crick had been seen groping towards an answer; if they had published a partly right solution and had been obliged to follow with corrections and glosses, some of them made by other people; if the solution had come out piecemeal instead of in a blaze of understanding: then, it would still have been a great episode in biological history but something more in the common run of things; something splendidly well done, but not done in the grand romantic manner.

(Stent 1981: 218)

This is very much in the spirit of Watson's own account. He and Crick in combination had had the breadth of vision – chemical, crystallographic, biological – and the methodological daring to solve the whole structure and show how it could perform its genetic function. Others, most notably Franklin, had contributed pieces to the jigsaw, admittedly crucial pieces, but still only pieces. Only Watson and Crick had put the whole thing together and shared in the moment of discovery.

Watson, in line with this interpretation, is careful to meet his scientific obligations by spelling out precisely what it was they had learnt from Franklin's work. In particular he describes the occasion when Wilkins had, without Franklin's knowledge, showed him the X-ray photograph of DNA that she was to publish in her *Nature* paper. 'The instant I saw the picture my mouth fell open and my pulse began to race.' The image could only have been made by a helical structure and on 'mere inspection ... gave several of the vital helical parameters' (1981: 98–9). Watson does not attempt to play down the importance of seeing this photograph. It had triggered off his second, and eventually successful, bout of model building. Nonetheless the general implication of his account is clear: Franklin's role had been a secondary one which was appropriately mirrored in the way their discovery and her supporting evidence had been published in *Nature*.

In contrast Sayre contends that the structure was in fact (*pace* Medawar) worked out 'piecemeal' – although Crick and Watson had chosen to announce it wholesale. Credit for the discovery ought to have been shared out amongst all those who contributed parts to the final construction: including of course Franklin, whose contributions stood on a level with Crick and Watson's, and who, unknown to them, was working slowly and patiently towards the solution. Instead Watson and Crick had claimed, and been awarded, credit for the whole thing. If they had wanted to announce the solution 'in the grand romantic manner', as a single achievement, they should have made an offer of co-authorship to Franklin (and also presumably to Wilkins) – otherwise they should have been satisfied with publishing a paper setting out the features of the structure they had discovered for themselves and allowed the rest of it to emerge 'unromantically', bit by bit, as others published papers identifying other elements and were accordingly given credit for their contributions. Sayre reads *The Double Helix* as 'a long and subtle rationalisation' of this demotion of Franklin from the status of co-discover to that of an unwitting supplier of some of the essential raw materials out of which the discovery was made and, after the event, a willing provider of confirming evidence for the Watson-Crick structure.

Watson and Sayre give credibility to their interpretations of Franklin's contribution to the discovery in identical ways: they both seek to demonstrate that the role she played was consistent with her commitment to a research style, a way of doing science, that reflected her particular intellectual powers and personality. Thus 'Rosy', as Watson calls her throughout his book, is portrayed in such a way as to make it impossible to believe that she could have pulled off an achievement 'in the grand romantic manner'. Watson and Crick had solved the helical structure intuitively, by building 'tinker toy' models. 'Rosy' was, Watson claims, stubbornly antihelical and regarded model building as frivolous and unprofessional. All her efforts were devoted to generating hard data by using orthodox crystallographic techniques. She was a highly skilled experimentalist, 'a good brain' (1981: 15), but lacked theoretical vision. She may have been, to use another of Medawar's phrases, 'groping towards an answer' but her work was 'data-driven'; she did not have the intellectual daring to make the imaginative leap that would have released her from her 'self-made anti-helical trap' (1981: 124) and taken her all the way to the double helix.

Watson's narrative is laced with references to 'Rosy's' appearance, manner and behaviour. As Watson portrays her, 'Rosy' had strong, but not unattractive features, wore no lipstick, had straight black hair, and dressed 'with all the imagination of English blue-stocking adolescents' (1981: 14). She lacked small talk. At a colloquium Watson attended she delivered her paper in a 'quick, nervous style', speaking without 'a trace of warmth or frivolity in her words' (1981: 43–4) and intimidating her audience into virtual silence. Generally, she was barely able to control her emotions, was prey to 'belligerent moods', sometimes 'positively aggressive' (1981: 59) and, on one occasion, 'in hot anger' appeared to be about to strike Watson (1981: 96). Her relations with Wilkins were impossible. She wanted him out of the DNA work altogether, obstructing his efforts to mobilise the King's team, refusing to discuss her results and rejecting all his attempts at reconciliation. The only person she seemed to get on with was her easy-going research student, Raymond Gosling.

It would be a mistake to suppose that Watson gives these personal details simply to add a little colour to his narrative. In his Preface he emphasises the strength of the association between personality and research style. As he describes them, 'Rosy's' methodological commitments were not dictated by the demands of the problem she was seeking to solve. They were rooted in her character: and it was her compulsive commitment to an inappropriate methodology and not Watson's opportunistic disregard for the proprieties of the recognition system that stood between her and a full share in the scientific prize of the century.

Sayre (1975) challenges this account of Franklin's scientific persona at every point. 'Rosalind' (as Sayre calls her) was not dogmatically antihelical – very early in her work she had thought it likely that DNA had a helical structure, and had only subsequently gone through an antihelical phase while she was concentrating her attention on the more difficult to read and less obviously helical photographs of the so-called 'A form' of DNA. Nor was she set against model building or obsessively committed to X-ray techniques. Rather, she had a pragmatic attitude to research techniques, being prepared to use whatever method promised to bring results. Finally, it was quite untrue that she lacked the theoretical vision to interpret her own results; indeed the reason why she had accepted the Watson–Crick model as soon as she saw it was not because, as Watson alleges, her own evidence was beginning to force her out of her antihelical prejudices, but because she had already started to think again in helical terms and was (as has since become clear) very close to working out the structure for herself.

Watson's account of 'Rosalind's' personality is, Sayre contends, as distorted as his account of her science. 'Rosy' is pure fiction: a character invented to play the 'wicked fairy' (1975: 22) to his 'lovable rogue' (1975: 194). Even the nickname 'Rosy' was an invention: '[it] was never used by any friend and certainly by no one to her face' (1975: 19); as indeed was virtually everything that Watson had to say about her appearance and manner. Watson did not draw 'Rosy' from life, but lifted her straight from social mythology: 'She was the perfect, unadulterated stereotype of the unattractive, dowdy, rigid, aggressive, overbearing, steely, "unfeminine" bluestocking, the female grotesque we have all been taught either to fear or despise' (1975: 21).

In essence, Sayre's case against Watson is that this transformation of 'Rosalind' into 'Rosy' was not an innocent misreading of her character, nor was it simply a reflection of a general prejudice on his part against bright women. Rather it was (as Sayre would have it) 'purposeful' (1975: 21). Watson robbed Rosalind of her true character to conceal another robbery. In the guise of 'Rosy', Rosalind Franklin simply could not be thought of as a serious contender in the race for DNA, still less as a co-discoverer of its structure. She was temperamentally too aggressive and too touchy to establish productive working relations with others and too compulsively committed to an inappropriate research methodology to find her own way to a solution.

Reputation building as story telling

The Sayre-Watson exchange gives us an unusual insight into the process of reputation building. It is plainly a process whose character is not caught, or at least not fully caught, by the Cole-Merton 'economic' model. Making a reputation involves more than publishing scientific papers, standing back, and waiting for the 'payment' to which, under the norms of scientific property, one is entitled. Reputations have to be made, they do not make themselves. Scientists, their friends and colleagues, their competitors and critics are all involved in the process of construction during which claims about a scientist's character, creative powers and achievements are made, examined, debated, contested, and confirmed or denied. The debate is not often conducted in books, but one can assume that it is constantly going on in the informal networks that support the day-to-day practice of science. It calls into play far more evidence than is contained in the published record and it results in the creation of a reputation that is a reflection not only of the individual's contributions to that record but of the whole professional persona with which the scientist has been endowed. The creation of the scientist as a character in this sense is a narrative, story-telling process. It forms a distinctive genre, with its own conventions and rules of composition. As the exchange between Watson and Sayre shows, it permits the story-tellers to draw on a wide range of cultural resources – a gallery of ready-made characters from popular mythology as well as from scientific folklore (which has its own hagiography and demonology).

Thus reputations are very far from being straightforward reflections of scientific achievement. They are complex cultural constructs. The utterly impersonal 'R. E. Franklin' whose unpublished work is acknowledged in the paper by 'J. D. Watson and F. H. C. Crick', and the regendered 'Rosalind E. Franklin', joint author with 'R. G. Gosling' of a supporting paper, both provide data for a collective biography aimed at establishing statistical linkages between publication records and reputations – in the attenuated sense that Cole gives this latter term. But it is by studying the transformation – whether through the medium of individual biography or of gossip among scientific colleagues – of these ghostly presences into the more substantial figures like 'Rosy' (supplier of indispensible data, but compulsive, volatile, misguided and, in the end, sadly limited) or 'Rosalind' (a genuinely creative experimental scientist) that we can get an understanding of how reputations in a fuller sense of the term are made and unmade.

If we look at reputations as being built up in this way – by telling stories that convey the character, particular competencies and achievements of scientists, rather than by counting and assessing the worth of their publications – we can perhaps begin to see why women, particularly highly productive women, find it more difficult to turn 'research productivity' into 'reputational capital'. As the case of Franklin amply illustrates, given the nature of the rhetorical resources that our culture puts at the disposal of scientific storytellers, women scientists are more likely to have their reputations talked down, towards 'Rosy', rather than up, towards (equally mythologised) 'Rosalind'.

References

Cole, J. R. (1987) *Fair Science: Women in the Scientific Community*, New York: Columbia University Press (originally published 1979).

Cole, J. R. and Zuckerman, H. (1984) 'The productivity puzzle: persistance and change in patterns of publication of men and women scientists', in M. W. Steinkamp and M. L. Maehr (eds) *Advances in Motivation and Achievement*, **2**, Greenwich, Connecticut: JAI Press.

Merton, R. K. (1957) 'Science and democratic social structure', in *Social Theory and Social Structure*, Chicago: Free Press.

Merton, R. K. (1988) 'The Matthew effect in science II: cumulative advantage and the symbolism of intellectual property', *Isis*, **79**: 606–23.

O'Neill, J. (1990) 'Property in science and the market', *Monist*, **73**(4): 601–20.

Parsons, T. (1954) *Essays in Sociological Theory*, Chicago: Free Press.

Pawson, R. (1978) 'Empiricist explanatory strategies: the case of causal modelling', *Sociological Review*, new series, **26**: 613–45.

Reskin, B. (1978) 'Scientific productivity, sex, and location in the Institution of Science', *American Journal of Sociology*, **83**: 1235–43.

Sayre, A. (1975) *Rosalind Franklin and DNA*, New York: W. W. Norton.

Stent, G. S. (ed.) (1981) *James D. Watson, the Double Helix: A Personal Account of the Discovery of DNA*, reprinted in a new critical edition, London: Weidenfeld & Nicolson (originally published 1968).

Zuckerman, H., Cole, J. R. and Bruer, J. T. (eds) (1991) *The Outer Circle: Women in the Scientific Community*, New York: W. W. Norton.

CHAPTER 9

Whose service is perfect freedom: women's careers in the Church of England

ALAN ALDRIDGE

In 1986, eleven years after the Sex Discrimination Act – from the provisions of which religious organisations were exempted – the Church of England opened the clerical profession to women. Hundreds of women who had previously served as deaconesses presented themselves for ordination as deacon. The Church now has over a thousand women serving in the diaconate: a rich resource of human capital for the professional ministry of the Church.

For the women themselves, ordination as deacon has been both momentous and frustrating. Whereas deaconesses were technically lay people, women deacons are unequivocally clergy. Women's divine vocation to serve the Church in Holy Orders has been recognised. They wear the symbols of clerical status – black cassock and clerical collar – and have the title 'Reverend'. Yet they cannot, at the time of writing, be ordained priest, and so are not permitted to perform the central liturgical functions which distinguish the profession and around which the worshipping life of the community revolves.

For the Church, women deacons present a problem. Since they are unable to celebrate the Eucharist – the most important ritual act in most Anglican parishes – deacons are less economically efficient than priests. By the end of 1989, there were 63 women deacons in pastoral charge of a congregation (Advisory Council for the Church's Ministry 1991: 17). Despite their position of responsibility, these women are dependent on priests to 'help' with the central act of corporate worship, a limitation which generates profound role problems.

Men almost invariably remain deacons for one year before progressing to priesthood; women are left behind with embarrassing rapidity. For centuries, the diaconate has been no more than a brief probationary period before men move one step up the hierarchy. There is clear evidence, to be discussed later in this chapter, that ordination to the diaconate has not diminished but intensified women's aspiration to become priests. In this uneasy situation, the Church of England faces the challenge of constructing satisfying careers for women.

On Wednesday 11 November 1992, the General Synod of the

Church of England voted in favour of the ordination of women to the priesthood. The approval of both Houses of Parliament will be legally required before the Royal Assent is granted. The Parliamentary timetable is open to challenge, negotiation and filibustering. At the time of writing it appears unlikely that ordinations will take place before the summer of 1994. For reasons to be examined in what follows, it is emphatically not the case that women's career aspirations will be met as soon as the priesthood is opened to them.

Sacred and profane in the Church of England

To understand the dynamics of the current crisis, it is necessary to focus on the fundamental duality of the Church and of discourse within it. On the one hand, the Church is a social organisation: a bureaucracy, governed by rational-legal principles, goal-oriented, developing and marketing goods and services to paying clients in a competitive society where resources are scarce. On the other hand, the Church is the antithesis of a social organisation: it is a sacred entity, governed by tradition and by its charismatic birthright, value-oriented, freely offering salvation to humanity through the sacraments entrusted to its stewardship. As a social organisation, the Church is staffed by salaried officials whose career development is an essential component of the efficient running of the enterprise. As a sacred entity, the Church is served by women and men whose divine vocation entails selfless purity of motive heedless of extrinsic reward.

To characterise the Church as a social organisation is to provoke the indignation of the faithful and the mockery of the faithless. Staff appraisal, personal action plans, ambition, promotion, career: these are not the terms in which the Church typically elaborates its personnel policies. The preferred realm of discourse is the sacred. In a classic sociological study, Kenneth Thompson (1970) analysed the Church's problems in confronting the imperatives of bureaucracy; reforming the structures of the Church on rational-legal lines has been arduous and hotly contested. Concluding his examination of the creation in 1919 of the Church Assembly, the precursor of the modern General Synod, Thompson writes:

Instrumental efficiency could best be attained by the fullest use of the criteria of formal rationality, but this had to be balanced against the need to follow a substantive rationality which took account of the ultimate goals and values of the institution. This, in turn, posed difficulties in a religious body which possessed goals and values which transcended mundane considerations; the means employed to further these could not be evaluated for their effectiveness by logico-experimental criteria. ... The bureaucratic forms of organisation appeared to symbolise principles and values inappropriate for a religious body, and those who exercised power in such an organisation were often denied a legitimate authority.

(Thompson 1970: 238)

In the Church today, there is widespread feeling, particularly among the clergy, that the General Synod's combination of formal democratic procedures and bureaucratic machinery is unfitting to a sacred theocratic organisation whose spiritual leadership should properly be the responsibility of bishops.

For many in the Church, not least clergymen, the religious professional is envisaged and celebrated as a free-booting idiosyncratic solo practitioner, not a salaried employee of the diocesan bureaucracy (Russell 1980, Towler and Coxon 1979). Carrying the argument a step further, Towler (1969: 449) argued that 'the Ministry cannot be considered as an occupation, as we currently understand that concept'. The fundamental point for Towler is that, unlike membership of occupational groups and especially professions, clerical status is ascribed rather than achieved:

The clergyman is an odd-man out in any sociological analysis of his position. He has a social position, but it is ascribed; it is comparable to that of a Knight of the Bath, or Earl or Doctor of Letters, each of which was relevant to the structure of an ascription-oriented society, but fundamentally irrelevant to contemporary social structure.

(Towler 1969: 448–9)

The contrast between the sacred and profane realms of discourse is shown in two reports commissioned by the Church of England: *Deacons in the Ministry of the Church* (House of Bishops of the General Synod of the Church of England 1988) and *Deacons Now* (Advisory Council for the Church's Ministry 1991).

It is instructive to compare the conclusions drawn by these two reports. First, *Deacons in the Ministry of the Church*:

At the end of this Report the recommendation is made that the Church of England make provision for, and encourage, men and women to serve in an ordained distinctive diaconate.

This conclusion is drawn from a consideration of scripture, tradition and contemporary experience which would seem to complement and affirm one another. Furthermore, the future ministry of the Church will be greatly enriched by the restoration of a diaconate after the model and pattern of Christ's diaconate. He came 'not to be served but to serve, and to give his life as a ransom for many' (Mark 10.45), to provide an example and support for the diaconal ministry of all – laity, presbyters and bishops. All who follow him are called to be 'servants for Jesus' sake' (2 Cor. 4.5).

The conclusions of *Deacons Now* are in a different genre:

The Church should be greatly encouraged by the very high level of positive impact which ordained women have had amongst congregations and in the local community. This Report underlines the significant contributions which are being made by many women of high calibre in the ordained ministry of the Church. We consider that the Guidelines provided in this Report are valid as an urgent theological and practical response to present circumstances, and as a basis for the future, irrespective of whether or not women are to be ordained to the priesthood.

We hope that the Guidelines for Dioceses and recommendations will assist dioceses in developing the ministry of ordained women for the benefit of the Church and of the deacons themselves.

Deacons in the Ministry of the Church is situated at the sacred pole. The report's discourse is conspicuously theological. Following customary Anglican methodology, its theology draws on three resources: Bible, Church tradition, and reflection on experience. The report is studded with references to the Christian scriptures. It contains an historical conspectus of the unfolding of the diaconate in the traditions of the Church of England, the Anglican communion worldwide, and in other Churches. The theological concept of *diakonia* – usually translated as 'service' – is frequently deployed and receives extended consideration. The report also dwells on what it calls 'the experience of the Church'. Deacons themselves were not, however, surveyed: it is, revealingly, not *their* experience which matters. The objective ontology of diaconate and priesthood is ultimately more important than the subjective feelings of deacons and priests.

Career is not treated in the report. What are described as 'some practical issues' – including the selection and training of deacons, their salaries, their relations with others in the hierarchy, and transfers to priesthood – are dealt with summarily in two of the report's one hundred and forty-four pages. The question of career is effectively suppressed.

Conversely, the paramount concern in *Deacons Now* is the career development of women serving as deacons. Crucial employment issues are highlighted: salaries, expenses, housing, maternity leave, pension entitlements. Detailed recommendations are made, and the Church of England and its constituent dioceses are urged to take seriously their responsibilities as employers.

The tone is comparatively secular: there are, for example, no citations of Biblical authority. The terms of reference given to the working party that produced the report deliberately excluded discussion of ordination of women to the priesthood. The report therefore displays a studied agnosticism on women priests; it argues that, whether or not the Church opens the priesthood to women, the challenge of women's career development is and will continue to be a matter of urgent importance.

Even so, it is very telling that the report does not ignore theology altogether. To have done so would have left the report open to the fatal charge of ignoring the Church's sacred mission. The working party's remit was not wholly secular, since it included a request 'to examine the theological, legal and practical reasons for placing them [women deacons] in senior posts'. Avoiding definitive theological pronouncements, the report maintains (1991: 45) that 'a theology can be provided which is compatible with the appointment of deacons to posts of senior responsibility'. At this point, *Deacons Now* refers to *Deacons in the Ministry of the Church*, arguing that the importance of

diaconal ministry calls for full incorporation of the principle of diaconate in the corporate structures and hierarchy of the Church.

The duality of the Church as sacred and profane may be represented as a set of binary oppositions.

Sacred	*Profane*	
Vocation	Ambition	
Virtue	Utility	} IDENTITY
Ontology	Function	
Calling	Occupation	
Ministry	Career	} PROFESSION
Voluntary principle	Paid employment	
Theology	Management science	
Tradition & charisma	Rational-legality	} LEGITIMATION
Mystical union	Bureaucracy	

In the schema above I have distinguished three levels at which
sacred and profane discourse operate: identity, profession and legitimation. Career has a critical location at the interface between individual identity and corporate legitimation.

Sacred discourse, which in the set of binary oppositions is usually
asserted as primary, has profoundly shaped the experience of women
serving as deacons. The impact may be traced at the levels of identity, profession and legitimation.

Identity

In sacred discourse, deacons are defined not by their functions within
the Church and society, but by their being, their ontological status.
They are unable to perform priestly functions not because they lack
talent or professional expertise, but because they are not priests.

A deacon's life is governed by the ideal of *diakonia* – service. The
virtuous qualities required of and attributed to deacons include hu-
mility, selflessness, obedience to authority, self-sacrifice, relative
poverty and unconcern for material rewards.

Profession

At the collective level, the vocation of a deacon is to Holy Orders,
which is a calling rather than an occupation. The Church does not
offer a career, still less a *cursus honorum*, but the opportunity to
exercise a ministry. The fact that so many people – including, as we
shall see later, women deacons – give their time and energy voluntarily, without salary or even reimbursement of expense, is seen not as
exploitation but as liberation.

Legitimation

Sacred discourse is, of course, theological. It is constituted by and appeals to the sacred scriptures, sacred tradition, the charismatic foundation of the faith and the transmission of charisma to the contemporary Church. The Church is not a bureaucratic organisation but a mystical union: the Body of Christ. Theological discourse – even when it applies to women – is largely in the hands of men, principally clergymen and academic theologians.

The dynamics of the dialectic between sacred and profane, and the ascendancy typically claimed by the sacred, is sharply illustrated by the vocation–ambition polarity.

The pre-eminence of the sacred: vocation versus ambition

Paradoxically, as the wider society has become more secular so the churches have become more religious. Processes of social differentiation have stripped away the churches' secondary social functions as educational, judicial and political agencies. Their core function as agencies of salvation remains: to diagnose the human condition in terms of a theodicy of evil and suffering, to offer the prospect of salvation and to provide access to its attainment (Wilson 1982: 27–52).

The distillation of religious institutions to their core religious functions applies at the level of the religious professionals themselves. Thus the public persona of the cleric is more overtly 'religious' than ever before (Martin 1978: 279). The contemporary stereotype of the cleric is of an other-worldly individual, a prayerful, pastorally sensitive man of great personal integrity and minimal worldly *nous*. Such a man is not motivated by material incentives, but called by God.

The modern understanding of the Anglican cleric's role derives from the Evangelical and High Church revivals of the nineteenth century, in both of which a strong professional commitment was prescribed (Crowther 1970, Haig 1984). The clergyman was defined as a sacred person irreversibly set apart by the 'indelibility' of his holy orders (Heeney 1976: 15). The new professionalism was to be cultivated not through reading Classics at Oxford or Cambridge, which were deemed to have become unsuitably secular *milieux* (Chadwick 1970: 504), but through professional training in highly specialised seminaries. The mid-nineteenth century therefore saw the foundation of theological colleges, typically tied to the worshipping life of the cathedrals: Wells, Chichester, Lichfield, Salisbury, Exeter, Gloucester, Lincoln and Ely. Thus the professional formation of the Anglican cleric became differentiated from the social and cultural life of the landed gentry. Hence the development of a professional subculture: 'the rectory culture', the butt of frequent witticisms. As Russell

(1980: 108–10) points out in his study of the development of the clerical profession, the growing preoccupation in the nineteenth century with 'liturgical science', involving scrupulous attention to the minutiae of ceremonial, was crucial to the clergy's attempt to redefine their role in terms of specialist professional priestcraft. Sartorial changes were significant. In the eighteenth century, distinctive clerical apparel had been widely abandoned by Anglican clergy except for formal occasions; by the 1880s the 'Roman' clerical collar had become universal (1980: 235–360).

The growing professionalism was deplored by some traditionalist commentators, who warned of the creation of a clerical 'caste' (Haig 1984: 18–19). This code-word signalled both condemnation of the new professionalism and longing for the old order, in which the clergyman enjoyed as of right a secure position in a stable local community ordered by deference to assigned social status. As Martin says (1978: 281), 'The parson (or "person") might be corrupt, hated, despised or even physically an absentee, but he was not, conceptually, a dispensable adjunct of the social order.' Holy Orders were necessary to social order.

One significant strand in the differentiation of the clerical role has been the emphasis on divine vocation. The intending cleric is required to demonstrate to the satisfaction of Church authorities that he, and now also she, has received a call from God to a particular order of ministry. It was during the nineteenth century that this new emphasis – which is now taken for granted – became prominent. It is seen in the flourishing early and mid-Victorian literature that offered guidance to aspiring and practising clergymen. No longer was the clerical profession presented, as it had been in eighteenth-century guides, as an option to be evaluated by rational weighing of costs and benefits. Calculative secular ambition was treated as wholly inappropriate; purity of motive was demanded. Set before the reader was 'an ideal priestly persona, that of an unworldly gentleman whose moral qualities placed him apart from the society to which he ministered' (Heeney 1976: 7). The clergyman's professional competence was to be built on the foundation of his calling from God.

Vocations for women

If clergymen are required to evince an appropriate sense of calling from God, what of women deacons? The critical factor here is that while the overwhelming majority of people in the Church of England have been eager to affirm women's vocations to the diaconate, many remain sceptical of or opposed to the proposition that God is calling women to be priests. The current focus on diaconate is, therefore, a coded debate about priesthood. Discussion of diaconate often serves as a convenient vehicle for 'bracketing' the problem of ordination of women to the priesthood. Here is the Bishop of Portsmouth, introducing the report *Deacons in the Ministry of the Church* to General Synod on 11 February 1988: 'Let me say at once that the report does not seek to engage in the debate about women in the priesthood, and certainly the recommendation for the recovery of a distinctive diaconate in no way intends that this order should be used to divert or satisfy the aspirations of those who hope to be priests.' In the same vein, the bishop commented in his summing-up that one woman speaker had 'raised the matter of the women deacons and their vocation possibly to the priesthood. I am grateful that this was not the issue that dominated the debate this afternoon; we could have gone down an important by-way on that, but it is not what we are about today.' The question of women's vocations to diaconate or priesthood is thus characterised as a distraction from more important issues.

The bracketing of the issue of ordination of women to the priesthood has been a recurrent feature of Church reports on the future development of the clerical profession. One example is *A Strategy for the Church's Ministry*, a substantial and wide-ranging report prepared by Canon John Tiller. Ordination of women to the priesthood is dealt with in a paragraph (Tiller 1983: 50). Tiller predicts that the priesthood will be opened to women at some time during the period under consideration, i.e. before the year 2023; there is also a broad hint that he would be in favour. He points out, however, that ordination of women priests would not in any material way alter his recommendations. If anything, it might jeopardise their implementation. He warns that a windfall of women priests could tempt the Church to prop up existing patterns of parochial ministry that stand in need of radical reform. So, despite his apparent advocacy of ordination of women to the priesthood, women are seen to be, here as in other Church debates, an awkward and rather distracting problem.

A muted group: women's experience of ministry

Theological reflection on women's ministry has been more abundant than evidence of women's own experience. Women in the Church of England, lay and ordained, have been what Shirley and Edwin Ardener termed a 'muted group' (Ardener 1978: 20*ff*). Their opinions have seldom been sought, and they have not had fora in which to articulate their own experience and perspectives.

Before women were ordained to the diaconate, their muteness was acute. The role of deaconess (Aldridge 1987) was compounded of anomaly, ambiguity and subordination. A deaconess was technically a lay person, licensed not ordained, in Orders but not in Holy Orders. Denied clerical status, deaconesses found most positions of responsibility in the Church closed to them. In the discharge of their day-to-day activities they were entirely dependent on the goodwill of the clergymen with whom they worked. The formal mechanisms of the Church took little account of deaconesses, and informal networks excluded them. Few in number and lacking support groups, they operated as isolated individuals.

In a series of in-depth interviews of a sample of deaconesses in 1985 (Aldridge 1987), I found among many respondents uneasiness and hesitancy in answering questions about their own vocation. In asking whether they felt called to the priesthood I was clearly raising a sensitive matter. One respondent evaded the question by emphasising that her calling was to chaplaincy. Some respondents gave complex replies; thus one who, having confessed at length to her own inadequacies and to emotional problems of menopause, concluded by saying that her reservations were probably 'total rubbish' and that 'as a younger person I would have been able to have coped better'. Others answered pointedly in the counterfactual, for example: 'If I had been a man I would have been a priest.'

Women's entry into the diaconate has contributed to a revolution of rising expectations. My 1989 survey (Aldridge 1991) of women deacons showed that the fundamental change experienced by deaconesses after their ordination as deacon was explicit incorporation into the clerical profession. The anomalies and uncertainties of the role of deaconess had been swept away; in particular, the legal fiction of the deaconess as a lay person was replaced by an unambiguous status in Holy Orders. The title 'Reverend', and the sartorial transfer from the blue cassock to clerical black and the clerical collar, have been of unforeseen significance to women's move into the public arena of clerical professionalism. Most lay people, even active churchgoers, are ignorant of the nice theological distinction between deaconess and woman deacon, and are sometimes unaware that blue is Mary's colour: but they do know a dog collar when they see one. Although some feminists have attacked the clerical collar as a symbol of women's masochistic subordination to patriarchy, my respondents typically saw it, less psychodynamically, as a crucial sign of professional recognition.

Growing confidence in the place of women's professional ministry in the Church of England, and in their own vocations to priesthood, was demonstrated in the replies to my 1989 survey of women deacons in four dioceses, as shown in Table 9.1.

The diaconate has evidently not proved a satisfying terminus to women's professional ministry. This is not surprising, for two main reasons. First, very few men voluntarily remain deacon; almost all move on to priesthood at the first available opportunity, which usually presents itself after one year. Despite the salience of *diakonia* in the sacred discourse of ministry, the diaconate is little more than a probationary period within the promotion structure. A stepping-stone for men but an impasse for women: only sacred discourse has

Table 9.1 Opinions of women deacons on ordination of women to the priesthood

	Yes	No	Uncertain
Are you in favour of the ordination of women to the priesthood?	99	0	1
Do you feel yourself called to the priesthood?	86	4	7
If the Church of England opens the priesthood to women in the near future, will you seek to go forward as a candidate for ordination?	82	3	13

	Strongly agree	Agree	Disagree	Strongly disagree
There are no valid theological objections to the ordination of women to the priesthood	89	11	0	0
The time is not ripe for the Church of England to ordain women to the priesthood	4	11	30	54

Percentage figures, n = 71.

protected the Church from anti-discrimination legislation. Second, deacons are defined by what they cannot do, by the priestly functions – celebration, pronouncing blessings and absolution – denied to them. Why remain a deacon if one could be a priest?

In my survey of women deacons, I asked whether former deaconesses had experienced significant changes in their ministry following ordination to the diaconate. Table 9.2 shows the pattern of response.

Table 9.2 Changes experienced by former deaconesses after ordination as deacon

	Much better	A little better	As before	A little worse	Much worse
Relations with male clergy	8	25	60	8	0
Relations with lay people	22	19	57	2	0
Involvement in corporate worship	15	19	57	9	0
Involvement in decision-making with other clergy	11	6	80	4	0
The resources provided	6	8	85	2	0

Percentage figures, n = 54.

The general pattern is that, following ordination as deacon, very few women find their position has deteriorated; some find it improved, but for the majority it is effectively unaltered. Women typically experience a more prominent involvement in corporate worship, and relations with fellow clergy and lay people improve. Equally striking is the relatively static position with regard to women's involvement in professional decision-making, and in the level of resources provided to support their work.

The national survey conducted for *Deacons Now* (Advisory Council for the Church's Ministry 1991: 87–8) found that, of the 999 women serving as deacons at the end of 1989, only 51 per cent were in receipt of a full stipend paid by the Church. Non-Church agencies paid the stipend of 8 per cent; 9 per cent received a part stipend or honorarium. This leaves 32 per cent in receipt of no stipend at all. Here is the material aspect of the sacred ideal of diaconal service. There appears to have been only a slight change since the opening of the diaconate to women; *Deacons in the Ministry of the Church* found that, of the 745 deaconesses identified in its survey in February 1987, 40 per cent were non-stipendary.

Since they are a muted group, it is difficult to know how many women are unhappy with their level of remuneration. On the one hand, the ideal of selfless giving should not be lightly dismissed as an exploitative sham, unless we are to count all religious ideals as ideology or false consciousness. On the other hand, given that deacons are less useful to the Church than priests, it is not surprising that overall they are paid less. One feature of the Church that distinguishes it from the twentieth-century ideal-type profession is that so many of its practitioners are unpaid volunteers. Other professions practice exploitation more covertly – through support staff, ancillaries, and of course housewives.

Deconstructing the sacred

My argument so far has turned on a set of binary oppositions between sacred and profane elements in the Church of England. Far from seeking to reify these polarities or treat them as universals, my aim is to contribute to their deconstruction.

The project of deconstruction is not just an intellectual pastime, but a practical goal which many women and men have set themselves in their engagement with the Church. This is manifest in the ferment within the Church of England over ordination of women to the priesthood.

In the dialectic between the binary oppositions, women have been historically encapsulated in the 'sacred' sphere. Since career and career aspirations ('ambition') are located in the profane realm, women's career development has been inconsequential.

Those who argue against ordination of women to the priesthood typically insist both on the binary oppositions and on the primacy of the sacred. They complain that pressure groups such as the Movement for the Ordination of Women fail to advance theological justifications for their cause. Theological arguments, rooted in the sacred domain, are upheld as essential.

But what is theology? In operation, theological arguments typically present themselves as incontrovertible assertions made by certain privileged categories of men. If women theologise, what they produce is feminist theology; and this is then portrayed as a contradiction in terms, given that feminism is branded as corrosive of the Christian faith. Historically, theology has been ring-fenced as a predominantly male discourse, one which has celebrated women's subordinate role.

The starting point for deconstruction is to focus on the second, subordinate terms in a set of binary oppositions; in this case, on the profane rather than the sacred (Culler 1983: 156–79). This is precisely what women deacons are doing. So, questions such as 'What does creation theology teach us about women?', or 'What does Paul's teaching on male headship say to the Church today?', or 'Can a woman be an icon of Christ?' are not the challenging questions. They are supplanted by other, career-related questions. Will the Church offer women a full stipend, and reimburse all their legitimate expenses? When women have pastoral charge of a congregation, what arrangements are made to ensure their role is not undermined? Can women be licensed to such senior positions as team vicar, residentiary canon or archdeacon? What career barriers are faced by those women deacons, currently 26 per cent of the total, who are married to serving clergymen? How can younger women be attracted into the profession? Will women have the same retirement and pension rights as men? And, crucially, can women be offered fulfilling careers without opening the priesthood to them?

That the Church has begun to address these issues is a direct consequence of women's admission to the diaconate. When women were deaconesses, they were encapsulated in a realm of sacred discourse which denied them a voice: women served, while men theologised their service. Women were a muted group whose aspirations remained private. Once women joined men in the clerical profession – albeit only in the junior grade – they entered a public arena. Men, as Jill Robson (1988) pointed out in terms different from those employed here, are able to move relatively freely between the two realms of discourse. Naturally, there are English social mores to be observed; one must not be too crass in discussing one's terms and conditions of employment and one's career prospects. Nevertheless, in a coded form men's careers are negotiated.

The binary oppositions of sacred and profane bore heavily on deaconesses. Paradoxically, although they were lay people in the constitution of the Church, their role was more sacred than that of clergymen. Now that women, as deacons, are recognised professionals, the sacred discourse of vocation and the profane discourse of career have become available to them. Attributions to women of 'stridency', 'militancy' and cognate derogatory terms carry ever-diminishing conviction and are becoming less frequent. Women deacons are now legitimately claiming, as men do, both a vocation and a career.

Towards priesthood

The aftermath of the General Synod's decision in favour of ordination of women to the priesthood is highly significant for the issues raised in this chapter. There has been scarcely any public debate on the prospects for women's career development. The Movement for the Ordination of Women has deliberately stood aside from controversy, for fear of alienating public opinion and jeopardising the decision of Parliament. As so often, women deacons find themselves obliged to wait on the decisions of others – most of whom are men.

Women's careers have already received one minor setback. The Additional Curates Society was founded in 1837 to offer financial support to deacons and priests working in poor urban parishes. The Society has informed its patron, the Queen, that it proposes to withdraw grants from any woman deacon who becomes a priest. Its Assistant General Secretary was quoted (*Church Times*, 19 February 1993) as offering this consolation: 'Actually, the amount given to these ladies is negligible, a mere £10,000 out of our total £350,000.'

Debate within the Church has focused not on women's careers but on the provision of safeguards and pastoral care for people who remain conscientiously opposed to the priesting of women. An umbrella organisation has been formed to ensure that people with principled objections to women priests will be able to remain within the Church of England. Adopting the title *Forward in Faith*, its campaign has been twofold: to secure guaranteed protection for individuals and parishes from unwelcome ministrations by women priests, and to ensure that bishops opposed to women priests will continue to be appointed.

The immediate reaction from the Vatican to the General Synod's vote expressed dismay. Following approaches from *Forward in Faith*, Cardinal Basil Hume, Archbishop of Westminster, has suggested that this may precipitate the historic crisis prayed for by devout Roman Catholics since the Reformation: the conversion of England to the true Faith.

Faced with issues of such sacred moment, the profane careers of women clergy can be represented as a distracting bagatelle. Events are confirming the opinion of almost all women deacons: the opening of the priesthood may be a necessary, but not a sufficient, condition of significant career development for women.

References

Advisory Council for the Church's Ministry (1991) *Deacons Now*, Advisory Council for the Church's Ministry.

Aldridge, A. E. (1987) 'In the absence of the minister: structures of subordination in the role of deaconess in the Church of England', *Sociology*, **21**(3): 377–92.

Aldridge, A. E. (1989) 'Men, women and clergymen: opinion and authority in a sacred organization', *Sociological Review*, **37**(1): 43–64.

Aldridge, A. E. (1991) 'Women's experience of diaconate', in *Deacons Now*, Advisory Council for the Church's Ministry.

Aldridge, A. E. (1992) 'Discourse on women in the clerical profession: the diaconate and language-games in the Church of England', *Sociology*, **26**(1): 45–57.

Ardener, S. (1978) 'The nature of women in society', in S. Ardener, (ed.), *Defining Females*, London: Croom Helm.

Bentley, J. (1978) *Ritualism and Politics in Victorian Britain*, Oxford: Oxford University Press.

Bradley, I. (1976) *The Call to Seriousness: The Evangelical Impact on the Victorians*, London: Jonathan Cape.

Chadwick, O. (1970) *The Victorian Church*, vol. 1, London: A. & C. Black.

Crowther, M. A. (1970) *Church Embattled: Religious Controversy in Mid-Victorian England*, Newton Abbot: David & Charles.

Culler, J. (1983) *On Deconstruction*, London: Routledge & Kegan Paul.

Haig, A. (1984) *The Victorian Clergy*, London: Croom Helm.

Heeney, B. (1976) *A Different Kind of Gentleman*, Hamden, Connecticut: Shoe String Press.

House of Bishops of the General Synod of the Church of England (1988) *Deacons in the Ministry of the Church ('the Portsmouth report')*, London: Church House.

Martin, D. A. (1978) *A General Theory of Secularization*, Oxford: Blackwell.

Robson, J. (1988) 'Ministry or profession: clergy doubletalk', in M. Furlong, (ed.) *Mirror to the Church*, London: SPCK.

Russell, A. (1980) *The Clerical Profession*, London: SPCK.

Thompson, K. A. (1970) *Bureaucracy and Church Reform*, Oxford: Oxford University Press.

Tiller, J. (1983) *A Strategy for the Church's Ministry*, London: Church Information Office.

Towler, R. (1969) 'The social status of the Anglican minister', in R. Robertson, (ed.) *Sociology of Religion*, London: Penguin.

Towler, R. and Coxon, A. P. M. (1979) *The Fate of the Anglican Clergy*, London: Macmillan.

Wilson, B. R. (1982) *Religion in Sociological Perspective*, Oxford: Oxford University Press.

CHAPTER 10

Women surveyors: constructing careers

CLARA GREED

Introduction

The construction industry is a major sector of the British economy employing over 2 million people ranging from higher professionals, managers and technicians, through to the skilled workers and labourers on site (Ball 1988, CISC 1991). The vast majority are men, suggesting there is an underlying 'problem' for women. Yet, strangely, this is an area which scarcely features in feminist literature, in contrast to the vast amount of material on women's employment areas such as nursing, social work and teaching. In this paper I will consider the factors which are likely to act as 'inhibitors' to a woman's chances of achieving a satisfactory career, with particular emphasis on the 'place' allocated to women within the structure of the property professions, their perceived role in professional practice, the image projected which discourages women from entering in the first place, and the mechanisms at work which limit women's progress. I will also highlight factors which might act as 'encouragers' (few though they be) such as the 'man'power crisis, positive role models, and the organisation of women's networks, concluding with recommendations for future improvements (compare GASAT 1991). This paper is based on my research on women surveyors (Greed 1991, the examples used are from this book), who make up less than 5 per cent of the fully qualified members of their profession, but many of the observations related to surveying are applicable to the property professions as a whole. Over the last ten years increasing numbers of women have become interested in surveying, and women now comprise over 20 per cent of students. The majority of women surveyors are young and have not even had their careers yet, although significant trends can already be identified which limit women's progress.

The 'place' of women in surveying

Surveyors give professional advice on all aspects of land use and property development; 80 per cent of all surveyors are employed in the private sector in professional firms, and 20 per cent in the public sector. The work of the surveying profession in Britain is not limited to land surveying, but includes the valuation, investment, transfer, development and management of land, and what is built upon it. My research is particularly related to 'chartered surveyors', that is those who belong to the RICS (Royal Institution of Chartered Surveyors). However, one cannot isolate surveyors from the wider construction fraternity within which they live and move, which includes architects, civil engineers and town planners, in which women comprise 6 per cent, less than 1 per cent and 16 per cent respectively of the fully qualified membership of the relevant professional bodies. 'Below' this there are semi-professional and technician levels in which the numbers of women are also small, whereas in the malestream of construction workers on site there are very few women at all.

Whilst more women are entering the profession, they are more numerous in some specialisms of surveying practice than others, the general principle being that women are more likely to be found in the lower status specialisms and thus are less likely to be in the right 'place' to ensure career progression and promotion. 'Horizontally' the RICS comprises within its scope many different specialist fields related to land and property. The surveying spectrum extends from technological areas where few women are found (for example there are only 6 mineral surveyors who are women in Britain) through to the quasi-technological areas such as quantity surveying in which over 3 per cent of practitioners are women, and across to the more up-market, commercial areas such as estate management where over 10 per cent of practitioners are women. A high proportion of women are found in residential estate agency work within the private sector, not all of whom are professionally qualified, this being seen as a low-status area by many women and men in the profession. At the other end of the spectrum, the smaller, more socially orientated areas of practice are found, such as housing management where up to 50 per cent of students are likely to be women. Indeed there is considerable debate amongst surveyors themselves as to whether housing managers count as 'real' surveyors. This is an example of the 'tilting' downwards of the status 'seesaw' which commonly occurs when the number of women increase in an area of employment (compare Reed 1991). But, it should be remembered that men are in the majority in surveying practice, even in the 'women's specialisms'. In housing most of the senior posts are occupied by men, and women are concentrated in the middle and lower levels (Hargreaves 1990).

Women are also segmented 'vertically' within the profession. Men have encouraged more women into the profession in order to compensate for the 'man'power crisis of recent years, caused by the declining numbers of [male] school-leavers, but they have a somewhat static 'fixed in time' view of the women they are employing, as if they will never grow old, will remain as willing assistants, or will conveniently leave when the present staffing crisis is over. There seems to be a double standard of not seeing the women as having long-term careers stretching ahead of them, and so they are less likely to be sponsored and supported on to the path towards partnership and seniority. In fact men surveyors have quite different expectations from Day One as to the future of male, as against female, entrants. For women the principle 'thus far and no further' seems to be the unwritten rule in the profession. But many of the women do not realise this, being beguiled by the impression of initial encouragement to pursue surveying as a career, only to find, too late, that all those careers pep talks which they had heard in college and out in practice, were never really intended to be for them but for their male colleagues alone.

Women's perceived role

Many women feel inhibited in their vertical career progression by the nature of the role which they are given. First, women are often seen as 'suitable' to deal with areas of surveying which relate to 'prettifying' the environment. They are often seen as suitable for areas related to landscaping and building conservation. A woman mining surveyor who wanted to be involved directly in mining extraction was told by her employer that she should work on spoil tip reclamation, because he thought landscaping with all those 'pretty trees and hedges' was more ladylike! Of course women may be seen as being 'attractive' in themselves. Many men have joked to me that 'attractive women make unattractive property more attractive' (this argument takes for granted that all buyers, sellers and clients are also males, of course). I have also come across a number of women who started off in fairly technological areas and found that they were gradually moved into public relations, publicity or sales. For example, a woman land surveyor found that she increasingly became the 'token woman' on display at exhibitions and conferences and eventually was encouraged to move over to the marketing side of her organisation.

Second, women are often given roles which have an element of 'caring', almost as an extension of the traditional female role as housewife and mother. A woman building surveyor was given the task of investigating building faults in some housing for the elderly because this was seen as more caring! Women are also seen as being good at 'property management' which is often seen as an extension of the housewife role of 'managing' the household. This is not management in the executive sense of high-power decision-making and power, rather it is concerned with looking after buildings and people. For example such women may be concerned with keeping the tenants happy in a shopping mall development, dealing with rent reviews, servicing contracts and public relations. In fact they might be expected to keep a watchful eye on the fabric of the buildings too, which requires as much technical and professional knowledge as would be required by a man in a more obviously technical role. Surveyors are always very conscious of their professional status, and have been known to describe themselves as 'property doctors' and, guess what, women surveyors have been known to be called (therefore) 'property nurses'!

The peripheral yet supporting role of women as 'helpers' can be seen in many other areas of surveying too. For example, increasing numbers of women are finding themselves working in 'property research'. They are the real 'back-room boys'. Paradoxically, women who often appear to be better qualified than the men they are servicing, using their not inconsiderable expertise and mathematical ability, have little say in the final decision-making. Interestingly property research is increasingly an area typified by short-term contracts, 'flexibility' and home working (parallels with women researchers in universities). Women will also be found as back-up helpers in other more technological specialisms. For example, a number of the women surveyors who appear to have specialised in quantity surveying or building surveying, on closer inspection will be found to be in ancillary roles. They may be involved in legal contract work related to the building process, or again in financial accounting; but seldom will they be found actually doing construction-related work on the building site. The trouble with most of these helper-type jobs is that they are not strategic decision-making or power-wielding roles which are necessary stepping stones to the fast track of promotion. Indeed women are often seen as so indispensable in their particular specialism that the view is taken that they cannot possibly be promoted without major disaster for the 'team'; an argument which is seldom raised in the case of men. Ironically, women engaged in such specialist work may not get the status or recognition they merit.

The third area which women are often seen as 'naturally' fitting into is anything 'social', especially anything to do with residential development. This includes not only public sector housing management but also private sector estate agency, where it also 'helps' if the women are 'attractive' as explained in point one above. In fact many professional women surveyors avoid estate agency because of its low-status image, being aligned to 'trade', and because, as women, they feel they will become trapped in this area. However, those women who have had to move around the country because of their husbands' careers often find that it is one of the easiest areas to get back into again.

Images and fortresses

Before even getting to the point of considering surveying as a career, many women have been the subject of many 'inhibiting' factors in their childhood, emanating from both home and school, disinclining them from entering the construction industry in any shape or form. In contrast many of the women who were in surveying had received active encouragement from their parents, but at the same time had had to contend with little support from their teachers in their 'unusual' choice. I have quite recent accounts of girls who expressed an interest in surveying being told, variously, that they were going through a rebellious phase; that they would be unable to have children if they had to lift heavy equipment on site; and being steered in the direction of librarianship instead. I found that many careers teachers (particularly women ones) had no idea what surveying was. Indeed they possessed very misleading, false ideas about the construction industry as a whole, which was generally seen as rough, dirty, and frankly rather 'common'. Clearly the problem is exacerbated by misinformed women as well as by the more frequently cited bias of some men towards women entering 'their' territory. Indeed young women still have to be fairly determined, even somewhat maverick in personality to press forward against such discouragements.

False images of surveying act as inhibitors to women contemplating a career in surveying. A surveyor is often seen by the general public as a man working on a motorway (have you seen those large motorway signs saying 'SURVEYING!', warning motorists that this is the next hazard ahead?); or as someone standing on a building site using a theodolite. These images reflect only one small part of the picture, but are significantly male. Such men are more likely to be surveying technicians. However, in recent years more inviting images have emerged, which reflect the true professional nature of surveying. Encouraged by the enterprise culture of the 1980s, and the ongoing emphasis on getting more women into science and technology, increasing numbers of women have been entering surveying. They have been able to see through the smokescreen of false technological images which swirls around the profession. The growth in women entrants has continued into the 1990s, albeit somewhat abated by the current recession in the property market leading to a reduction in the job market.

Only a certain type of woman is attracted to and accepted into the 'fortress' of surveying, and it should not be assumed that she is likely to be feminist. A woman's personal motivation will influence both her 'suitability' and her staying power when/if things get rough, and therefore will influence the nature of her future career progression. Some women enter surveying because they are genuinely interested in buildings and land, but these tend to be the minority. Indeed a specific detailed interest in a particular aspect of professional work may be interpreted as a minus factor, indicating that someone is more suitable to be employed at a technician rather than professional or managerial level. Take note any careers advisors reading this book! Women are often wrongly encouraged to gain technical skills to compete with the boys, and in the process they disqualify themselves from a professional-level career. A GCSE in 'Surveying' can destine one to a bleak, boring life out in the cold on site as a low-grade technician. A range of reasonably average A levels in mainstream academic subjects is much preferred, with the exception that for the more technological areas of surveying one needs maths and science.

I found from my research that women are more likely to be encouraged to be a surveyor because they want to be 'a professional', and are attracted by the perceived independence and status this brings. Many were attracted by the role model of the 'business woman', the bourgeois feminist (Hertz 1986). 'More' women does not necessarily mean 'better' (Greed 1988) either for women in the profession or for women in society if the women promoted have a limited awareness of urban social and environmental issues, and have not developed any sort of women's consciousness. In discussing career 'success' and 'progress', one must not confuse the personal success of individual women with progress for women in society as a whole. If the women who are most likely to be promoted are the least likely to question the status quo, and have little wider social or environmental awareness, one can hardly argue from a broader structural perspective that their career success has necessarily been in the interests of women and men as a whole. This is a 'touchy' issue, as one does not want to appear 'disloyal', but which nevertheless needs to be raised.

Once women had overcome these hurdles and applied to college, I found that generally they were welcomed, and there seemed to be little overt discrimination at this stage. It was generally considered that more women on a course would raise the standard of the course by making the boys work harder, and compete with the women (parallels with the argument for 'mixing' schools). The pressure this might put upon the women was not recognised, in fact encouragement for the wrong reasons could act as an inhibiting burden. Since this paper is about careers rather than education, which I discuss elsewhere (Greed 1990, 1991) I will not go into this aspect here. However, in respect of 'careers' it is of significance that many women lecturers (few though they be) stressed that the way in which they were treated in college employment structures (in terms of promotion, childcare, level of respect) was a silent object lesson which was bound to influence students' perception of 'women's place' in surveying. I would argue that the way that women lecturers, rather than female students, are treated in college is a better measure of equal opportunities. Relatively speaking, male and female students are more 'the same', than adult men and women to whom society still gives very different burdens and responsibilities. Also for lecturers, college is their workplace and site of their career for several years

(Greed 1990) whereas students are rather like fast trains rushing through college on their way to elsewhere. Women students have told me they will put up with anything for a short while if it's the only way of obtaining the right qualifications for their desired career.

Career progression

Once over the hurdles of getting into, and surviving a college course, women surveyors can then look forward to a lifetime of further potential obstacles and inhibiting factors! (Some would say, 'why bother', it is so much easier to go and do a more 'girl-friendly' career, and save oneself a lot of worry and trouble.) Many young women enter surveying with great enthusiasm and have every intention of being highly successful and having life-long careers ending up as senior partners. Unfortunately the male perception of the women's future careers is often poles apart from that of the women themselves. Women are still, typically, seen as the helpers in the work and career progression of others, not as people who will have careers themselves. Let us now see how this works out in practice, 'longitudinally' by giving an overview of women's career progress within surveying. Even allowing for the fact that most women surveyors are young, and many are under the age of 30, women do not seem to achieve proportionately as many higher posts as the men. But, at the early stage, straight out of college, women seem to find no difficulty getting jobs. It is rumoured that some employers prefer them because they work harder. Several women surveyors commented that firms seem to allow the male entrants more time and 'tolerance' to grow up and mature in the job, whereas the women are expected to be competent from day one.

Whilst at the first interview the 'treat them all the same' principle appears to be at work, the situation may change if women seek another job interview after a couple of years in their first post. Women frequently reported questions being asked about whether they were married, if they had, or intended to have children. For a man this seemed to be a plus factor but for women a minus factor. Opportunities abound for younger women surveyors, but it is less so for older women as the pyramid narrows. When it comes to employers looking at the pool of potential candidates for further promotion, 'it's as if the women don't exist' (as many of the women I spoke to in the course of my research commented). I would go as far as to say that the women are recruited on the basis of completely different criteria to meet short-term manpower needs and that their employers have very different expectations of them. These factors might not manifest themselves for several years, as everyone is a 'junior' until their late 20s. I have come across many women who have sailed along thinking everything is wonderful and then find that they have been overtaken by men whom they had discounted as relatively unimportant (Greed 1991: 133).

Some women surveyors reach associate partnership level by their early 30s, which in surveying provides a pool of possible talent from which promotion to full partnership is made. Women have commented to me that a log-jam is developing as the new wave of women surveyors reach their early 30s and are not promoted further but left at this lower management level. Many women see men younger than themselves being picked up and promoted whilst they stay put. There is a general feeling amongst the women, that the men are likely to be groomed for partnership earlier, whereas women after an initial climb upwards are shunted horizontally into specialist areas rather than continuing up vertically. The men are seen as being given bigger car allowances, an outward 'sacramental' sign of their greater inner value. Although a few women have now broken through to partnership level, there are partners and partners. Also there are the women who have gone it alone, and set up their own businesses as sole practitioners, often out of sheer exasperation, or become 'consultants' (arguably a euphemism for professional women's semi-unemployment, with some notable exceptions) who may survive on intermittent, low-status work.

Exclusionary mechanisms

I became fascinated with the dynamics at work within the surveying profession, which determined which sort of people reach positions of seniority. There seem to be different 'rules' and 'forces' governing the career progression of men, as against women. It was helpful to see the world of surveying as a subculture. 'Subculture' was taken to mean the cultural traits, beliefs and attitudes, the lifestyle peculiar to surveying (Joseph 1978). One of the most important factors seemed to be the need for a person to fit into the subculture. It was important to be the 'right type'. Gender is a major factor in determining this, and in affecting 'who' receives what sort of treatment. Women as 'outsiders' have been particularly conscious of exclusionary mechanisms being used against them, but often their experiences have been dismissed as being too 'personal' and therefore of little importance. Indeed, women surveyors themselves have, in the past, suppressed such feelings, and have been unwilling to share their experiences with others so as not to be seen as 'weak' or 'feminist' and therefore the 'wrong sort'.

The need for identification with the values of the subculture would seem to block out the entrance of those people and alternative ideas that are seen as 'different'. The concept of 'closure' as discussed by Parkin (1979: 89–90) in relation to the power of various subgroups protecting their status was an important theme. This is worked out on a day-to-day basis with some people being made to feel awkward and wrong and others being welcomed and made to feel comfortable in the world of construction (Gale 1989). It is a major hypothesis of this study that one should not see all the little occurrences of everyday life (i.e. the encouragements and discouragements) as trivial, or irrelevant, but as the very building blocks of the subculture, and therefore as key 'encouragers' or 'inhibitors' in women's career progress. All these 'little' factors would determine 'who', male or female, would be in the right 'place' within the profession with the power to make policy decisions to shape the property world, the built environment, and the nature of the profession itself for the future. Even if women had different or better ideas (or even written equal opportunities statements) it would make little difference if they were not in positions of influence or power within the professional structures to implement their proposals. I concluded that there was a need for fundamental changes both in perceptions of male surveyors towards their female counterparts, and in the nature and organisation of the profession itself. The need for women themselves to 'improve' by being more assertive, better qualified and more organised (factors which are so often stressed as if it is the women's 'fault') to me seem quite secondary to the need for fundamental changes in male attitudes and institutions.

Encouragers and reforms

There are not many encouraging factors about surveying which might be built upon to improve the situation for women. Wider societal issues such as the 'man'power shortage have given women a valid 'excuse' for being admitted, but this might prove shortlived in view of the current recession in the construction industry. Women have also been encouraged by the role models of pioneer women who have entered male-dominated professions and companies, giving them a 'right' to be recognised in the business world, and in particular giving an alternative 'image' of what a surveyor might be like. However, there are equally signs of growing gender-based segmentation within erstwhile male professions, for example with more women entering housing rather than mainstream surveying. So no sooner do women gain a footing and get the right qualifications, than the men 'move the goal posts', or redesign the pitch altogether.

Individual, tough, determined women have soldiered on admirably, and opened up new paths, out of desperation coming up with ad hoc solutions to childcare problems and other practicalities. But with greater numbers of women entering surveying more fundamental structural changes (as against individual solutions) are needed. Nevertheless the experiences of the pioneer women, their respected status, and the networks they have established amongst other like-minded women are a very valuable basis for further change. Some of these 'forerunner' women have proved ideal to sit on professional working parties, set up by the male-dominated professional bodies (somewhat belatedly) to consider possible change. It is encouraging that in recent years 'special' committees have been set up in town planning, surveying and housing dealing with 'women's issues', and impressive reports have even been produced under the auspices of the professional bodies which say all the right things (implementation is another matter of course) (RICS 1990).

At the wider structural level, I would argue that there is still much room for a change in the image and nature of the land-use professions, although it is a chicken and egg situation. Unless there really are more women in the profession, and they are being treated better, young women will soon see through the inevitable publicity photographs showing happy women on building sites as mere sham. Equally important for future generations is the need for fundamental changes in the socialisation messages put out by schools and parents about women's role and potential. This should be backed up in higher education by better provision for women lecturers and mature women students as a normal right, not as a 'special extra'. The male 'ethos' of higher education, which many women find so off-putting, needs transforming, because so much of higher education 'by default' is still organised around the needs of the fancy free, sport-loving, male school-leaver, at a cost of non-allocation of resources to the needs of women. The content of courses, the ways of teaching (especially the sorts of examples used in technical subjects) and the organisation of courses all require a fundamental overhaul.

There needs to be an underlying change in the professional cultures and employment structures of the construction world. This would involve valuing women's particular skills and characteristics as plus factors, not as disabilities. This, in turn, might result in more women being promoted and thus attaining positions in which they might shape the future of the profession more to the advantage of other women: whilst having more fulfilling careers themselves too. There is much room for practical changes to enable women surveyors to be 'surveyors and women' at the same time, without tearing themselves apart in the process. More flexible approaches to day-to-day working; better childcare provision (tax allowances would particularly help women surveyors, as they mainly work in the private sector and some as 'associate partners' are not entitled to maternity benefits); more accommodating career progression routes based on women's life cycles rather than on continuous, linear, male patterns; and less competitive models of professional practice and management (to mention but a few) all need to be taken on board. In conclusion, everything is linked, individual women cannot have 'better careers' unless structural changes are made to the profession, and many of these cannot be accomplished unless there are attitudinal and governmental policy changes in society.

References

Ball, M. (1988) *Rebuilding Construction: Economic Change in the British Construction Industry*, London: Routledge & Kegan Paul.

CISC (Construction Industry Standing Council) (1991) 'Final report to CISC for the construction industry occupational mapping exercise for technical, professional and managerial occupations', London: The Building Centre.

GASAT (1991) 'Action for equity: the second decade. Report of the sixth international gender and science and technology conference', Melbourne: Melbourne University with Curtin University, Perth.

Gale, A. (1989) 'Attracting women to construction', *Chartered Builder*, September/October, London: Chartered Institute of Building.

Greed, C. (1988) 'Is more better?: with reference to the position of women chartered surveyors in Britain', *Women's Studies International Forum*, 11(3): 187–97.

Greed, C. (1990) 'You're just imagining it, everything's all right really, don't worry about it: the position of women in surveying education and practice', *Gender and Education*, 2(1): 49–61.

Greed, C. (1991) *Surveying Sisters: Women in a Traditional Male Profession*, London: Routledge.

Hargreaves, K. (1990) 'Gains and losses of 100 years of women in housing', Paper from *Women and the Built Environment Conference*, South Bank Polytechnic, London: Housing Employment and Register and Advice.

Hertz, L. (1986) *The Business Amazons*, London: André Deutsch.

Joseph, M. (1978) 'Professional values, a case study of professional students in a Polytechnic', *Research in Education*, 19: 49–65, May.

Parkin, F. (1979) *Marxism and Class Theory: A Bourgeois Critique*, London: Tavistock.

Reed, R. (1991) 'Compositor: a job fit for a woman?' Paper presented at Ninth Annual International UMIST–Aston Labour Process Conference on the Organisation and Control of the Labour Process, Manchester: University of Manchester.

RICS (1990) *Report of the Working Party on Equal Opportunities*, London: Royal Institution of Chartered Surveyors.

CHAPTER 11

Gender and secondary headship: managerial experiences in teaching

JULIA EVETTS

In teaching in schools women are concentrated in certain sectors and predominate at the lower promotion levels. Nearly all teachers and headteachers of nursery and separate infant schools are women. The majority of primary teachers (81 per cent in 1990) are women, yet 51 per cent of primary headteachers are men (DES 1990). In secondary schools 52 per cent of teachers and 80 per cent of headteachers are men. In teaching women are marginalised less through numerical under-representation but more through ghettoisation and concentration in women's enclaves such as class teaching in general and particularly teaching in nursery and infant schools. In teaching, as in all careers, women are under-represented in senior positions which involve management tasks and which are achieved as a result of career promotions.

In secondary teaching, promotion has come to be identified with management. The responsibilities of management and administration differentiate more senior promotion positions from the classroom- and pupil-orientated functions of other teachers. Senior positions in schools do not necessarily reflect length of teaching experience or quality of teaching expertise. Promotion (under the old structure of scale positions and the current system of incentive allowances) is allocated for the taking on of managerial tasks and administrative responsibilities. The 1971 Burnham settlement, which revised the promotion ladder in teaching, included an agreement to drop the assumption that promotion would necessarily involve the acceptance of additional administrative and managerial responsibilities (Saran and Verber 1979). But this has not affected promotion patterns. In the organisation of secondary schools virtually every promotion allowance involves some administrative/managerial responsibility (West-Burnham 1983).

Women's under-representation in positions of management in schools has been well documented both in Britain (Acker 1983, 1989) and in the USA (Shakeshaft 1987). However, in teaching some women do succeed in achieving career promotions into managerial positions. Such women are an interesting group in terms of their co-ordination of career and gender identities. For the minority of women who do achieve secondary headships, they and their schools are more visible and likely to be subject to great observation and scrutiny. Kanter (1977) claimed that where women are only a few, they get extra attention, are the subject of more gossip, stories and rumours, and are always in the spotlight. Ball (1987) described the additional pressures on women who are highly visible as a result of their minority position. Acker (1980) explained a fear of visibility where some women have attempted to play down, hide and minimise traits or behaviours that might be seen as feminine and therefore as inappropriate in a managerial role.

In the summer of 1990, I conducted career history interviews with twenty secondary headteachers, ten men and ten women, from two Midland educational authorities in England. The sample was unusual only in the fact that half were women. For the women headteachers the sample of ten was 66 per cent of the population of women heads of secondary schools in the two authorities. For the men headteachers ten represented a sample size of about 8 per cent. In other respects the career history heads could be regarded as representative in that their schools varied in size from unit total group eight to unit total group twelve. Also, the heads' lengths of time in headship posts had varied from one year to twenty. The over-representation of women in this research was intentional since one objective was to explore gender differences in the experience of careers in teaching. Using the career history material it was possible to examine gender differences in headship styles and in management strategies. It was also possible to begin to explore the range of experience of career and gender identity for women headteachers.

Career and gender can be experienced as problematic if the managerial responsibilities of headship are perceived as being at odds or in conflict with gender identity. Cultural contradictions have been perceived as inherent in career and management positions for women (Kanter 1977, Chapman 1978, Marshall 1984). Women who enter the world of career and promotion into management are taking part in social relationships determined by masculine values. Career, promotion and management as presently constituted are areas where the values of scientific rationality, bureaucratic objectivity and hierarchical authority can be at odds with the caring, subjective, relational values which are supposedly important to women. It is possible that promotion-successful women will become absorbed by the managerialist values and structures which they have had to learn to operationalise in order to succeed. We have to ask, therefore, what happens to women who do manage, who have built careers and achieved promotions?

The answer to this question is important. It is intended to explore this in a preliminary way by considering the experiences of some women headteachers. Can women headteachers operationalise a different style of headship? Are their schools different kinds of social organisations? Can gender liberate and transform headship or does the headteacher role neutralise gender identity? Are there gender differences in managerial leadership styles and in the experience of being a headteacher?

Leadership styles: gender differences

When researchers have focused their attentions on gender differences in management, then the question of leadership 'style' becomes the point at issue. Gender differences in terms of the definitions of objectives, perceptions of the organisation and task completion, are not significant, but in terms of manner of execution of tasks and style of leadership, gender becomes an important differentiating variable. The concept of leadership *style* needs some preliminary explanation. Ball (1987: 83) gave the following definition:

A style is a form of social accomplishment, a particular way of realising and enacting the authority of headship. It is eminently an individual accomplishment, but at the same time it is essentially a form of joint action.

In his analysis of the micro-politics of schools Ball expressed the organisational task of the head (1987: 82) as the need to achieve and maintain control (the problem of domination), while encouraging and ensuring social order and commitment (the problem of integration). Heads manage their schools in different ways according to Ball: some rely on their own leadership qualities; others emphasise their bureaucratic responsibilities. Some heads manage by means of personal influence and conviction; some through authority and control; while others manage through committee structures and hierarchies of delegation. Heads give indications to others, to staff, pupils, parents, advisers, governors, as to their preferred or intended style by means of verbal, non-verbal and written communications, in face-to-face encounters, informal and formal meetings. When the leadership/management style is acceptable, then joint action can proceed. When the style is unacceptable, however, then relationships become strained and conflict may develop.

The difficulties of demonstrating gender differences in leadership style have been discussed by Shakeshaft (1987). She argued that there might be substantial contrasts and contradictory findings between studies which used observation and work diaries compared with the findings of studies which used specially devised questionnaires involving measurement of leadership perceptions. Her own analysis (Shakeshaft 1979, 1985) using a Leadership Behaviour Description Questionnaire found no differences between males and females on twelve dimensions of leadership behaviour: representation, demand reconciliation, tolerance of uncertainty, persuasiveness, initiation of structure, tolerance of freedom, role assumption, consideration, production emphasis, predictive accuracy, integration and superior orientation. However, other researchers using research techniques such as observation *have* found gender differences.

Most of the research into gender differences in leadership styles had been American. Such research has been fairly small-scale, however, and relatively inconclusive. Adkison (1981) suggested that female compared with male principals were more likely to involve themselves in instructional supervision, to exhibit a democratic leadership style and to concern themselves with students. Such differences confirmed Shakeshaft's analysis of the head as educational leader and master teacher compared with the head as manager and administrator. Cochran (1980) noted that women principals were more effective at resolving conflicts, at motivating teachers, and at acting as representatives rather than directors of a group.

The question of leadership style and of gender differences is one which is difficult to handle empirically. The results of quantitative testing procedures designed to be used on large samples have found few significant differences between male and female heads in their perceptions of leadership or their rankings of the task performances of headship. However, qualitative studies, usually small-scale, but considerably more detailed, *have* suggested gender differences in style. The question of 'leadership style' is difficult for researchers to take over and to define operationally. A style of leadership is a manner of working, an approach, a feeling, a method and a way, and as such it is elusive and intangible, problematic to measure and to demonstrate.

There are difficulties, therefore, in demonstrating gender differences in management and leadership style. For a number of years, researchers argued that there were no significant differences. Shakeshaft (1987) claimed that it was not difficult to demonstrate ways in which men and women did the same things when they managed. The women would not have been selected for management unless they could complete the tasks and comprehend and master the managerial culture. Shakeshaft also argued that to claim no difference has been a political strategy used by both supporters and opponents of the need to encourage more women into senior positions. For women's advocates the no differences argument enabled them to refute notions that women would be less effective than men as managers. For opponents, it was politically desirable to report no differences since it was then possible to explain the small numbers of women in educational management by reference to the lack of demand from larger numbers of women in that they refused to apply and put themselves forward for such positions.

The lack of success of such 'no difference' arguments, in terms of increasing the proportions of women in educational leadership posts, led Shakeshaft (1987) to take up a different position. She argued that there *are* differences and that in certain organisations, like schools, feminine styles of leadership and management are more appropriate and effective. Similarly Gray (1987: 299) claimed that if schools as organisations 'are perceived as needing to be caring, nurturing, maintaining, supporting, understanding, they will be seen to require a form of management that for many is essentially a stereotype of femininity'. While warning against stereotyping by gender, Gray argued that management needs to draw on 'intuition, calculated risk taking, aesthetic considerations, dependence on colleagues, messiness and incompleteness'. These were for Gray the 'feminine' aspects of all personalities since in terms of stereotypes he claimed ' "real" men do not make mistakes!'.

In Britain, there have been several attempts to describe the leadership styles of headteachers (Lyons 1974, Peters 1976, Weindling and Earley 1987). Qualitative researchers have provided useful insights into the way a headship style is negotiated (Burgess 1983, 1984, Ball 1987, Gillborn 1989). Few, however, have alluded to *gender* differences in leadership style. Indeed significant differences have usually been denied (Weindling and Earley 1987, Hall *et al.* 1986). So what happens to the women who do achieve promotion to the senior management positions of secondary headship?

The analysis of the responses from the career history headteachers demonstrated a great deal of variation both amongst the women and amongst the men headteachers. There were differences in the career history headteachers' leadership and management styles but few of the differences were gender-related. It is important to note that some of the male heads emphasised collegial relations and participatory forms of management in schools while some of the female heads were inclined towards hierarchy and authority in management. Significant differences in styles of leadership are not difficult to demonstrate in general, although the clear linkage of style with gender is more problematic. Ball (1987) analysed four ideal-type categories of leadership style (interpersonal, managerial, political-adversarial and political-authoritarian) and in his subsequent elaboration and illustration of these styles, he does not mention gender differences. Perhaps we should conclude from such an omission that gender was not a significant variable in differentiating these types.

What is significant, however, is an emphasis on style rather than on gender. Stereotypes of masculinity and femininity are not helpful except in so far as they better enable us to assess what are the best qualities and styles in any individual, whether man or woman (Archer and Lloyd 1982). Similarly with managerial and leadership styles, the objective in demonstrating differences is not to enable us to claim that either women or men make the best headteachers. However, where differences are demonstrated we are then in a better position to ask which, in that time and at that place, is the best style of management and leadership in the organisation that is the school. The most important criterion of good management is that it should relate to the organisational needs of the institution. Such needs are both structural (continuity and replacement) and cultural (including working relations and practices). In the case of headship of secondary schools, therefore, we need to ask which aspects of managerial and leadership style best suit the needs of schools in the current economic and political climate. This is a much more intriguing and relevant question. Our answers in terms of most appropriate style will vary from school to school and area to area. Opinions will differ and may even conflict. In addition, circumstances will alter as external conditions change the needs of the organisation that is the school.

Experiencing headship: gender differences

If it is difficult to demonstrate conclusively that there are consistent gender differences in styles of headship, it is not difficult to show gender differences in the *experience* of headship. Analysis of the experiences of the holders of particular occupational positions and the effects of work roles on worker identities has been an important contribution of interactionist research. Such a viewpoint concentrates on how people construct meanings and understandings in everyday relations and activities at work. Woods (1983) explained such an approach in respect of teachers (and pupils) in schools and the study by Lortie (1975) of the American schoolteacher is regarded as a classic analysis of teacher experiences. In considering the experience of headship, it is important to consider the process of *becoming* a headteacher and the everyday experiences involved in *being* a head. In respect of both of these, there are significant gender differences.

Becoming a headteacher

The process of becoming a headteacher is one of adult socialisation into a managerial identity. It involves assuming the tasks and responsibilities of headship and developing a management structure which is worked at and realised in each encounter (Goffman 1971, Ball 1987). There has been little research on becoming a *head*teacher although there have been a number of studies of *teacher* socialisation which have concentrated on the early years in teaching (Hanson and Herrington 1976, Taylor and Dale 1971, Lacey 1977). Lacey elaborated a model of teacher socialisation using the notion of strategy in order to emphasise the teacher's own impact and input into the process of assuming a teacher identity. Nias (1984) used the concept of self in order to examine the definition and maintenance of self in primary teaching.

In the process of becoming a headteacher most heads will have been well prepared for their headship tasks and responsibilities as a result of a succession of career moves and promotions into management. The various positions on the promotion ladder of the teaching career prepare heads for the duties of headship and their experience of different schools makes them aware of the differences in style of leadership of particularly headteachers. The perceptions of career through individualistic success in competition for promotion posts and the increased responsibility and authority acquired through successive promotion achievements are common to all heads' experiences.

Gender differences in experience are likely to become more obvious as the higher levels of promotion ladders are reached, however. Although the competition for headship is severe since there are few posts available, this is nevertheless a competition in which women feel at a disadvantage. In the career history group of headteachers, Miss Hollis explained the difficulties she had in achieving a headship post:

I took about five years to persuade this authority that I was worth appointing as a head. I should think I applied for certainly a hundred jobs. I'm not bad at writing applications; I had my references taken up; I know my references were supportive. The inspectors came into my school and said, 'Keep on applying, you should get there.' And I never got a sniff of an interview either in this authority or anywhere else. I mean I then had all the qualifications. I had written books. I'd had a diverse experience. I would apply and boom. So much so that I actually started to make enquiries with the Equal Opportunities Commission. I don't go through life thinking 'discrimination', women aren't going to get there; but my experience was such that there had got to be something wrong here. Nobody was saying to me well what's wrong with you is that you're short of this experience or you don't get on well with people or whatever. They were all saying you're very capable, you get on well with people, you'd make an excellent head. Blah, blah, blah, end of story. . . .

So I started to think about the selection of heads and I was appalled when I started to compare notes about what had happened to friends and colleagues. I couldn't see anything consistent at all. So I wrote a paper on the subject of what would be an appropriate system for recruiting heads and I sent this to the Director of Education. . . .

And sure enough his secretary rang me and said he would like to see me. So I went to see him and had a most civil discussion about the selection of deputies for heads, and I think that was the first time he had ever seen me. He accepted full responsibility for why I hadn't been interviewed; he said he wasn't going to hide behind the inspectors – though I actually think it was the inspectors. . . .

And interestingly, within three months, I was interviewed and I was appointed as a result of my first interview.

Although Miss Hollis met the criteria of merit, achievement, wide experience and an ability to manage and lead, she felt there were additional problems for her because she was a woman. Many men are also unsuccessful in the competition for headship posts but for them gender is not a factor in their failure to achieve promotion. Several of the heads reported the widely held view that the appointment of a woman head by selection panels was regarded as more of a risk. The lay members of selection panels, such as parent governors in particular, would advise caution and conservatism in headteacher appoint-ments. In this way gender could override other merit-determined criteria in selectors' decisions. Anti-discrimination legislation was little help since appointment decisions could always be couched in terms of merit and explained as gender-neutral.

Being a head

The experience of headship also refers to the everyday activities involved in *being* a headteacher. Such experiences also vary accord-ing to gender. For men headteachers there are likely to be few prob-lems arising from gender identity. A headmaster's *style* might result in conflict in school if the style does not meet the expectations of staff, pupils and parents. But for men the conflict arises from style and not from gender. Similarly some women headteachers experi-ence few difficulties associated with gender. In the career history group, Mrs Grainger explained how, for her, gender was unproblem-atic in her achievement of a headteacher identity:

I am very much *not* a feminist except that I totally believe in female equality. It's an issue sometimes that I discuss with the women on my staff because there are women on my staff who care about being called 'chairperson' or get twitchy if they see a letter addressed to 'the headmaster'. They mind that we still have about a million report forms that we'll be using up to the year dot that say 'headmaster' on the bottom and (they) would prefer that I just threw them all in the bin and wasted them all.

I care not one jot for any of that. I think it utterly boring. I work in a sphere where every time there is a meeting of the headteachers, secondary heads in Pennington, there are only seven female secondary heads and eighty-one men. And of course I've arrived late at a meeting sometimes and been walking along a row looking for an empty space and one of them will say 'Sit here, if you like Joan' (patting knee) and I'll say 'Well you might like it for ten minutes but you wouldn't like it for longer than that' or 'I'll find a better lap than yours' or something. 'Cause I think it's funny, I actually think it's quite a compliment. I'd start to worry if I didn't get remarks like that because as a female I like clothes, I like perfume, I like jewellery, I like men. Apart from that I live my life as if I were a man. And it doesn't occur to me not to; it doesn't occur to me that it's a problem. But I don't know why it doesn't and I would dearly love to know why it doesn't because I'd like to instil that in the girls here in school.

In this extract, this headteacher perceived no difficulties in reconcil-ing her gender and headship identities. Her gender was important to her sense of self and well-being but it was not perceived as problem-atic in the way she wished to run her school.

For other women heads, however, gender did intrude in their ex-periences of headship. Amongst the career history heads, Mrs Cooper had kept a log of sexist comments, harassment and embarrassment which she had experienced. These experiences were not confined to school but also intruded at heads' and local education authority meetings, at social gatherings, and professional association conferences:

At my first meeting with other heads in the Authority I was conspicuous as one of only eight women heads in a force of seventy-eight and was asked by a male head, 'Do you know why they appointed a *woman* at (your school)?' He had no idea that was offensive. An adviser thought that the LEA now had a 'lot of women heads'. In school in another context a fairly senior colleague said, 'Presumably you were appointed for your ideas.' I quickly got used to being welcomed as the *wife* of a head at heads' meetings and to comments on my clothes and looks. During a lunch-time off-the-record discussion a woman deputy head known to me was discussed. The reason for her non-appointment to headship was advanced: her dress was too flamboyant and she wore heavy make-up and jewellery! Typically I was asked one evening (by the male chair of governors) whether I was going to change my clothes. I was wearing casual trousers and a sweatshirt-type top for a community association meeting.

I got used to being accused openly of being 'too soft' when dealing with difficult pupils because I listened to them and did not usually raise my voice. A male head of year followed such a comment with the remark that of course I knew more about girls than he did.

On the telephone I frequently met disbelief when I clarified my identity after a query. I was usually taken for a secretary; after clearly stating that I was the head I was asked 'the head of which department?' on one occasion. Face to face, a computing salesman used my first name without asking, while the superintendent of parks and gardens greeted me with 'Hello, young lady!' and the caretaking supervisor risked 'you are gorgeous!'

For this woman head, gender was intrusive and prominent in her experience of headship. Such experiences were common amongst the career history women heads and were felt by some to interfere in managerial relationships in schools. Another women head, Mrs Ince, had taken steps to try to ameliorate some of the difficulties which she felt women experienced in managerial arrangements in schools:

I have come to see how weighted the scales are against women in management in that almost all my dealings are with men. Almost all the officers I deal with are men; a large number of my senior colleagues at school are men and most of my fellow heads are men. I think that I have only allowed myself to really become aware of that as I have become more confident in being a head and when just occasionally I found myself interviewing with only women on the panel. It suddenly occurred to me what a different experience that is and that men have that experience practically all the time.

I have recently felt able to make a very deliberate effort to encourage women in the school to look at themselves as potential managers. We have talked a lot about our difficulties, about our strengths and the fact that the whole business of competitive interview actually suits men a great deal better than women. A lot of business is decided at meetings and that meetings, on the whole, suit men, large formal meetings particularly.

It seemed then that, for the women heads in the career history group, gender was a part of their experiences of headship and for some of these women gender was intrusive in managerial relations in schools and in perceptions of headship identity. Whereas for men heads, their gender is positively associated with increased managerial responsibility and authority in their schools, for women heads gender can be intrusive in managerial arrangements and a constant threat to headship identity. Gender can intrude in the process of becoming a headteacher, if women feel there might be discrimination in selection processes. And gender can intrude in the experience of being a head, if the women's minority status results in difficulties in managing staff, children and parents as well as in dealings with school governors and local education authority officials.

Discussion

This paper has examined, first, the question of gender differences in style of headship of secondary schools and, second, the different ways in which gender and headship can be experienced. Research evidence has confirmed significant differences in headship style but the association of such style differences with gender is less conclusive. It is important in this connection to remember the comments of Scott (1986) concerning the ahistorical nature of arguments which attempt to assert that the differences between men and women are universal and unchanging. It is more appropriate and indeed optimistic to assume that notions of masculinity and femininity are historically and societally specific and hence are able to change and be changed. If style rather than gender is the critical variable, then we are in a better position to be able to determine which, at any particular time and any particular place, is the best style of management in the organisation that is the school.

In respect of the experiences of men and women headteachers, this paper has explored the different ways in which a career history sample of twenty men and women headteachers experienced gender and headship. For the men headteachers, gender was unproblematic in negotiating a headship and leadership style. For some women heads gender was likewise unproblematic. For other women heads, however, gender was intrusive both in becoming a head and in the experience of headship.

The cultural power of sex-role stereotyping needs to be acknowledged for this is the source of the managerial conflicts for some women headteachers. Stereotypes are sets of beliefs about the personal attributes of a group of people. These attributes are generalised from direct experience, from culturally transmitted information or some combination of both. There is increasing awareness that stereotypes reflect a group's work roles and the kind of activities in which we see them engaged (Eagly 1987). Thus sex-role stereotypes arise in response to the sexual division of labour and occupational segregation in home and workplace. When women are absent from senior management positions or only a minority of women hold such posts, as in the headship of secondary schools, then women are not characterised in terms of their authority and leadership abilities but rather in terms of their identities as *woman* headteachers. Furthermore, sex-role stereotyping causes us to make the mistake of attributing occupational segregation to personality differences. Thus we assume that the nurturant and submissive behaviour of (female) secretaries results from women's personality characteristics, not the role requirements imposed by the work situation (O'Leary and Ickovics 1992). These gender stereotypes, deriving from the sexual division of labour, come to constitute normative beliefs to which people tend to conform or are induced to conform. This is the cultural power and force of sex-role stereotyping which results in the double-bind for women in management positions in schools and elsewhere.

I have noted in this paper that there is clear evidence that headteachers manage in diverse ways, have a wide variety of personality traits and leadership styles and skills. There are differences in style between headteachers, but few of these differences are consistently gender-related. I have also indicated that gender differences in the experience of headship stem primarily from women's minority status. For the minority of women who do achieve secondary headships, they and their schools are more visible and likely to be subject to greater observation and scrutiny. The women heads in the career history study frequently referred to the double-edged aspect of being more visible. At least they and their schools were noticed and remembered; the women's 'deviant' gender status ensured such recognition. At the same time, these women felt that they were constantly on trial; as representatives of their gender they were fearful to put a foot wrong since their mistakes would be used to condemn all women headteachers (although similar mistakes by men are not used to argue the unsuitability of men for headship). Such pressures were acute and constant. The additional pressures on women who are highly visible as a result of their minority position have been discussed by a number of researchers (Kanter 1977, Acker 1980, Ball 1987).

Some of the women heads in the career history group were troubled by the intrusion of gender into their professional work relationships and responsibilities. Only the promotion of more women into senior management positions in schools (and elsewhere) will shatter the stereotypical conceptions of men as managers and women as assistants. O'Leary and Ickovics (1992) have suggested, following Eagly (1987), that the way to minimise the power of sex-stereotyping is to emphasise the *other* identity such as headteacher or manager. By removing the gender link we might eventually be able to avoid the cultural stereotyping deriving from the sexual division of labour. The critical question will then become headteacher management style and how appropriate styles can be operationalised by both men and women headteachers.

References

Acker, S. (1980) 'Women, the other academics', *British Journal of Sociology of Education*, **1**(1): 68–80.

Acker, S. (1983) 'Women and teaching: a semi-detached sociology of a semi-profession', in S. Walker and L. Barton (eds) *Gender, Class and Education*, Lewes: Falmer Press.

Acker, S. (1989) (ed.) *Teachers, Gender and Careers*, Lewes: Falmer Press.

Adkison, J. (1981) 'Women in school administration. A review of the literature', *Review of Educational Research*, **51**(3): 311–43.

Archer, J. and Lloyd, B. (1982) *Sex and Gender*, Harmondsworth: Penguin.

Ball, S. J. (1987) *The Micro-Politics of the School*, London: Methuen.

Burgess, R. G. (1983) *Experiencing Comprehensive Education*, London: Methuen.

Burgess, R. G. (1984) 'Headship: freedom or constraint?', in S. J. Ball (ed.) *Comprehensive Schooling: A Reader*, Lewes: Falmer Press.

Bush, T. (1990) *Managing Education: Theory and Practice*, Milton Keynes: Open University Press.

Chapman, J. B. (1978) 'Male and female leadership styles – the double bind', in J. A. Ramaley (ed.) *Covert Discrimination and Women in the Sciences*, Boulder, CO: Westview Press.

Cochran, J. (1980) 'When the principal is a woman', ERIC microfiche ED 184–247.

DES (1990) *Statistics of Education: Teachers in Service in England and Wales*, London: HMSO.

Eagly, A. H. (1987) *Sex Differences in Social Behaviour: A Social Role Interpretation*, Hillsdale, NJ: Lawrence Erlbaum.

Gillborn, D. A. (1989) 'Talking heads: reflection on secondary headship at a time of rapid educational change', *School Organisation*, **9**(1): 65–83.

Goffman, E. (1971) *The Presentation of Self in Everyday Life*, Harmondsworth: Penguin.

Gray, H. L. (1987) 'Gender considerations in school management', *School Organisation*, **7**(3): 297–302.

Hall, V., MacKay, H. and Morgan, C. (1986) *Head Teachers at Work*, Milton Keynes: Open University Press.

Hanson, D. and Herrington, M. (1976) *From College to Classroom*, London: Routledge & Kegan Paul.

Kanter, R. M. (1977) *Men and Women of the Corporation*, New York: Basic Books.

Lacey, C. (1977) *The Socialization of Teachers*, London: Methuen.

Lortie, D. (1975) *School-teacher: A Sociological Study*, Chicago: University of Chicago Press.

Lyons, G. (1974) *The Administrative Tasks of Head and Senior Teachers in Large Secondary Schools*, Bristol: University of Bristol.

Marshall, J. (1984) *Women Managers*, Chichester: Wiley.

Nias, J. (1984) 'The definition and maintenance of self in primary teaching', *British Journal of Sociology of Education*, **5**(3): 167–80.

O'Leary, V. E. and Ickovics, J. R. (1992) 'Cracking the glass ceiling', in U.

Sekaran and F. T. L. Leong (eds) *Womanpower*, Newbury Park, California: Sage.

Peters, R. S. (ed.) (1976) *The Role of the Head*, London: Routledge & Kegan Paul.

Saran, R. and Verber, L. (1979) 'The Burnham unit total system', *Educational Administration*, **8**(1): 113–37.

Scott, J. (1986) 'Gender: a useful category of historical analysis', *American Historical Review*, **91**: 1053–75.

Shakeshaft, C. S. (1979) 'Dissertation research on women in educational administration: a synthesis of findings and paradigm for future research', *Dissertation Abstracts International*, **40**: 6455a.

Shakeshaft, C. (1985) 'Strategies for overcoming the barriers to women in educational administration', in S. Klein (ed.) *Handbook for Achieving Sex-equity Through Education*, Baltimore: John Hopkins University Press, pp. 124–44.

Shakeshaft, C. (1987) *Women in Educational Administration*, Beverly Hills and London: Sage.

Spencer, A. and Podmore, D. (1983) 'Life on the periphery of a profession: the experience of women lawyers', Paper presented to British Sociological Association, University College, Cardiff.

Spencer, A. and Podmore, D. (1987) (eds) *In a Man's World*, London: Tavistock.

Taylor, J. K. and Dale, I. R. (1971) *A Survey of Teachers in their First Year of Service*, Bristol: University of Bristol School of Education Research Unit.

Weindling, D. and Earley, P. (1987) *Secondary Headship: The First Years*, Windsor: NFER – Nelson.

West-Burnham, J. (1983) 'A discussion of the implications for secondary school management of a static career structure', *School Organization*, **3**(3): 255–62.

Woods, P. (1983) *Sociology and the School*, London: Routledge & Kegan Paul.

CHAPTER 12

Women in higher education administration in the USA

DIANE M. DUNLAP

Introduction

The number of women in senior academic leadership positions is increasing slowly but is still very small. In 1982, the American Association of University Professors (AAUP), reporting on 2,500 American institutions of higher education, found that at Harvard University, for example, women were only 4.2 per cent of full professors and at Princeton 3.2 per cent. Senior academic administrators are traditionally appointed out of this available pool. These elite institutions were identified as leading examples of a pervasive pattern in American higher education of few women as senior professors and even fewer as academic administrators.

In Britain, Bradley (1989) has reported that 17 per cent of the full-time academic staff and only 3 per cent of full professors are women. Thus, less than 3 per cent of the pool of qualified full professors are women who could be senior academic administrators.

Yet, enough women are promoted each year into senior academic administrative roles in the USA, Canada and Great Britain, that it is not completely unheard-of for a woman to be a formal academic leader. Despite the small numbers of women in the senior faculty of higher education institutions, there are women who are senior academic administrators and who have had very successful careers. However, it has been estimated that as many as 95 per cent of western higher education students are served by white men in all three top administrative roles (e.g. president, chief academic officer, dean) (Sandler and Hall 1986). While there are enough female leaders that it is not a rare exception to see a woman in a senior leadership role, there are still few who successfully cross over the many hurdles necessary even to be considered for such a role (Aisenberg and Harrington 1988, Clark and Corcoran 1986, Swoboda and Vanderbosch 1983).

What are these successful women administrators like? How do they describe their career development? Is there one pervasive career pattern that is peculiar to women as leaders and, if so, does it apply to all types of higher education institutions?

It is these and related questions which have been the focus of my research on women in senior academic administrative roles in the last ten years. I have interviewed and observed (1990) both male and female administrators in different work settings (e.g. business, industry, government, non-profit health, schools, colleges and universities), and I report here findings from a sub-sample of fourteen women who were senior academic administrators in Canadian and US research universities at the time of interview.

I limited the broader study from which this sample is drawn to women in comparable roles in comparable institutions who were identified by their peers as 'very successful leaders'. I interviewed each participant for from three to six hours and observed them in their work setting doing different administrative tasks and working with faculty and administrative groups. I used their description of their work, their formal written job description (if any), and my observations to determine if the roles were 'comparable'. I focused on one type of institution, the large research-oriented American university.

Part of the reason for drawing such a tight boundary around the sample is that there are considerable differences between administrative roles and between types of institutions (e.g. technical college, national college, teachers' college, research university, etc.) in different locales (Twombly 1986, 1990). Even where the same job title is used, one person's role on one campus may differ significantly from another person's role under the same job title on a different campus.

The results of the study are presented after a brief introduction to early research in this field.

Early research and assumptions

Early study of traditional academic administrative careers typically assumed an orderliness at the individual level. Wilensky (1961) described this orderliness as 'a succession of related jobs arranged in a hierarchy of prestige, through which persons move in an ordered (more or less predictable) sequence'. Most studies assumed this linear progression as the normative career path. This assumption automatically identified all people who did not fit the path as deviant or abnormal. Included in this category are most women, non-traditional men, and members of ethnic and cultural minorities (Cohen and March 1986, Moore 1984).

As long as an orderly, planned progression is identified as the normative career path, the orderly path can act as a series of 'filters' which exclude people at any filtering level because their career path, prior to entering the new level, does not follow the prior perceived normative pattern.

In their classic study of the academic world, Caplow and McGee (1958) noted that women, in particular, could not look forward to 'normal' academic careers. Women administrators tended to be found mostly in non-academic administrative roles (e.g. a dean of students or other student services role), there was considerable variation in the patterns of prior work, and less predictability for future work roles. Caplow and McGee identified alternative routes for academic career patterns, but found all such indirect routes to be 'less desirable'.

This sort of assumption has a direct negative impact on most women, since the years of doctoral study and research productivity that are essential for tenure and thus for the first administrative assignments in a 'normal' career come in the years that most women marry and have children. If the 'normal' academic pattern were to be followed by women, it would be at the direct expense of a 'normal' personal life or at great cost to provide a family support system for the 'absent' wife and mother. Under either scenario, the woman is leading an 'abnormal' life in some way (Welch 1990, Armour *et al.*, 1990).

Disciplines

Later studies suggested differences in administrative careers by discipline (Biglan 1973, Eble 1978, Moore 1984, Moore *et al.* 1983, Pfeffer and Moore 1980, Wilke 1983, Carroll 1990). Each academic discipline is, in effect, a national or international market for each specialised faculty position, whereas administrative appointments are more likely to be viewed as local roles. Wilson and Shin (1983) have argued forcibly that discrimination against women in higher education is embedded in hierarchical college curricula, with the highest levels of discrimination occurring in disciplines where income, power and prestige are perceived as the highest ranking among disciplines.

Look at physical science and engineering as an example of differences in disciplines (Zuckerman 1987). In a 1990 National Science Foundation report, it was noted that women account for only 9 and 4 per cent of these fields, respectively, even though their enrolment has grown substantially in the last fifteen years. King in his chapter in this volume notes that entry and advancement within science fields is controlled by core sets of male scientists. Atkinson and Delamont (1990) cited '. . . mastery of the indeterminate' and 'failure to share the habitus'. They found men disproportionately represented in leadership positions and the highest amounts of prejudicial attitudes against women in curricula ranked high on all stratification dimensions.

Administration as a career

Because academic administrative careers have traditionally developed out of careers focused first on the faculty role, there are few early extensive studies of higher education administration as a career. What study there was typically equated all institutions and positions: research universities, community colleges, vocational colleges, chairpersons, division heads, programme directors, deans, academic vice-presidents, support positions, presidents, etc. (Moore and Sagaria 1981, Green and Kellogg 1982). This occurred even though types of jobs were quite different and were sometimes described as such (Mattfield 1972). That positions were equated across very different institutions in very different cultural and social contexts further masked unique characteristics of particular roles.

Types of institutions

Where institutional type is acknowledged, differences have not always been found in career patterns. Twombly (1986) found differences in patterns, while Carroll (1990) did not. Twombly suggests that most administrative movement within higher education takes one of four forms: moving to positions at the same institution that have greater responsibility or status; having a position at the same institution evolve into a position of greater responsibility; leaving one institution for a higher position at another institution; and accepting a lower position at an institution that has higher status. Her work at this stage still assumed horizontal career paths, but took into consideration institution type. She showed that the 'normal' pattern was not normal for most administrators, even in different types of higher education institutions, and even for single-sex and historically black institutions where there might be unique reasons to predict some normative pattern.

Gender

Most early studies of administrative careers in academe did not sort by male and female, since women were latecomers to formal education and to non-sex-segregated paid work like academic positions (Nivea and Gutek 1981). The few studies reporting on gender focused on the faculty role and career advancement as faculty members (Blackburn and Havighurst 1979, Bowen and Schuster 1986). Menges and Exum (1983), for example, found that while one-third of all men who received a doctorate in history from 1970 to 1974 were full professors in 1980, less than one-eighth of the comparable women graduates were professors and even less had served in any administrative role. By 1981, women represented more than half of the undergraduate and graduate students in American universities, yet received only 31.5 per cent of awarded doctorates and represented less than one quarter of junior faculty members nationwide (Hewlett 1986). Finkelstein (1984) reported that while female representation in faculty ranks grew by more than 7 per cent during the 1970s, it is now at a level equivalent to that of the 1930s.

Such differential advancement and retention reduces the number of women eligible for academic administrative posts (Rausch *et al.* 1989). While females represent more than half of the total population and more than half of the students in colleges and universities today, they are underrepresented at all professorial levels and for subsequent academic administrative positions.

While gender has not historically been identified as a variable important to study in higher education, there is ample evidence that gender does mark a significant difference in career progression for men and women. For example, Mann (1990) used four broad settings in her study of faculty: (1) schooling, (2) work outside academia, (3) the academic career, and (4) life away from work. Personal variables were found to be particularly significant: marriage, divorce, relocation, children, family-of-origin, geographic concerns, illness and buying a home were all reported at a high level as causing problems in faculty career progression. She found that married women listed a higher proportion of life-away-from-work events than unmarried women and all men, married or unmarried. When only faculty who had children were considered, 68 per cent of the women and 20 per cent of the men reported such events as critical to their careers. Women and men were equally likely to list births as critical career events, but the continued presence of children at home affected females significantly more than males.

There is an additional gender issue in other research on leadership that has not been well addressed in study of higher education administrative leadership. Kanter (1977) has reported that women often find it difficult to manage other women and that it is more problematic for women to manage men since gender expectations are in conflict with administrative expectations. Yet Dunlap and Schmuck (in press) have reported many studies that document women's success in administrative roles. I have also argued that preferred administrative power roles in educational settings have changed, and success can no longer be determined by old, predominantly male norms of leadership (Dunlap and Goldman 1991, Goldman *et al.* 1993). As role expectations change, so may the impact on men and women in those roles.

Summary

Early research has produced limited study of academic administration careers, with even more limited application to today's institutional realities. What is characteristic of today's higher education is multiple career systems within rapidly evolving institutions, ill-defined career paths, multiple entrance (and exit) points to careers, and lack of explicit criteria about specific career tracks. Since early studies did not distinguish difference by type of position, career path, discipline area, administrative track, gender/family/ethnicity, or by locale, there is much to learn about different career paths in higher education. If differences exist by any of these variables or combination of variables, they have not been apparent because they have not been singled out for study. It is possible that such a set of complex, interrelated variables might affect most men and women differently, might look different for different roles in different settings, might differ by the discipline of origin of the administrator or by the structure of work at each campus. Each of these factors will be discussed individually and then as they work together to complicate our understanding of career paths for women in higher education administration.

Results of the study

In this study, I focused on a group of fourteen women administrators and asked each of them to describe their career development in administration. This is a form of critical events research that falls within the broader framework of life history methodology. Baldwin (1979) and others have successfully used this technique to study faculty careers. It is a way of examining how an individual's school history, pattern of work outside academe, work inside academe, and life away from work have affected career development. Discussion is divided into nine areas: role identification, skills acquisition, gender and power, career development, early focus, balance of work/family, access/opportunities, aspirations/expectations, and mentors.

Role identification

These women described a successful progression through faculty ranks, as might be expected when interviewing people in roles that have historically required such progression. Eleven of the women were married; nine had had children. While the majority told one or more stories of difficult times with family or financial responsibilities interfering with career, they all reported successfully overcoming those difficulties.

Despite ten or more years in substantially full-time administration, these women continued to define themselves in terms of their primary field, e.g. biologist, historian, sociologist, etc.

Well, I never planned to be an administrator. I had wanted to be a biologist since I was a child. I concentrated on science through high school and college. I got a good research fellowship for graduate school and my only question was whether I was going to be a full-time researcher or a researcher and a teacher. I never gave administration much thought.

I knew I was good at organising things. What professional woman isn't? But it came as kind of a surprise when the men in my department asked me to take a turn as chair of the department and then that led to being dean. I still think of myself as an historian; I still write and read in my field and I go to my professional meetings, even though it is harder to keep up with my other responsibilities.

The women described their professional careers as bifurcated; first they had a successful faculty career, and then a successful administrative career 'happened'. They also typically described their administrative successes in terms that downplayed their roles and ascribed success to circumstances.

I didn't seek the position, but when I saw that they wanted me to do it, I took it and I did a pretty good job. Of course, it was because lots of key faculty pitched in and helped when it was needed. There were lots of problems I couldn't have solved without their help.

Administration is not a big thing. It is mostly listening to people and using your common sense. I guess I do well because I'm lucky.

I've had the good fortune to be part of a successful period of time on our campus.

These women are active participants in the accepted ritual conceit of claiming faculty status first, and then subsequently downplaying one's role and one's actions in administration. Until the last few decades, higher education administration was typically, politely viewed as an unplanned career embedded within a primary planned career. Administrators were seen as senior faculty who had been successful in their primary career as a professor and, for some peculiar reason, were drafted to occupy a 'temporary' administrative post. This embedded career was generally said to 'evolve without conscious forethought' as a natural consequence of success as a faculty member among one's peers (Green and Kellog 1982, Graham 1973). So, even though a majority of faculty spend part of their academic career in administration (Astin 1981), becoming an administrator has been viewed as a fortuitous, but not predictable, event not particularly worthy of study beyond occasional reporting of an unique individual's academic life.

This myth of a 'normal career' of unplanned ascendence has masked a considerably more complex reality. It masks competition for power, and even the acknowledgement that such competition might be a 'fitting' thing for a faculty person. Keeping ambition for, and preferred occupancy of, administrative roles a silent topic has also masked the under-representation of many people in administration. Politely not discussing administration has created silences about the effects on women, non-traditional white males, and minorities; about career paths by type of institution and type of role; about differences in academic careers by the discipline area in which the faculty member is housed; and about alternative routes 'to the top'.

Interestingly, the 'normative' administrative career pattern does not apply even to the men who have administrative careers. Moore and her colleagues (1983) tested the supposed normative career ladder for academic administrators in the United States and found that 76 per cent of the presidents studied did not fit the 'normal' pattern.

In fact, higher education administration is not one career, but is a family of careers, where many of those who become administrators of colleges and universities have not been and do not plan to be faculty members. It does not take deep study to identify different tracks of lifelong administrative commitment at any campus: dean of students, director of admissions, academic dean, vice-president for research, athletic director, student union director, etc. Yet, the myth of one 'normal' pattern persists.

Skills acquisition

Most of the women in this study appeared to want to brush aside discussions of coping strategies or skills acquisition as being something they, and others, do as a matter of course and therefore not worthy of being a primary topic of discussion. None of the women seemed to find their skills acquisition strategies unusual, and more than half noted surprise that the question was asked.

When I pursued the question into specifics of, for example, budget management, or long-range strategic planning, all the interviewees were quickly forthcoming on how and where they had acquired skills necessary to be successful at budgeting or planning.

Oh, I see what you mean. I've never really thought about it that way. Doesn't everybody do that? I mean when you move into a new job situation, or something comes up that changes the institution, then that's what you do – you find out what you need and you find out where to get it. That's why I like working in a university; you can get to almost anything you might need to know by just going down a hallway and asking around.

I haven't done much formal training since my doctorate, if that is what you mean. And I haven't done many workshops or administrative institutes or that kind of thing. I keep up with management trends, as well as the literature in my field. But, no, I guess I'd have to say that the thing I do most is I have friends and colleagues, some here and some in my professional associations, who I talk with and I learn from them and they learn from me. I experiment a lot. Lots of what you need is just good common sense.

In fact, most respondents became quite animated in describing acquisition skills, once they had stated that it was 'something everyone did'. I often had the sense that many of these capable administrators looked at determining what they needed to know and then finding the fastest and most cost-effective way of getting that knowledge, before anyone else, as 'entertainment'. Part of the challenge of administrative work was like playing a game where you only had part of the rules and part of the tools; the 'fun' was finding out what you needed and getting it before anyone else did.

Villadsen and Tack (1981) found successful higher education administrators who are women using many successful coping strategies to deal with potentially conflicting work and personal responsibilities. The women experienced conflicts in scheduling, etc. to which they often found ingenious solutions. Many of them reported, however, that the expectations of others were often more difficult to resolve than the actual problems themselves. When pressed for examples, the women in my study reported similar perceptions.

The biggest problem I have is more that my campus colleagues think I don't know something, or that I can't understand it, or that I wouldn't be interested, and I have to continually intervene and keep in touch to keep from being left out of the conversation entirely. This isn't skills, is it? This is prejudice.

I like solving problems. What 'pisses me off' is the people you have to solve around. Knowing how to do something is seldom an issue for me. Figuring out the politics to get it done is where the action is.

Gender and power

When I asked what they perceived people's opinions about a woman in their role, replies typically downplayed both gender and power as issues.

I don't think it makes any difference. I just sort of lead the group to some conclusion when we have a problem. Being male or female doesn't have much to do with anything, and I don't think that most people think much about it.

Well, there hadn't been a woman in this (role) before, but that was just because we hadn't had a woman in the department until a few years ago.

Whoever is [in this role] doesn't have much control over events or people. I'm at the mercy of the faculty, just like every man before me.

Differences between men and women can also be seen in individual aspirations. Male faculty have expressed greater confidence, greater career and performance satisfaction, and more interest in going into administration than female faculty (Sorcinelli and Andrews 1987). These successful women administrators appear to be overcoming difficulties in management of men and women, in that their peers identified them as successful managers. Yet, their talk significantly understates their success.

Career development

When I asked them about career development, their answers yielded five distinct themes: early faculty focus, balance of work and family, access and opportunities, aspirations and expectations, and mentors.

Early faculty focus

All of the women in this study described an early career focus on graduate work and subsequent development of a successful faculty career. Twelve of them reported not thinking about serving in an administrative role in advance, but being willing to 'take their turn' as head or chair when others asked them to do so. Most of them continue to describe themselves as faculty first, and administrators second.

Balance of work and family

There appeared to be no pattern in whether they were single or married, or in whether they had children or other dependent responsibilities. Whatever their family or financial circumstances, they successfully negotiated the early career stages. When asked, each of them readily identified many women colleagues who were not successful at each stage because of 'birth of a child', 'partner took another job', 'had to leave studies to earn money', 'lost a fellowship', 'became ill', etc. They often used words like 'lucky' to describe their own negotiation of a difficult stage in their career or family. Once they had made a conscious commitment to administration as a late career track, many of them did talk about conscious planning for balance between work and non-work needs. Examples include timing of a partner's retirement, timing of a promotion to coincide with a last child leaving home, etc.

Some of the women administrators in this study talked about 'prevention' of conflicts as a coping strategy, but it was not the primary theme of their career development. Women in Villadsen and Tack's study (1981) reported marrying late, marrying an understanding fellow professional, and limiting the number of children in the family as the best 'preventive coping strategies' in forging a successful career. The women in this study seemed to either be less planful about achieving this balance, or simply reflect a changing societal norm where there is a broad expectation that young women balancing family and career is not unusual or impossible.

While 68 per cent of faculty in Muller's study (1990) included some aspect of life away from work in describing critical events in their careers, the variance was found in personal variables rather than in rank or disciplinary areas, or, for that matter, in academic variables in general. Married women reported a higher proportion of life-away-from-work events than unmarried women and all men. Muller described the successful professionals as 'survivors'.

The women in my study appear to be Muller's survivors, but they ascribe the most critical events in their careers to the at-work variables described in this chapter.

The most critical event in my career was opportunity, and support from key people on campus when the opportunity occurred. That had a lot more to do with my promotion than my skills, abilities, or readiness. My family would have helped me adjust to whatever I needed to do.

I've been lucky. I am healthy and so is my family. We have been able to get through some of the years that tears other families apart, and still keep very interesting professional lives. But the biggest difference came in opportunity at work; if opportunity doesn't happen, it doesn't matter how ready you or your family are.

In Muller's study, women were concentrated in lower faculty ranks, were less likely to have tenure, and were less likely to be married. When these statistics are combined with a general societal institutionalised expectation that aspirations and expectations *ought* to be different for men and women, under-representation is not necessarily defined as a 'problem'. While the demographics in Muller's study, and in this one, seem to speak quite loudly on their own, it should not seem surprising that the way in which these very successful women describe their career paths echoes a broad set of institutionalised norms of expectation.

Access and opportunities

These women regularly used works like 'lucky', 'fortuitous', and 'godsend' to describe the complex balance between often conflicting responsibilities that they negotiated throughout the early years of their faculty careers. Most of them described family responsibilities in addition to the demands of long work hours. The majority also described some type of unpaid work, church or leisure activities that they balanced along with work and family.

They frequently noted that they were 'fortunate' at many critical stages such as tenure, promotion, book publication, etc. They would describe an 'opportunity' that occurred, and someone who helped them take advantage of it. Eleven of the fourteen argued that they were first promoted because no qualified male was available, wanted the position, or was acceptable to the faculty. Nine of the eleven said that all three conditions had to occur for their first promotion to happen; if a qualified male was available, wanted the position, and was acceptable to his peers, a woman would not be automatically considered for leadership.

Some made the argument of male preference for the first department head/chair position into which they were promoted. They argued that the first administrative position was because there wasn't a qualified man; subsequent positions came because they had that first chance to show what they could do, and people got 'used to' their leadership. Others made the male preference argument for later promotions in the administrative hierarchy as well.

Yes, I became chair because the 'boys' were fighting with each other, and I seemed the safest bet. They didn't think I could really do the job, and some of them thought I would be easier to manipulate to do the work our peers wouldn't let them do directly. So, at first, I got to be chair because I was the most preferred bad alternative. Then, well, I guess they liked what I did because nobody wanted to throw me out later.

The first time I was chair it was because our 'natural' leader was on sabbatical. Plus, there was a big budget problem and some of the other guys didn't want to be responsible for dealing with it. They had to argue me into it, actually. I didn't want to do it either.

In my case, 'chance' had a lot to do with the first time. I was there, and I was ready, and nobody else wanted it. They didn't complain, or make sexist remarks, or anything. But, if one of them had been ready, it would have been a different story.

Seven of the eleven women who talked about male preference did not recall 'lobbying' for the first position. Nor did they count their administrative career from their first administrative appointment.

That is a related point. Only one woman counted the beginning of the administrative phase of her career as the department chair/head role. Most of these women described that role as 'taking their turn' at some of the 'dirty work' that faculty have to do now and then for their collegial group. It was only with the acceptance of subsequent appointments that they acknowledged a new primary career path in administration. That acknowledgement was typically made with references to the unplanned nature of the promotions and with reference to their original primary faculty discipline.

I didn't know that this was going to happen in my career. I had planned to be a scientist, not an administrator who used to be a scientist. I didn't really figure out that I had changed directions permanently until I was asked to be (the vice-president), and I knew I couldn't return to my research later.

I still think about myself as an historian who has taken some time out to 'help the cause'. Pretty amusing when I notice that I have been doing this 'temporary' work for almost twenty years.

Aspirations and expectations

Acknowledgement of a 'career' in administration was also typically retrospective and not extended to the future. While most of the women readily acknowledged that they were seen as successful administrators, they appeared immediately uncomfortable when asked about future administrative aspirations.

Who knows what will happen next? I try to do my job, and I'm ready to go back to teaching any time. I don't think that anyone can plan the future.

Do I want to be present? I don't know. I've never thought about it [from a senior vice-president who was covering responsibilities for the president's office while the president was ill].

Oh, I know I've been doing this for more than a decade, but I wouldn't say I have a career in administration. This is just something I have enjoyed doing, and that the institution needed to have someone do. I don't know what or who the institution will need next, and I plan to spend the rest of my work life here, so I don't 'plan' a 'higher' position.

The social norms of faculty being faculty, and not seeking administrative power, appear to be at work here in the way these very successful senior administrators both have a successful career progression as administrators, but talk about their career as being non-administrative. I believe that this is compounded by the pervasive social norm that women do not seek overt power. In these interviews, this combination of pervasive norms added up to a pattern of silence or awkward speaking for these women.

I suppose I do have a career in administration ... if you look at it that way. I don't. I have spent most of the last fifteen years in administration. But this isn't a career. I just don't think about it that way. This [university] is my home and it has just worked out that I have been able to be useful. It could have been anyone.

My career is [in my faculty field]. Administration just happened. I am good at it, and I think it is a good way for me to contribute during my 'golden years'. But a career is something you plan, isn't it? I didn't plan this.

When I pressed this person on whether she was 'good at' the administrative roles, or maybe even 'better at' them than others, she replied:

Yes, I am very good at this. Administration requires a keen eye, an ability to work with people, endurance and friends around you. Who could have guessed that I would turn out to be good at this?

Another very capable senior administrator on the same campus replied:

Career? My career is as a faculty member. Becoming an academic administrator is something your peers decide. So, I can do it for a while. Then, I go back to being a faculty member.

When I asked this woman what she wanted to do next, however, another picture emerged.

I've had a good chance to see what happens in a president's office during the last six months, and I've been talking with the other [leaders on campus and in the region], and we've decided to try and position me in a presidency. I have a contribution to make, and I think that the timing is right for a lot of reasons.

During these interviews, and in follow-up conversations, I continued to be amazed at the ability of obviously capable, dedicated administrators to say one thing and do another. I do not mean that these administrators are devious; I mean that the pervasive nature of institutionalised norms bring even these most astute people to actions and words that are amazingly contradictory on the surface.

Mentors

One of the 'opportunities' frequently described by these women as part of their success was identification of one or more mentors in their administrative progression. Typically, the first mentor was a male administrator who told them they could be effective administrators and subsequently helped them with local campus politics, specific management skills or strategic manoeuvring. Seven identified more than one mentor. Only two said that they sought out the first mentor, but eight said they sought other mentors as they progressed through administrative positions.

The biggest influence for me was when [a senior administrator] began to give me projects to do, and talk to me about taking charge in a formal way. He also really paved the way when I was ready.

I wouldn't have made it through the first six months if I hadn't had 'friends in high places'. That sounds cliché, I know, but I needed help behind the scenes and [they] provided it for me.

Mentors played a critical informal role for most of these women. This role included advice and instruction on how to negotiate the 'unwritten rules' of power in order to progress in the administrative career. In her 1990 study of faculty, Mann found that there were significant ways in which career tracks differ for men and women faculty, especially where multiple life events were considered. Men were much more likely to have access to temporary administrative responsibilities than women, regardless of institutional type or discipline. This access was often through nomination from a senior administrator. Since administrative appointment was often with unclear guidelines and process, many women were not familiar with possible options for administrative appointment.

Muller (1990) argues that such 'hidden passages' affect women and minorities more severely than white men who more typically have direct access to career movement. While Muller does not list administrative assignments as a 'hidden passage', they clearly fall within her definition of alternative routes through a faculty career as 'means by which an individual opts for a certain form of professional activity to allow greater flexibility or freedom to accommodate families and careers in the context of pursuing very demanding professional roles' (1990: 6). This marginalisation of women within the faculty careers that form the pool from which academic administrators are drawn applies to both access to administration, and to continuing problems with promotion once entry is achieved (Hewlitt 1986).

The women in this study found mentors, or mentors found them, and they were helped to negotiate the formal and informal passages necessary for a successful administrative career. This finding is consistent with other studies of women and mentoring (Johnsrud 1990).

Conclusions

What are these successful women administrators like? How do they describe their career development? Is there one pervasive career pattern that is peculiar to women as leaders and, if so, does it apply to all types of higher education institutions?

These women are as varied in personality and style as the general population. They begrudgingly acknowledge that administration is part of their basic faculty career track. They reported similar complex patterns of career development that screen out most women before reaching the pool from which senior academic administrators are selected. And, despite all odds, they successfully negotiated difficult and complex paths to senior administration.

I was impressed by the ability of these women to negotiate a complex series of obstacles to (a) complete required graduate education, (b) achieve entry into the faculty profession, (c) negotiate all performance hurdles required for promotion and tenure, (d) maintain simultaneous work and family responsibilities, so they can (e) be ready to understand an additional career avenue available to them through administration when it appears, and (f) be flexible enough to seek new knowledge and skills not formally available to anyone, often in the face of (g) lack of understanding of the difficulty of their task by themselves and those around them. All of this occurred for these successful female administrators in a normative atmosphere of often narrow and conflicting views of what is acceptable or preferred behaviour for a woman, a professional, and an academic administrator.

I have described several pervasive patterns identified through interviewing and observing these administrators. First, even these very capable achieving women continued to downplay their accomplishments by their choice of self-describing language. I do not think that they are unaware of their capability or of their achievement. I believe they are walking the fine line of manners of what is acceptable to themselves or to others as women and as academic people. How they see themselves as women and as faculty influences how they talk about what they do and how they determine what constitutes appropriate discussion of power. How their colleagues and family see them as individuals, as females, as academics, and as administrators, also influences how they see themselves and how they determined appropriateness of behaviour and description of behaviour.

Second, I believe that the ability of these women to negotiate successfully excellent leadership actions, alongside strong norms of silence on issues of power and aspiration, is indicative of slowly changing gender and power expectations. While these women represent a relatively small percentage of people in comparable administrative roles, none of them described their roles or career paths as being 'extraordinary'. Nor did their peers identify them as 'extraordinary', just because they were women. For example, most of their peers did not remark on my request to name a successful senior administrator who was female as an unusual or peculiar request. This lack of comment occurred in spite of the fact that, in some states and provinces, people had trouble thinking of any females who met the definition of senior academic administrator in a large research university. If a woman occupied the role, she was almost automatically identified as successful. If no woman was identified, the only comment typically made was, 'I never noticed that before' or 'I wonder how long that has been true because I'm sure we've had some before'. Even where representation did not exist, there seemed to be changing expectations that there would typically be representation of women in senior positions.

Clearly, women and their colleagues in senior academic administrative positions have much to teach us about how women professionals view themselves, how others view them, and how success in a career can be achieved. Even in this small sample, it is apparent that different career tracks look different for different roles in different settings, differ by the discipline or origin of the administrator, and by the structure of work at each campus. Based on the findings of this study, it is possible to predict that such a set of complex, interrelated variables might affect most men and women differently. Certainly, additional research can help us learn more about how some people are able to negotiate complex roles and thrive in less than supportive environments.

References

Aisenberg, N. and Harrington, M. (1988) *Women of Academe: Outsiders in the Sacred Grove*, Amherst: University of Massachusetts Press.

American Association of University Professors (1982) *Annual Report*.

Armour, R., Fuhrmann, B. and Wergin, J. (1990) 'Racial and gender differences in faculty careers', paper presented at the annual meeting of the American Educational Research Association.

Astin, H. S. (1981) 'Academic scholarship and its rewards', Invited address delivered at the annual meeting of the American Educational Research Association, Los Angeles, CA.

Atkinson, P. and Delamont, S. (1990) 'Professions and powerlessness: female marginality in the learned occupations', *Sociological Review*, **38**(1): 90–110.

Baldwin, R. G. (1979) 'The faculty career process–continuity and change: a study of college professors at five stages of the academic career', Unpublished doctoral dissertation, University of Michigan, Ann Arbor.

Biglan, A. (1973) 'The characteristics of subject matter in different academic areas', *Journal of Applied Psychology*, **57**: 195–203.

Blackburn, R. T. and Havighurst, R. J. (1979) 'Career patterns of US male academic social scientists', *Higher Education*, **8**: 553–72.

Bowen, H. R. and Schuster, J. H. (1986) *American Professors*, New York: Oxford University Press.

Bradley, H. (1989) *Men's Work, Women's Work*, Cambridge: Polity Press.

Caplow, T. and McGee, R. G. (1958) *The Academic Marketplace*, New York: Basic Books.

Carroll, J. B. (1990) 'Career paths of department chairs in doctorate granting institutions', Paper presented at the annual conference of the American Educational Research Association, Boston, Massachusetts.

Clark, S. M. and Corcoran, M. (1986) 'Perspectives on the professional socialization of women faculty: a case of accumulative disadvantage', *Journal of Higher Education*, **57**: 20–43.

Cohen, M. D. and March, J. G. (1986) *Leadership and Ambiguity: the American College President*, 2nd end, Boston: Harvard Business School Press.

Dunlap, D. M. (1990) 'Differences between men and women administrators in four settings', Paper presented at the annual meeting of the American Educational Research Association, San Francisco, CA.

Dunlap, D. M. and Goldman, P. (1991) 'Rethinking power in schools', *Educational Administration Quarterly*, **27**(1): 5–29.

Dunlap, D. M. and Schmuck, P. (1994) *Women Leading in Education*, New York: SUNY Press.

Eble, K. E. (1978) *The Art of Administration*, San Francisco: Jossey-Bass.

Finkelstein, M. J. (1984) *The American Academic Profession*, Columbus, Ohio: State University Press.

Goldman, P., Dunlap, D. M. and Conley, D. T. (1993) 'Facilitative power and nonstandardized solutions to school site restructuring', *Educational Administration Quarterly*, **29**(1): 69–92.

Graham, P. A. (1973) 'Status transition of women students, faculty, and administrators' in A. Rossi and A. Calderwood (eds) *Academic Women on the Move*, New York: Russell Sage Foundation.

Green, M. F. and Kellogg, T. (1982) 'Careers in academe: confirming the conventional wisdom', *Educational Record*, Spring 40–3.

Hewlett, S. A. (1986) *A Lesser Life: The Myth of Women's Liberation in America*, New York: William Morrow.

Johnsrud, L. K. (1990) 'Mentoring between academic women: the capacity for interdependence', Paper presented at the annual conference of the American Educational Research Association, Boston, Massachusetts.

Kanter, R. M. (1977) *Work and Family Life in the United States: A Critical Review and Agenda for Research and Policy*, New York: Russell Sage Foundation.

Mann, M. P. (1990) 'The impact of life events on faculty careers', Paper presented at the annual conference of the American Educational Research Association, Boston, Massachusetts.

Mattfeld, J. (1972) 'Many are called, but few are chosen', Paper presented at the annual meeting of the American Council on Education, ED 071 549.

Menges, R. J. and Exum, W. H. (1983) 'Barriers to the progress of women and minority faculty', *Journal of Higher Education*, **54**: 123–44.

Moore, K. M. (1984) 'The structure of administrative careers: a prose poem in four parts', *Review of Higher Education*, 8(1): 1–13.

Moore, K. M. and Sagaria, M. A. (1981) 'Women administrators and mobility: the second struggle', *Journal of NAWDAC*, 44(2): 21–8.

Moore, K. M., Salimbene, A. M., Marlier, J. D. and Bragg, S. M. (1983) 'The structures of presidents' and deans' careers', *Journal of Higher Education*, 54(5): 500–15.

Muller, C. B. (1990) 'Hidden passages to success in the academic labor market', Paper presented at the annual meeting of the American Educational Research Association, Boston, Massachusetts.

National Science Foundation (1990) *Women and Minorities in Science and Engineering*, Washington, DC: National Science Foundation.

Nivea, V. F. and Gutek, B. A. (1981) *Women and Work: A Psychological Perspective*, New York: Praeger.

Pfeffer, J. and Moore, W. L. (1980) 'Average tenure of academic department heads: the effects of paradigm, size, and departmental demography', *Administrative Science Quarterly*, 25 September 387–406.

Rausch, D. K., Ortiz, B. P., Douthitt, R. A. and Reed, L. L. (1989) 'The academic revolving door: why do women get caught?' *CUPA Journal*, Spring, 40(1): 1–16.

Sandler, B. R. and Hall, R. M. (1986) 'The campus climate revisited: chilly for women faculty, administrators and graduate students', Project on the status and education of women, Association of American Colleges, Washington, DC.

Sorcinelli, M. D. and Andrews, P. H. (1987) 'Articulating career goals: a comparison of male and female university faculty', *Journal of NAWDAC*, 50(1): 11–19.

Swoboda, M. J. and Vanderbosch, J. (1983) 'The society of outsiders: women in administration', *Journal of NAWDAC*, 46(3): 3–6.

Twombly, S. B. (1986) *Theoretical Approaches to the Study of Career Mobility: Applications to Administrative Career Mobility in Colleges and Universities*, San Francisco: Jossey-Bass.

Twombly, S. B. (1990) 'Career maps and institutional highways', in K. M. Moore and S. B. Twombly (eds) *Administrative Careers and the Marketplace*, San Francisco: Jossey-Bass.

Villadsen, A. W. and Tack, M. W. (1981) 'Combining home and career responsibilities: the methods used by women executives in higher education', *Journal of NAWDAC*, 44(3): 20–25.

Welch, L. B. (1990) *Women in Higher Education*, New York: Praeger.

Wilensky, E. (1961) 'Orderly careers and social participation', *American Sociological Review*, 26: 521–39.

Wilke, P. K. (1983) 'The relationship of the reward structure, sources of stress, and productivity in a land-grant university', Unpublished dissertation, Washington State University.

Wilson, K. L. and Shin, E. H. (1983) 'Reassessing the discrimination against women in higher education', *American Educational Research Journal*, Winter 20(4): 529–51.

Zuckerman, H. (1987) 'Persistence and change in the careers of men and women scientists and engineers', in L. S. Dix (ed.) *Women: Their Underrepresentation and Career Differentials in Science and Engineering*, Washington, DC: National Academy Press.

CHAPTER 13

Women in management careers: opportunities and outcomes

LYNN ASHBURNER

Introduction

What does a career in management mean for a woman? The issues raised by this question are illustrative of the wide range of constraints which serve to minimise the participation of women at higher levels within all types of careers and all types of organisations. The concepts of both career and of management, as they exist in current literature, are viewed predominantly from the norm of male experience. Early concepts of work were seen purely in male terms, but the influence of research on women and work and of feminist theory has broadened the perspective now taken within sociological studies (Beechey 1986). The early focus on men, usually in manual work with full-time and continuous employment patterns, no longer predominates. Studies of work now encompass both peripheral workers; the part-time, home-working, contractual and temporary; as well as unpaid labour in the domestic and voluntary spheres.

With women firmly established in the world of work, the concept of career needs to be re-examined. This continues to be viewed in the narrow terms of a typically male employment profile; a full-time and continuous work pattern, recognised promotion stages plus, in some cases, the early attainment of professional or related qualifications. The consequence is that women are marginalised when it comes to seeking a career.

Dex (1987) in her examination of the Women and Employment Survey (WES) (Martin and Roberts 1984), shows how the concept of career has developed within the sociology of work. Where 'career' is conceptualised as a work history it is predominantly descriptive and could accommodate women. However the literature on careers has focused on the production of career typologies which are predominantly prescriptive and, being in the mainstream of occupational studies, have concentrated exclusively on men. The WES data uniquely offered the opportunity to identify patterns of women's occupational experiences over time. Such an empirical base is necessary before a meaningful set of career types can be constructed which include both men and women.

Analysis of women's career paths suggests that even where women are not marginal in numbers, they are marginal when it comes to career progression. Concepts such as cultural duality can be offered as ways of explaining or understanding women's position but they also serve the purpose of suggesting that the 'problem' then lies with women. An alternative way of understanding how women relate to the concept of career is to challenge the concept itself and see why it excludes women, with the result that the 'problem' now lies with the concept.

What are the opportunities for women who seek management careers? McRae (1990) suggests that opportunities for women have never been greater. Of the 1.7 million new jobs predicted by 1995, 1 million will be in the professional and related occupations (IER 1989). The likelihood of women taking up a major share of these new jobs is increased by the continuing trend among women to gain professional and higher level qualifications (Crompton 1986), and by data which show that the growth rate in numbers of women in professional and related occupations has doubled that of men (IER 1989). Data (*Social Trends* 1991) show that 45 per cent of students studying for business degrees and social administration are women, compared with 10 per cent in 1973. Entry is now posing less of a problem than career progression.

Womens' expectations are changing. As an increasing number of women are spending most of their working life in employment (Martin and Roberts 1984), more are looking for work which takes them beyond the low-skilled and part-time mass markets which employers offer to women. The prospect of a career, which usually involves the attainment of qualifications, is one area where women have always tried to compete equally with men. Armed with equal qualifications, the question of equal ability would appear to be answered. However, the promotion policies and processes within many organisations remain rife with indirect discrimination (Ashburner 1988). The management career ladders within organisations and professions exemplify these processes well.

This chapter begins by considering the gendered nature of management work and the participation pattern of women in management. The question is whether men and women can be viewed as similar or different in relation to their ability to manage, and recent literature, which has produced conflicting analyses, will be examined. The nature of management work needs to be explored in relation to the myths and realities of perceptions of gender difference.

Second, the chapter will examine organisational processes which influence the structure of career patterns. This will draw on recent literature and the author's own research within the finance sector, to examine the particular problems faced by women who aim for management careers.

Thus we have the dual problem in analysis of the need both to redefine the main concepts in use, as well as to increase our understanding of the roles, structures and processes which exist in organisations. The chapter will conclude with a discussion on the importance both of redefining career and understanding the position of women in employment.

The necessity for the development of gender as a category of analysis is emphasised. In studying careers an analysis of the process of interaction between the individual and the organisation exposes not just the ways in which social forms and processes are reproduced but also the ways in which they might be changed.

Management

The problems encountered by women seeking careers in typically male professions have been outlined by other contributors to this book. Given the pattern of women's position in the hierarchies of most organisations, management as a career is no different. Management can be viewed as a career in itself but for many professional women, a move into management may represent promotion. Alban-Metcalfe and Nicholson (1984) show that female managers were more likely to be 'specialists' than 'generalists'.

Management may literally mean 'the management of others' but in many organisations 'management' remains a descriptive term for a position in the hierarchy which denotes a level of responsibility rather than a supervisory role. It is problematic to define 'management' since management structures, responsibilities and levels of qualification required, differ between employment sectors. However in terms of process, gender forms a constant variable and by studying women in management it is possible to understand those processes which are integral to all working environments, which result in low numbers of women in senior positions.

Women in management

Women are most likely to be managers in those occupations which are still traditionally female such as catering and retail (Alban-Metcalfe and Nicholson 1984). Higher percentages of women are employed in service organisations such as education, health, training and professional services. Wilson (1991) has shown that more women end up in the public sector because of even more limited opportunities elsewhere. They are also more likely to be found in certain managerial occupations such as training, office administration and personnel.

Given the difficulties in defining management and comparing 'management' posts across organisations, data on the number of women in management is problematic to produce. The Hansard Commission (1990) calculated that in 1988 women accounted for 11 per cent of general managerial staff, rising to 25 per cent of managerial jobs outside general management.

While women are attaining managerial posts at lower levels in organisations it remains difficult for them to reach upper and senior management positions (Asplund 1988). In 1988 only 5 per cent of members of the Institute of Directors were women and of its 35,000 members in 1991 only about 6 per cent were women (Howe and McRae 1991). This may not be representative since the membership of the Institute comes mainly from small and medium sized firms. Eighty per cent of the companies in the Hansard survey (1990) had no women on their main board and with the inclusion of subsidiary boards, the figure was less than 4 per cent.

With less than 1 per cent women chief executives and with so few in key positions in organisations, it is inevitable that the structures and value systems, which set the rules and culture of organisations, are dominated by men.

The process of marginalisation which is experienced by many women in the professions (Spencer and Podmore 1987) can also occur within the management hierarchies of organisations. It is, however, only one of several strategies which serve to restrict the progress of women. In those employment sectors which are highly feminised, the lack of women in senior management cannot be blamed on their marginality. The continuation of male domination of management is less to do with the scarcity of women than to do with organisational culture which sets both the requirements for progression and the predominant management style.

Management style

Of the numerous studies which have compared men and women managers most have concluded that there are far more similarities than differences in terms of efficiency and performance. Where differences do occur they are due to attitudinal factors, the low proportion of female managers and individual life circumstances.

Studies of management style have produced apparently differing conclusions. Many writers believed that it was more important for women to stress their similarity to men and to minimise the differences, which might be used as excuses for their lack of promotion. However, other writers believed that it was important to acknowledge the differences between men and women as managers. This was not just to show that women might be more suitable in certain roles and environments but also as an attempt to raise the issue of the assumptions being made about 'management'. The argument was that the definition of what management is should be changed, not just to accommodate more women, but to increase organisational flexibility by broadening the predominant value system. It may be significant that it was a woman, Mary Parker Follett (1926) who laid down the foundations of modern management, developing the work of the classical school by stressing the centrality of democratic social relationships, 'creative collectiveness' and participative management.

Stereotypes in management values

What are termed 'male' and 'female' values are not necessarily attributable to men and women individually but form the basis of stereotyping. The male stereotypes usually focus on attributes such as independence, competitiveness, focus, control, ambition, activity and attention to specifics. For women they comprise attributes such as interdependence, co-operation, acceptance, receptivity, ethics and perception of wholes. Whereas in an ideal world any set of polarities would be seen as complementary, in the world of management male stereotypes have predominated and have influenced the structures, processes and policies within organisations.

Difference is not important

Alban-Metcalfe and Nicholson's (1984) study of the members of the British Institute of Management highlighted the main differences between men and women managers. Women managers, for example, were more likely to be unmarried and have no children, when compared to their male counterparts. A study by Nicholson and West (1988) of 2,300 British managers showed that women managers were younger, lower paid, more highly educated, occupied lower levels of management, were less likely to be married and twice as likely to be divorced or separated. The differences that were found bore no relationship to the traditional stereotypes of male and female characteristics.

Kakabadse and Margerison (1987) studied women chief executive officers, 29 from the USA and just 6 from the UK, to see what behaviours were instrumental in their career development. The characteristics identified for women were similar to men, but there were some differences in ranking. Female CEOs placed greater emphasis on personal drives such as a desire to seek new opportunities, whilst men considered a width of business experience more important. Women recognised the necessity to use political skills in the organisation and placed greater emphasis on communication, managing people, handling different people in different ways and delegation; listening to others and ensuring that others understood what they were doing.

Research from Australia (Gold and Pringle 1988) shows that factors in management promotion were also similar for women and men. Since the women studied had few dependents, the most significant fact hindering their promotion was organisational attitudes; women were aware that they should not be seen as too outspoken.

They conclude that the popular myth that women managers have a more casual attachment to work was not true.

Difference is important

Marshall's study of women managers (1984) recognised the pressure on women to acquiesce to male norms in order to gain promotion. She argues that the differences between men and women managers are important and that the strengths and characteristics that women bring to management should be recognised and valued in their own right. Marshall (1985) believes that although the surface structure of organisations has become more accepting of women since the early 1970s, the deep structure of valued characteristics and behaviour is still largely patterned by male values. Muting femaleness to gain organisational acceptance has negative consequences for women as well as for organisations since it fosters uneven personal development and reinforces those male organisational values which penalise women.

Women who do not fit easily into organisations as they are now structured do not necessarily adopt the male value systems. Instead they may find their experience of work reduces their commitment to their career, or they may just leave. As organisations make efforts to recruit and promote women, the issue of retention becomes increasingly important. In technology-related careers Cockburn (1986) found a highly masculine-gendered social environment which women did not fit into easily. Those that tried either had to accept being seen as not a 'typical' woman or avoided it by leaving.

Another important 'difference' in the way that men and women manage relates to how management is defined. As Skinner (1988) shows, when it is seen as a specific hierarchical position, no account is taken of management work in non-management roles; most notably done by women in support roles. She argues that increased flexibility in management structures, away from quasi-military hierarchies, would facilitate greater organisational effectiveness. New forms of work structures would reduce the element of 'control' and recognise the need for co-operation and the benefits of individual accountability and responsibility. Women's work experience might then be recognised in the formal requirements for career progress.

Is difference important?

Since many of the differences found between men and women managers are, for the women concerned, negative in nature, such 'difference' becomes an important issue, as it contributes to the difficulties faced by women and hampers their career prospects in management.

The consequence of highlighting the differences between men and women, far from further marginalising them, is to challenge the view that women do not conform to the 'norm', and to put the emphasis onto the issue of changing management style and structures. Minimising differences avoids any challenge to the predominant male value systems.

Organisational processes

The cultures, policies and processes of organisations have direct and indirect effects upon the way employees interact with the organisation and upon individual progress and careers. As organisations seek to change or adapt policies, for example in the area of equal opportunities, it is important to understand the extent to which such policies are capable of being effective.

Established organisational cultures and traditional management attitudes, plus the predominance of a male value system, can undermine the intentions of equal opportunity policies. Cockburn (1991) shows how policies to target women in the 'fast lane' may be used by employers to limit equal opportunity action to that which is relatively low cost and has advantages for the organisation. Although it might help a few privileged women it also serves to divide them from the remainder. Value changes may be a longer-term prospect but without them the instigation of new policies alone is unlikely to be effective.

Previous studies have considered women in management careers. The Women and Management action research project carried out at Ashridge Management College (1980), showed that the small number of women reaching management was related to an organisation's structures and policies. The resultant guide for managers, *No Barriers Here?* (Manpower Services Commission 1981), has yet to become out-dated. An Industrial Society report in 1981 looked at the lack of women in industrial management and it concluded that the problems for women were the same across all employment sectors. The issues identified by the research into building society employment practices followed similar patterns and this analysis of how gender strategies become embedded within general management strategies has relevance for all employment sectors.

The research

Research which was carried out within the building society sector between 1985 and 1989 (Ashburner 1987) will be used to illustrate how organisations which call themselves 'equal opportunity employers' were rife with processes which were directly and indirectly discriminatory. It will also show how such processes affected the management career chances of women employees when compared to men. Underlying these organisational features were management attitudes to and expectations of women employees. These, together, formed women's experience of work which was an important factor influencing their progress through the hierarchy.

The requirements for a 'career' within the building society sector were similar to those in other employment groups; continuity of employment, the increasing importance of qualifications, mobility and the need for specific work experience.

Employment practices within building societies

The building society sector was chosen for the research because it had several features which might be viewed as conducive to the progress of women. The percentage of women employees continues to increase (74 per cent in 1989), creating a highly feminised workforce where it might be supposed that marginalisation was less likely to occur. Historically the entry requirements for men and women were very similar since the nature of the work required a higher level of qualifications than for more routine clerical work. Counter staff needed several O levels and preferably A levels, and took on average two years to acquire the range of necessary knowledge and skills.

Women entered societies on similar terms to men but they experienced differential career progression patterns because of discriminatory attitudes and policies. The EOC's investigation of the Leeds Building Society in 1985 found that the society had been directly discriminatory in many areas, including its promotion procedures. The Leeds was viewed as fairly typical of the whole sector and this report awakened awareness that such practices were no longer acceptable.

The late 1980s were a watershed in the employment practices of building societies with the introduction of computerisation on a very large scale. This reduced the need for counter staff to have specific knowledge and skills, opened jobs up for lower qualified and lower skilled staff, and led to a dramatic increase in the use of part-time staff.

At the same time financial services legislation had led towards greater integration of building societies with the rest of the finance sector. With increased competition their need for external recognition of their professional status led to a growing demand by societies that employees who wanted a career should become professionally qualified.

Changing career structures

These factors combined and led to the major societies introducing greater formalisation of career structures. With the increasing use of technology, the rate of employment growth declined and meant a reduction in career opportunities, and more restrictions on promotion. Some societies also introduced management trainee schemes rather than relying totally on promotion from within.

When recruitment is done through male networks as was the case in one case-study society, and where promotion is at the discretion of management it offers few prospects for women since the requirements for management are not specified. A formalised and open career structure should improve women's chances since it means that women who want a career at least know what they have to achieve.

Qualifications, recruitment and promotion

The requirement for qualifications at recruitment, and for management trainees to take the building society professional qualification (which is similar to professional banking qualifications) should in theory enable women to compete on equal terms with men. Within the case-study societies this was not the case. In one medium-sized society there was a marked contrast between how the society treated their male management trainees and those female cashiering staff with similar qualifications. The male management trainees spent only one year gaining general experience before attaining their first management post. The female employees similarly qualified had worked with the society for between two and nine years and had not been told they were eligible for the professional examinations and were not viewed as potential management.

Where there was no separate system of recruitment into management, as in one of the major building societies, the system whereby men were promoted ahead of women was maintained by consistently recruiting men with higher qualifications than women. Women who did not follow the typical pattern for women employees of leaving to start a family were able to gain promotion but not on equal terms with the men. Women had, on average, to work twice as long before they could reach the next grade.

By the time the women had reached lower management positions they were viewed as 'too old' to begin the process of gaining qualifications and were instead seen to be blocking the male career route. Women who were recruited on a similar basis to men and who had the same aspirations were viewed very differently within this society where there was a male stereotype of management.

The solution to the apparent blockages in the career system was to redefine the management career route in very precise terms. A distinction would be made at recruitment between career and non-career staff. The requirements for career staff were that they made a long-term commitment, gained further qualifications, and were prepared to be mobile. Such features could be presented as an encouragement to those viewed as management potential but as a discouragement to those who did not align themselves with this typically 'male' profile of a career. The effect would be to prevent all women not on the career route from moving beyond the lowest grade.

Requirements of a management career

A long-term commitment, qualifications, mobility and specific work experience were the main requirements for a management career in most building societies. It is becoming less important for managers to remain within a single organisation, although there remains an expectation of continuity of employment. The almost complete absence of career break schemes and the minimum maternity leave provision was sufficient to ensure that only women who did not have children progressed through the hierarchy, however slowly.

At recruitment, career staff were told of the requirement for geographical mobility. In interviews with men and women in the three case-study societies, all those women who sought a career were prepared to be mobile. Most men, especially those who were similarly without children, were also potentially mobile. However, there was a significant minority of men who were not prepared to be mobile because of family commitments such as children's schooling and wives' careers. In reality only those men who wished to move for a promotion had actually done so. Others had found promotion at different branches within the same geographical locality. It needs to be questioned why mobility is stated as a requirement to new employees when it is not essential for career progression and it may serve to discourage more women than men.

Variations on the theme of 'necessary' work experience before promotion is granted, exist within many occupations. In insurance, Collinson and Knights (1985) showed how progression to management required sales experience but women were not employed in sales as this included evening work and visits to clients' homes. In the building society sector the equivalent is contact with outside professionals. The argument at the turn of the century, that women cashiers in banks would be unacceptable to the customers, has developed into that of the unacceptability of women negotiators to the business and financial customers of the society.

No women were found in those positions where contact with clients outside the branch office was required. One women who had, in the absence of the manager, temporarily taken on this role, had found no problems of acceptability or in dealing with male clients. This convention is accepted without any logical basis and disadvantages any woman who seeks promotion.

The similarity between these 'requirements' for a career, of continuity of employment, mobility and specific experience, is that none had any relationship to the specific work required by the management task. All were imposed disciplines which served to restrict the profile of those who were viewed as eligible to have a career in management.

Men's attitudes and women's experiences

Even when a woman could show continuity of employment, mobility, relevant work experience and qualifications these were no guarantee that she would be promoted on a par with her male colleagues. One personnel manager actually stated that his society had a policy of not promoting women because it did not project the image the society wanted.

In another society the experience of one woman shows how such generally held attitudes manifest themselves. She had A levels and a teaching qualification and had expressed her desire for a career at recruitment, but after ten years with the society, while most of her male contemporaries were main branch managers on grade ten, she was only on grade four and had been moved to 'manage' a sub-branch. As she said:

When I was recruited I was told that if I wanted a career this was the place. After a couple of years I felt that that was such a lie. I feel really bitter, that I'd been told that and then I spent two years sitting at the counter. It was very boring as there was no chance to learn other things. Men were never kept there that long, especially if they had my qualifications.

Not only had she not been given the same opportunities as male colleagues, she had also been 'promoted' to a job within which she had no opportunity to gain relevant experience. She had been told that there was no opportunity for further promotion.

Even those women who were taking the professional exams expressed doubt about the reality of their ambitions as they observed that there were no women in any senior positions and they saw the problems being faced by other women. All three of the women interviewed saw their ultimate career as being outside their present society. Women's experience of work and lack of career progression led them to adopt one of several observed coping strategies. Here strategy is being used with reference to the powerless; not in the context of planning of careers but in the context of coming to terms with their experiences of inequality. The women interviewed had developed a sense of resignation, realism or rationalisation about their situation which led them either to modify their career plans or accept the position they were in. Several were contemplating resignation whilst others shifted the focus of their attention on to the domestic sphere, or more challenging outside interests. Experienced women employees are a valuable resource and their loss had clear financial implications for an organisation (Ashburner 1991).

With regard to what organisations required of career staff, those women interviewed at the outset of their careers saw themselves as no different from the men. They were aware of all the requirements and had similar ambitions and expectations as their male colleagues. Interviews with longer serving women showed that it was their experience of work which had modified their attitudes over the years.

Conclusion

Challenging the concept of career

A career is no longer seen as something chosen at the beginning of one's working life, but as a broader development of skills and experience within a chosen field which encompasses the whole employment life cycle (Hall 1976). For Schein (1978) the essence of the career development perspective was the focus on the interaction of the individual and the organisation over time. Whether within a single organisation or moving between jobs, success was a move up the hierarchy, increasing salary and with more freedom to select one's own projects. The unbroken nature of this process and the necessity for full-time employment are not mentioned as they are clearly assumed.

Exactly how research into careers and managerial mobility is developing to accommodate women is an important issue. A recent study by Gunz (1989) on career cultures in different organisations and how career paths are developed, is an in-depth study which still addresses issues as if all managers were men. He surveys 'the kinds of things that are known about managers' careers', even discussing management styles, and yet ignores one of the basic variables – gender.

The problem of accommodating women into the concept of career is one which needs to be tackled in all spectrums and not just in the world of work. If teaching depends upon existing research and if the status quo is not challenged then new research will exhibit the same limitations, ad nauseam.

It is becoming increasingly important for organisations to question the validity of the concept of the unbroken career, or linear progression. Silverstone and Ward (1980) show that the women in the professions they studied had invested considerable time and effort in training for demanding careers which they perceived as a long-term commitment. This is increasingly becoming the case for women who seek a career in management but, by itself, it is not enough.

Pressure is coming from many directions for increased flexibility in all aspects of work organisation, employment patterns and careers structures. As Charles Handy said (1989), many jobs and skills are having shorter life cycles as new technology and new skills emerge, and retraining is becoming integral to an increasing number of employment sectors. He maintained that work structures needed to be more flexible with the emphasis on the outcome of work and not on where or how it is done. Such developments would challenge traditional career paths and patterns of working and would increase opportunities for women.

Opportunities and outcomes

Success for women seeking a career needs to be measured in terms of outcomes not opportunities. Merely wooing women back to work will not increase the status of the work they do. The organisational processes, attitudes and value systems which prevent women from developing a career need to be challenged. Davidson and Cooper (1992) conclude that unless government and organisations initiate substantial change, the position of women in management, in the 2000s, will improve only marginally.

Arguments about inequalities will have little influence in a system of power relations where that power will not be shared or ceded willingly. In the increasingly complex world of business, co-operation and not competition is becoming more important and some organisations are broadening their person profiles for management jobs to include so-called female values. If this results in increased opportunities for women, they should be able to enter organisations without having to compromise their value systems or be marginalised. Organisations would benefit from increased flexibility and a greater range of skills and experience within their management ranks and, equally, male managers would be released from their own confinement to a particular stereotype.

A gendered concept of career

The problem of cultural duality for women cannot be overcome in the long term by encouraging women to adapt to the career demands of their work. A more beneficial focus for both women and organisations is for there to be increased flexibility in what is required for career progress. Women *and* men would then be freer to re-evaluate their relationship with employment.

The concept of career must adapt to ensure that the realities of men and womens' work histories are encapsulated into the career typologies of the future. Organisations should not just reduce the level of prescription within career paths, but also recognise the interrelationship with patterns of work organisation, culture and management styles. Without gender as a category of analysis, research on careers will have a limited perspective, and organisations will limit their potential.

References

Alban-Metcalfe, B. and Nicholson, N. (1984) *The Career Development of British Managers*, London: British Institute of Management Foundation.
Ashburner, L. (1987) 'The effects of new technology on employment structures in the service sector', PhD Thesis, Aston University.

Ashburner, L. (1988) 'Just inside the counting house: women in finance', in A. Coyle and J. Skinner (eds), *Women and Work: Positive Action for Change*, Basingstoke: Macmillan.

Ashburner, L. (1991) 'Men managers and women workers: women employees as an under-used resource', *British Journal of Management*, **2**: 3–15.

Ashridge Management College (1980) 'Employee potential: issues in the development of women', Institute of Personnel Management.

Asplund, G. (1988) *Women Managers – Changing Organisational Cultures*, Chichester: John Wiley.

Beechey, V. (1986) 'Women and employment in contemporary Britain', in V. Beechey (ed.) *Women in Britain Today*, Oxford: Oxford University Press.

Cockburn, C. (1986) 'The relations of technology', in R. Crompton and M. Mann (eds) *Gender and Stratification*, Cambridge: Polity Press.

Cockburn, C. (1991) *In the Way of Women: Men's Resistance to Sex Equality in Organisations*, Basingstoke: Macmillan.

Collinson, D. and Knights, D. (1985) 'Jobs for the boys: recruitment into life insurance sales', in *Occupational Segregation by Sex*, EOC Research Bulletin **9**, Spring, Manchester: EOC.

Coyle, A. and Skinner, J. (eds) (1988) *Women and Work: Positive Action for Change*, Basingstoke: Macmillan.

Crompton, R. (1986) 'Women and the "service class",' in R. Crompton and M. Mann (eds) *Gender and Stratification*, Oxford: Basil Blackwell.

Davidson, M. J. and Cooper, C. L. (1992) *Shattering the Glass Ceiling: The Woman Manager*, London: Paul Chapman.

Dex, S. (1987) *Women's Occupational Mobility: A Lifetime Perspective*, London: Macmillan.

Equal Opportunities Commission (1985) *Formal Investigation Report: Leeds Permanent Building Society*, Manchester: EOC.

Follett, M. P. (1926) Papers in H. C. Metcalf and L. Urwick (eds) (1941) *Dynamic Administration: The Collected Papers of Mary Parker Follett*, London: Pitman.

Gold, U. O. and Pringle, J. K. (1988) 'Gender-specific factors in management promotion', *Journal of Managerial Psychology*, **3**(4): 17–22.

Gunz, H. (1989) *Careers and Corporate Cultures: Managerial Mobility in Large Corporations*, Oxford: Basil Blackwell.

Hall, D. T. (1976) *Careers in Organisations*, San Francisco, CA: Scott, Foresman.

Handy, C. (1989) Conference speech: 'Harnessing the female resource', The Women's Education Conference, 11 July.

Hansard Society (1990) *The Report of the Hansard Society Commission on Women at the Top*, London: Hansard Society.

Howe, E. and McRae, S. (1991) *Women on the Board*, London: Policy Studies Institute.

Industrial Society (1981) 'Women in management – onwards and upwards? A survey outlining the position of women today', Special Report: The Industrial Society.

Institute of Employment Research (1989) *Review of the Economy and Employment 1988/89*, University of Warwick: IER

Kakabadse, A. and Margerison, C. (1987) 'The female chief executive: an analysis of career progress and development needs', *Journal of Managerial Psychology*, pp. 17–25.

McRae, S. (ed.) (1990) *Keeping Women In: Strategies to Facilitate the Con-*

tinuing Employment of Women in Higher Level Occupations, London: Policy Studies Institute.

Manpower Services Commission (1981) *No Barriers Here?* Sheffield: MSC.

Marshall, J. (1984) *Women Managers: Travellers in a Male World*, Chichester: Wiley.

Marshall, J. (1985) 'Paths of personal and professional development for women managers', in *Management Education and Development*, **16**(2): 169–79.

Martin, J. and Roberts, C. (1984) *Women and Employment: A Lifetime Perspective*, London: HMSO.

Nicholson, N. and West, M. (1988) *Managerial Job Change: Men and Women in Transition*, Cambridge: Cambridge University Press.

Ryan, M. and Medlam, S. (1984) 'Blocks to women's career development in insurance', Unpublished report sponsored by the Further Education Unit: FEU.

Schein, E. H. (1978) *Career Dynamics*, MA: Addison Wesley.

Silverstone, R. and Ward, A. (1980) *Careers of Professional Women*, London: Croom Helm.

Skinner, J. (1988) 'Who's changing whom? Women, management and work organisation', in A. Coyle and J. Skinner (eds) *Women and Work: Positive Action for Change*, Basingstoke: Macmillan.

Social Trends (1991) London: HMSO.

Spencer, A. and Podmore, D. (eds) (1987) *In a Man's World*, London: Tavistock.

Wilson, P. (1991) 'Women employees and senior management', *Personnel Review*, **20**(1): 32–6.

CHAPTER 14

Midwifery: a career for women?

JULIA ALLISON AND GILLIAN PASCALL

Midwife – the very word suggests a woman. This endures, despite men midwives of the last century, and equal opportunities legislation of the present. Midwifery is a rare example of a women's career where both practitioners and command hierarchy are overwhelmingly female. Midwives, supervisors of midwives, the Royal College of Midwives, the English National Board – at all levels women predominate, in practice, decision and control. There are other 'women's professions'; social work and nursing are clear examples where women have a major history and contemporary presence, but here male dominance of the hierarchy is either established or becoming so. Midwifery is alone as a profession of women run for women and by women.

Perhaps the word midwife also suggests the catch. The domestic division of labour shows that wives' area of authority is circumscribed; it is paralleled by a division of childbirth labour which contains women's area of competence.

Midwifery careers are like others in the difficulties they pose for combining paid and unpaid work: indeed the need for 24-hour cover intensifies the problems. The historical pattern of midwifery practice extracted a great price in midwives' readiness to submerge private lives beneath the overwhelming needs of women in childbirth. But in midwifery these problems have not produced the gender hierarchies characteristic elsewhere. There is room for career in midwifery for women, in the traditional male sense of a ladder which they climb (though women with fewer family responsibilities have advantages). But when midwives write about midwifery, the salient issue is not the hierarchy of their own profession, but its relation to obstetrics.

Competition and career in the health professions

One key to understanding women's position as midwives is to analyse their place in the wider division of health care, understood in terms of medical dominance and of gender.

Medical dominance can no longer be seen as the unchallenged underpinning of western health care systems (Freidson 1975, Elston 1991). Managers now vie for supremacy, and midwifery is one among several occupations – health visiting, nursing, pharmacy, physiotherapy, radiography – which seek to establish autonomy and status as professionals, and challenge medicine's authority. But until recently the NHS has supported medicine's claims, and intellectual and institutional frameworks have made others subordinate.

Control of research – which defines health care – is fundamental to control of health practice, and medicine is ahead of nursing and midwifery here; it thus makes the ground rules for the practice of medicine and related professions.

Professional relationships have more to do with hierarchy than with partnership. Nursing and midwifery certainly claim areas of competence and autonomy but the daily practice of both is of deference. This deference has institutional backing – in the way hospitals and general practices are managed; political backing through medicine's role in health policy-making; and some legal backing in the form of less positive protection of midwives' autonomy.

Feminists have argued that gender has been crucial in the establishment of the health professions and the subsequent development of professional relationships (Doyal 1983, Leeson and Gray 1978, Stacey 1988). Medicine was established as male, nursing as female (Carpenter 1977, Gamarnikow 1978). Maternity care has been disputed by female and male midwives and more recently by midwives (predominantly female) and obstetricians (predominantly male) (Donnison 1977/88, Garcia *et al.* 1990, Oakley 1984). Women's contemporary presence in medicine and men's in midwifery have modified these distinctions. But gender remains significant in questions of access to professional occupations; the division of professional labour; control over professional practice; and the wider division of health care labour.

The division of childbearing labour

The hinge for the division of labour in childbirth has been a concept of normality. Female midwives had and have responsibility for normal delivery; men have been associated with the abnormal. This generalisation does not apply to every delivery, practitioner, period, or country (for example, higher-class women in seventeenth-century France might enjoy the prestige of being delivered by a male midwife, even without expected abnormality (Donnison 1977/88: 33). In practice, too, the definition of normality has been highly variable. But the conceptual division is widely applicable.

It has a bearing on the seventeenth century, when female midwives in London complained of inadequate colleagues who 'oftimes through ignorance do send for him (Chamberlen) when itt is none of his work, and so to the damage of the partie both in body and purse do highly increase his profitts'; and who complained of Chamberlen himself that 'he lacked the necessary experience of natural labours, he himself delivering none "without the use of instruments by extraordinary violence in desperate occasions"' (Donnison, 1977/88: 27). It applies again in the eighteenth (1720), when men invented and monopolised the forceps (Donnison 1977/88: 34).

In 1902, the relationship was formalised in the Midwives Act, which established the midwifery profession. The Central Midwives Board was to register and regulate midwifery practice: this body was dominated by medical men. Its rules required the midwife to call a doctor in emergency (Donnison 1977/88: 182).

In Britain today, midwives have at least theoretical autonomy in respect of normal delivery and a duty and responsibility for ante-natal care, intra-natal care, including the delivery of women who do not want a medical attendant, and post-natal care of women in normal childbirth; they retain a responsibility to call a doctor where they suspect abnormality.

These examples illustrate the significance of the concept of normality, as the division between obstetrics and midwifery and the legal basis of the division of labour. The concept also divides two ideas of childbirth, as a natural event or a condition requiring treatment. On either side are also technological and cultural differences. Restricted in the use of instruments, midwives traditionally developed skills to avoid their need (Donnison, 1977/88: 206). Alternatively, obstetrics' claim to childbirth rested on instrumental intervention. Culturally distinctive approaches to childbirth followed. These are generalis-ations which do not always hold. There are obstetricians associated with 'natural childbirth' (Odent 1984, Savage 1986); and midwives who have learnt to practise under the wing of obstetrics. But the concept of normality in childbirth is central to debates about who attends women and how they should be attended.

A normal delivery?

The widening field of obstetric care has therefore required a changing concept of normality. Until the Second World War medicine laid claim to a minority of births, thus implicitly accepting the normality of the majority. Since the 1970s conventional obstetric wisdom has been that birth is only normal in retrospect – encompassing 100 per cent as the domain of medicine. This idea has taken root in mid-wifery history: 'The problem is that no one can confidently define a labour as normal until it is complete' (Dingwall *et al.* 1988: 171).

The practice of childbirth changed with the concept. Managed childbirth became standard: the routine use of drugs to start and speed labour; electronic foetal monitoring; epidural anaesthesia; epi-siotomy. Applying such techniques to the majority implied that birth was best treated as an abnormal event, under obstetric management (for a critique of the application of these practices to potentially normal deliveries see Chard and Richards 1977).

Second was the changing place of delivery. In the pre-war period most women delivered at home, were attended by midwives and did not require a doctor. The pivotal period was post-war, when home births became a minority. Obstetric management techniques in the 1970s depended on hospital delivery for nearly all, and in the 1990s the UK hospital confinement rate is 99 per cent.

Most babies are still delivered by midwives; but the hospital context is significant for professional relations between midwives and doctors. Women giving birth at home rarely had or have a doctor present. In hospital obstetricians are ever-present as a background, if not at the delivery. Midwives may still claim autonomy, but the hospital hierarchy has doctors at the top: obstetricians make policy about the way babies will be delivered; midwives carry out that policy in practice. Midwives may thus be reconstituted as obstetric nurses, embracing in their daily practice the idea that birth cannot be defined normal until it has happened, thereby defining midwifery out of existence.

Safer childbirth for everyone – or obstetrics versus midwifery?

These developments may be interpreted as progress: midwives' relative ignorance has given way to the superior knowledge and skill of obstetricians, itself part of a scientific explosion. Maternal and infant mortality rates are ever lower and these trends must be seen as interrelated.

Alternatively these developments represent a demarcation dispute between two gendered groups – a dispute in which medical and male authority has been extended and entrenched; improvements in maternal and infant mortality would have happened anyway, having more to do with wider social changes – such as better nutritional standards, fewer births at safer ages – than with changes in procedures.

The debate is complex – involving international and home/hospital comparisons, historical and epidemiological interpretations (Campbell and Macfarlane 1987, Chalmers 1978, Enkin *et al.* 1989, Macfarlane and Mugford 1984, Tew 1990). The view that changes in practice have been implemented without adequate assessment has gained authoritative support in the National Perinatal Epidemiology Unit's review of the evidence. The recent House of Commons Health Committee report drew on this work to conclude that 'it is no longer acceptable that the pattern of maternity care provision should be driven by presumptions about the applicability of a medical model of care based on unproven assertions' (HCHC 1992: xii). The committee obliged the Royal College of Obstetricians and Gyneacologists to admit that 'there is no conclusive evidence that hospital delivery is safer than home' (HCHC 1992: xi).

The Nottingham Birth Register Study – 1956–88

Recent investigations into childbirth in Nottingham in the period of change to obstetric management shed light on two key questions. What is 'normal' in childbirth? And can we know the normal only in retrospect? The first question lies at the very foundation of the division of labour between midwives and obstetricians; assumptions about the second have been a crucial justification for removing autonomous practice from midwives.

The research

This section draws on a study of domiciliary midwifery care in Nottingham during a period when home delivery was commonplace. It uses registers which midwives were required to keep of every delivery attended; these are a rich source of data containing more detail than exists in national statistics. The process of analysing the data has recently begun, and results are provisional.

Record-keeping was common to home and hospital deliveries, though only the former are described here. Births recorded in hospitals included women booked for hospital birth and those who were home booked but transferred in labour. Births recorded by district midwives included women selected for home birth, those booked for hospital who failed to arrive, those refused a hospital booking and those who failed to book at hospital or home.

For reasons which will be discussed later the particular foci of the data in this chapter are unattended births, births which took place at home or some other unintended venue before the arrival of the midwife. Throughout this century, the term BBA – born before the arrival of the midwife – has been used for such births. Prior to the implementation of the National Health Service in 1948, BBAs recorded by certificated midwives were mostly home-booked women who had precipitate labours. Other women, who did not engage a certificated midwife or doctor or book at hospital, were cared for by a maternity nurse, family or friends, and no detailed accounts of the circumstances of the birth were kept. By 1948 every pregnant woman was entitled under the NHS to engage a district midwife and general medical practitioner, or have hospital maternity care. The catchment for BBAs therefore widened to include hospital-booked and unbooked births, and it becomes possible to compare the three groups.

Details of the BBAs attended by thirteen district midwives who practised at some time during the period 1956–88, in that area of Nottingham which prior to the 1972 re-organisation was defined as 'City of Nottingham', have been extracted from their personal birth registers. Between 1956 and 1988 approximately 50,000 births occurred at home. The thirteen midwives whose registers have been used undertook 9,561 births, i.e. one fifth of total births. Of those 9,561 confinements 510 (5.3 per cent) were BBAs.

Of the 510 BBAs, 349 occurred to women booked for home birth, 95 to women booked for hospital, and 66 to women who had not booked a place of birth nor had any antenatal care. They represent a rare group of women who gave birth without professional assistance or intervention.

Many questions could be asked of this data, but here we focus on two. First, where was the line of 'normality' drawn during this period? Under what circumstances and with what complications were women booked for home and hospital birth? Second, we ask about the selection process, about the accuracy with which midwives predicted complications and the need for hospital confinement.

Both these are vital to the division of labour between obstetrics and midwifery. As already argued, the concept of normality underpins this division. Equally, the prediction process is at the heart of any division which gives genuine autonomy to midwives over 'normal' labour. Unless complications can be predicted in advance, we shall not know who should deliver which babies where. Indeed, the idea that birth is normal only in retrospect, comprising the justification for 100 per cent hospital confinement, is another way of saying that safe predictions are not possible. All babies should be born under obstetric supervision so that no one need discriminate in advance.

Normal deliveries?

These 510 women are far from a straightforward selection in the 'low risk' category who could be expected to do well at an unattended homebirth. Many had medical, obstetric and social circumstances not to be found in a UK sample today.

Selection for place of birth using criteria related to age, parity, maturity of pregnancy, obstetric, medical and family history was complicated by many factors, including gestation at booking and social class. The midwives' registers regularly give age, parity and maturity of pregnancy, with occasional additional relevant information in the remarks column. Table 14.1 gives all the relevant infor-

Table 14.1   **Number of women who fell outside today's criteria for a home birth**

	Outside criteria	Total	%
BBAs booked for home birth	175	349	50
BBAs booked for hospital birth	54	95	56
Unbooked BBAs	52	66	79
Total	281	510	55

mation available, but it is only a sample of what was available to the midwife. We have no insight into the height, stature, weight or haemoglobin levels of these women: more than shown here would actually have fallen outside today's criteria for home birth. Fifty-five per cent of women in the sample fell outside today's criteria for a home birth. Almost as many home-booked women fell outside today's criteria as did the hospital-booked. Among the unbooked 79 per cent had factors which put them outside the criteria for home birth.

In addition some women in all three categories had more than one factor which contra-indicated a home birth (Table 14.2). Twenty-six

Table 14.2   *Women who fell outside today's criteria for home birth by two or more causes*

	Outside criteria	2 or more causes	%
BBAs booked for home birth	175	31	18
BBAs booked for hospital birth	54	21	38
Unbooked BBAs	52	20	38
Total	281	72	26

per cent of women who fell outside today's criteria for a home birth did so by two or more causes. Amongst them were 15- and 16-year-olds with premature labours, a 38-year-old gravida 15 premature birth, a 36-year-old gravida 7 pre-term twin delivery. The most extreme case was a 34-year-old primigravida with known heart disease being treated for ascites (presumably the pregnancy), whose pregnancy had gone undiagnosed. She spontaneously delivered a 6 lb 12 oz baby at home sustaining a third-degree tear. The child fell to the floor and the cord snapped. The woman refused to be transferred to hospital and mother and baby were successfully nursed at home.

Selecting for home and hospital

The selection process is vital to a system involving a choice of place of birth and birth attendant. It has been difficult to assess the quality of selection and the quality of care because of the inter-connections between the two and the number of transfers during delivery. But the focus on babies born before an attendant arrived allows us to examine the selection process aside from the chief confounding factors. Since mothers and babies had no care, and there was no time for transfer, we are left with data which clarify the quality of prediction for home confinement. Midwives had the key responsibility of making assessments, though mothers and doctors would have played some part.

Perinatal and maternal death are the traditional yardsticks for measuring success in childbearing. In addition, the incidence of complications can help to illustrate how 'risky' a situation was even though the eventual outcome may have been favourable (Table 14.3). In Table 14.3 social and domestic complications include inad-

Table 14.3   Complications by intended place of birth following BBA (%)

Complication	Home	Hospital	Unbooked
Social/domestic	0	17.9	25.7
Mother only	1.4	6.3	4.5
Baby only	4.9	13.7	42.4
Mother/baby	0	5.3	6.1
No complications	93.7	56.9	21.2
Total	100 (349)	100 (95)	100 (66)

equate heating or assistance, which would necessitate transfer to hospital. Medical complications include post-partum haemorrhage, retained placenta, etc. The complication rate of those booked for home delivery is much lower than for either of the other groups. A similar picture emerges from studying the deaths, though it should be borne in mind that the numbers are much smaller (Table 14.4). The

Table 14.4   Perinatal mortality rates by intended place of birth following BBA

Place	BBAs	Births	Perinatal deaths	PNMR
Home	349	349	1	2.9
Hospital	95	96*	5	52.0
Unbooked	66	69*	7	101.0
Total	510	514	13	25

* Includes some twin births.

perinatal death rate in the home-booked group was very low at 2.9 per 1000 births. This is despite the fact that almost as many home-booked women fell outside today's criteria as hospital-booked. The hospital-booked group had a perinatal death rate of 52.0 per 1000 births. Some but not all of the difference between the home and hospital group is explained by the slightly higher number who had contra-indications to home birth, or two or more complicating factors. The unbooked group had the highest percentage of women who fell outside today's criteria for a homebirth and the highest perinatal death rate at 101 per 1000 births. However the difference in the proportion of women in each group who fell outside today's criteria for a homebirth is hardly an explanation for the huge outcome differences, in terms of complications and perinatal death.

We may further examine these diverse outcomes through what is known of the causes or circumstances of these thirteen deaths (Table

Table 14.5 **Cause/circumstance of perinatal death in a group of women who had BBAs**

Intended place	Age	Parity	Gestation	Cause/circumstance
1 Home	23	6	36	5 lb 2 oz baby, transferred to SCBU died 4th postnatal day, reason unknown
2 Hospital	20	primip	?	SB anencephalic
3 Hospital	24	3	?	macerated SB
4 Hospital	30	?	30	1 lb 5 oz macerated SB
5 Hospital	20	3	?	macerated SB
6 Hospital	?	?	28	SB 3 lb 4 oz
7 Unbooked	30	2	30	SB ?weight
8 Unbooked	27	4	36	36 week twin pregnancy, both BBA. Twin 1 6 lb 4 oz alive. Twin 2 5 lb 8 oz DOA of midwife ?cause.
9 Unbooked	16	primip	?	SB 3 lb 14 oz
10 Unbooked	19	2	25	1 lb 1 oz died in SCBU
11 Unbooked	28	3	?	?weight SB
12 Unbooked	32	5	?	?weight SB
13 Unbooked	?	6	28	SB

(For home booked BBAs, women and babies transferred to hospital were returned to district midwife care. But for hospital and unbooked women there may have been later perinatal deaths of babies transferred to hospital, unknown to the midwife. Thus perinatal deaths for hospital and unbooked BBAs may have been greater than shown.)

14.5). Table 14.5 gives no evidence of poor decisions about the place of delivery or that place of birth or even lack of attendant contributed to the outcome. The first death is inadequately explained, but that does not indicate that it would have been avoidable had the birth been booked or delivered in hospital (had the mother time to get there).

These data show an overall perinatal mortality rate for the BBAs that is high by present standards of perinatal mortality in Britain (though not by the standards of the early part of the period represented) at 25 per 1000 births. But for women booked at home the associated perinatal mortality rate was only 2.9 per 1000, despite the fact that half fell outside today's criteria for a home birth, and all delivered without attendant. The success of midwives in selecting for home births seems evident in all the above data.

Detailed description of women who delivered at home gives a different picture from that usually offered in debates about home and hospital delivery. The good results of home deliveries at this period have often been explained as a result of their supposed 'safety' relative to the hospital group. But the home deliveries described here are not only of relatively socially deprived women – many are also of women who fall outside today's definition of normal, safe deliveries. The social factors which so confound comparisons between midwife and obstetric care do not fall so clearly in the midwives' favour as is usually assumed. Hospital obstetricians did undertake cases referred by midwives as needing specialist care, and therefore more likely to experience problems. But midwives undertook a more mixed and socially deprived caseload than is usually assumed; and they received their own 'transfers' in the form of unbooked and hospital-booked BBAs. Midwifery care was given to mothers and babies with a line of normality very different from today's.

The contemporary politics of midwifery: obstetric nurse or midwifery professional?

The first 44 years of the National Health Service have seen a gradual erosion of the position of midwives. At first the competition was with General Practitioners; more recently the shift to hospital practice has left GPs behind, and brought many midwives into the orbit of obstetric care (Kirkham 1987). Domiciliary midwifery has nearly declined to ante-natal and post-natal nursing – but not quite: in Britain, midwives still deliver most babies, and women are entitled to their services (Kitzinger 1988). The role of the medical profession in decision-making at every NHS level, from patient care to government reports such as the Peel (Ministry of Health 1970) and Short Reports (HCSC 1980), has been critical in reducing the midwife's area of competence. Indeed such trends have been seen as a confirmation of midwifery's already inferior position as a branch of nursing practice, with the implication that they are nearly irreversible (Dingwall *et al.* 1988). But a number of winds of change have recently been blowing up into a gale, with the publication of the House of Commons Health Committee report on the Maternity Services (HCHC 1992), chaired by Sir Nicholas Winterton. The gale may blow midwifery back into a central role in a maternity service based on a robust assessment of the normality of childbirth for most women and babies.

First the winds

The politicisation of maternity care is evidenced by the quantity and range of submissions to the Winterton Committee. The women's movement has had its impact in radicalising both service-users and midwives. Growing consumerism in health is another factor. On the professional side are alignments between several interests – paediatricians, GPs, community health providers – who have reason to resist the view of maternity as an obstetric specialism. The development of a group of radical midwives has supported experimentation with midwifery-based forms of maternity practice.

Intellectual challenge to obstetric dominance has been crystallised in the work of the National Perinatal Epidemiology Unit at Oxford (Enkin *et al.* 1989). Their evaluation of evidence about current practices has given authority to the questioning of many obstetrical procedures, and of the assumption of abnormality in childbirth.

Educational developments are also significant. While midwifery lags well behind obstetrics, a surge in academic qualifications among nurses and midwives is enhancing their claim to specific areas of research, knowledge and competence.

Medical dominance is also under challenge from the managerial movement in health care. Managers' concern with costs may come into conflict with obstetricians' claim to control the majority of deliveries. Some local managers are already fostering the development of midwifery teams to play a larger role. The process may be speeded by NHS reforms, in particular the provider/purchaser split: a midwife-based service may be increasingly attractive to economy-minded purchasers.

Independent midwifery is another strand. Some midwives are working outside the NHS in order to offer a more autonomous midwifery practice. Such a service will tend to serve a social minority, but it provides a pattern of care which some public authorities are emulating.

Now the gale

The flow of official reports endorsing an obstetric-based model of maternity care has been reversed by the House of Commons Health Committee report on Maternity Services (HCHC 1992). A view of maternity care that has long seemed politically peripheral – even dangerous – now has the full endorsement of a Select Committee of eleven MPs (including two women) chaired by Sir Nicholas Winterton. The committee has drawn extensively on the evidence of consumer and professional groups, as well as on the scientific work of the National Perinatal Epidemiology Unit at Oxford. Its trenchant report proposes a maternity service based on a newly professionalised midwifery, and is worth substantial quotation.

The committee starts from a premise about the normality of childbirth:

We made the normal birth of healthy babies to healthy women the starting point and focus of our inquiry,

(i)

moves to a criticism of current orthodoxy:

We believe that the debate about place of birth, and the triumph of the hospital-centred argument, have led to the imposition of a whole philosophy of maternity care which has tended to regard all pregnancies as potential disasters, and to impose a medical model for their management which has had adverse consequences in the whole way in which we think about maternity care,

(xii)

and concludes that maternity care should be centred in the community:

That the majority of maternity care should be community based and near to the woman's home; and that obstetric and other specialist care should be readily available by referral from midwives or GPs.

(lxxx)

Midwifery is to be the instrument for achieving these targets:

We are persuaded that the key to the development of a pattern of maternity services which is more flexible and responsive to women's needs is a reassessment of the role of midwives.

(lxxi)

Detailed proposals about midwives' professional status involve: rights to refer to obstetric or paediatric specialists, midwives to have responsibility for normal deliveries in hospital while senior house officers function as trainees, involvement in the training of junior doctors, autonomy over midwifery's own training, access to research funding. On midwifery, the committee concludes:

We recommend:
– that the status of midwives as professionals is acknowledged in their terms and conditions of employment which should be based on the presumption that they have a right to develop and audit their own professional standards;
– that we should move as rapidly as possible towards a situation in which midwives have their own caseload, and take full responsibility for the women who are under their care;
– that midwives should be given the opportunity to establish and run midwife managed maternity units within and outside hospitals;
– that the right of midwives to admit women to NHS hospitals should be made explicit.
. . . We hope that when the recommendations of this report have been implemented and tested, perhaps by the end of this century, we will have reached a position where midwives will be fully acknowledged as an independent profession deserving the status that goes with such a position, and that this will be acknowledged by statute.

(lxxii)

These proposals represent a radical departure from previous reports on maternity care – especially from the report of its predecessor, the Social Services Committee (HCSC, 1980) – and a radical re-alignment of maternity services. Finally, they represent a radically new role and professional status for midwives.

Conclusion

The argument of this chapter has been that midwifery is highly unusual as a career for women in retaining a hierarchy that women can climb. But the challenge to the autonomy of women in midwifery has come from a male-dominated obstetrics profession.

That challenge has been highly effective: hospital delivery and obstetric management have demoted midwives and fragmented their work. Lacking autonomy in practice, midwives have found their professional status fragile.

The obstetric challenge has drawn on a changing definition of normality in childbirth, and on the proposition that births are only normal in retrospect. Evidence from the Nottingham Birth Register Study shows a very different idea of normality in practice – and in apparently safe practice – from that which we now have; and it shows midwives making accurate predictions about the suitability of home and hospital confinement. It adds weight to the argument that the shift to obstetric control of childbirth had more to do with politics than with careful assessment of evidence.

The contemporary politics of maternity care are suddenly more open. The House of Commons Health Committee has responded to the voices of consumers, to the evidence of the National Perinatal Epidemiology Unit and to health professions beyond obstetrics. Its proposal for change depends on re-establishing midwifery as the key profession for normal childbirth.

The committee do not clarify their own concept of normality. But they recommend that the majority of maternity practice should be in the community, and that consumers should have a more real choice. If all the proposals were implemented professional advice about normality would come from midwives. Midwives will certainly be involved in selection if the HCHC proposals are carried through, and may take comfort in the task from the success of earlier generations.

It will take more than one select committee report to shift maternity practice to a normality-based approach, to realign the health professions, and to instate midwives as full professionals in control of the majority of maternity practice. House of Commons Select Committees are not noted for their impact on policy. However, all-party membership, and a foundation in professional and consumer movements and in current research, suggest a significant political shift. We think the report represents a turning point for maternity politics and the fortunes of midwives.

Women in the profession should be conscious that improving status may have consequences. The evidence of other 'women's professions' is that revitalisation will draw men into the hierarchy. The development of social work, with roots in two women's worlds – philanthropy and local authority childcare services – and its present managerial domination by male Directors of Social Services – is one such example. There are others from closer at hand within nursing: the most immediate of these is the submersion of nursing management within general management resulting from recent NHS reforms. The Sex Discrimination Act has opened the door to men in midwifery, and positions in the hierarchy of a new midwifery will be attractive.

References

Campbell, R. and Macfarlane, A. J. (1987) *Where to be Born? The Debate and the Evidence*, Oxford: National Perinatal Epidemiology Unit.

Carpenter, M. (1977) 'The new managerialism and professionalism in nursing', in M. Stacey, M. Reid, C. Heath and R. Dingwall (eds) *Health and the Division of Labour*, London: Croom Helm.

Chalmers, I. (1978) 'Implications of the current debate on obstetric practice', in S. Kitzinger and J. A. Davis (eds) *The Place of Birth*, Oxford: Oxford University Press.

Chard, T. and Richards, M. (eds) (1977) *The Benefits and Hazards of the New Obstetrics*, London: Heinemann Medical.

Dingwall, R., Rafferty, A. M. and Webster, C. (1988) *An Introduction to the Social History of Nursing*, London and New York: Routledge.

Donnison, J. (1977/88) *Midwives and Medical Men: A History of the Struggle for the Control of Childbirth*, London: 1st edn Heinemann Educational Books, 2nd edn Historical Publications Ltd.

Doyal, L. (1983) 'Women, health and the sexual division of labour: a case study of the women's health movement in Britain', *Critical Social Policy*, 7: 21–33.

Elston, M. (1991) 'The politics of professional power: medicine in a changing health service', in J. Gabe, M. Calnan and M. Bury (eds) *The Sociology of the Health Service*, London and New York: Routledge.

Enkin, M., Keirse, M. and Chalmers, I. (1989) *A Guide to Effective Care in Pregnancy and Childbirth*, Oxford: Oxford University Press.

Freidson, E. (1975) *Profession of Medicine*, New York: Dodd, Mead.

Garcia, J., Kilpatrick, R. and Richards, M. (eds) (1990) *The Politics of Maternity Care*, Oxford: Clarendon Press.

Garmarnikow, E. (1978) 'Sexual division of labour: the case of nursing', in A. Kuhn and A. Wolpe (eds) *Feminism and Materialism*, London: Routledge & Kegan Paul.

HCHC (1992) (Winterton Report) *House of Commons Health Committee (Second Report): Maternity Services*, London: HMSO.

HCSC (1980) (Short Report) *House of Commons Social Services Committee (Second Report): Perinatal and Neonatal Mortality*, HMSO: London.

Kirkham, M. J. (1987) *Basic Supportive Care in Labour: Interaction with and around Labouring Women*, PhD Thesis, University of Manchester.

Kitzinger, S. (ed.) (1988) *The Midwife Challenge*, London: Pandora.

Leeson, J. and Gray, J. (1978) *Women and Medicine*, London, Tavistock.

Macfarlane, A. and Mugford, M. (1984) *Birth Counts: Statistics of Pregnancy and Childbirth*, London: HMSO.

Ministry of Health (1970) (Peel Report) *Domiciliary Midwifery and Maternity Bed Needs: the Report of the Standing Maternity and Midwifery Advisory Committee*, HMSO: London.

Oakley, A. (1984) *The Captured Womb*, Oxford: Blackwell.

Odent, M. (1984) *Birth Reborn*, New York: Pantheon.

Savage, W. (1986) *A Savage Enquiry: Who Controls Childbirth*, London: Virago.

Stacey, M. (1988) *The Sociology of Health and Healing*, London: Unwin Hyman.

Tew, M. (1990) *Safer Childbirth? A Critical History of Maternity Care*, London: Chapman & Hall.

Gender and Career: Identifying the Issues

Gender and Career: Identifying the Issues

In this section, Chapter 15 draws together the findings of the different chapters in the book in an attempt to reach some conclusions. Three themes and issues are discussed which would seem to be those identified as most critical by the contributors to this volume. These are, first, the problems which combining paid and unpaid work continue to pose for women's careers. Second, management and particularly hierarchical management is identified as a handicap to women's career progress, since stereotypes of effective management would seem to be at odds with cultural perceptions of what it means to 'be feminine'. Third, the dilemmas which discourse and language themselves pose for women's careers are analysed and discussed. The final chapter ends with an examination of the changes currently under way in the professions and work organisations generally which are altering the contexts in which careers are constructed.

CHAPTER 15

Career and gender: the conceptual challenge

JULIA EVETTS

There have been recent examinations of the different models of career used in social science research (Gunz 1989, Evetts 1992). The concept of career in paid work was developed in the sociologies of occupations, organisations and the professions, and it is from such contexts that the hierarchical assumptions of promotion progress through organisational layers and levels were attached. For interactionist researchers, in contrast, the emphasis in action research was on how individual actors influenced and developed their own social worlds in formal organisations and other institutions. Thus deviants, mental patients, prisoners and housewives also had careers (Becker 1963, Goffman 1968, Taylor and Cohen 1972, Finch 1983). In researching women's careers, use was made also of feminist concepts in order to explore and account for the substantial gender differences in careers.

For a period, researchers interested in women's careers had an uneasy relationship with feminist writers since their concerns were with women who were relatively privileged. Such women were receiving well paid salaries; many could afford their own transport and pay for help with housework, childcare and responsibilities for elderly relatives; their occupations were secure and their careers safe, if unspectacular. Compared with their less privileged sisters, it was difficult at first to argue that the position of such women needed different explanatory theories and concepts. Similarly with writers on work and the professions, it was problematic initially for researchers on women's careers to argue that gender was a significant differentiating factor. It was necessary to demonstrate first that women's work in careered occupations required different explanatory concepts to those developed for men.

It was probably not until the 1980s, when statistics of women's marginalisation in careered occupations became more widely recognised and acknowledged, that researchers began to develop their own ideas and concepts to explore the issue of women and career. The chapters in this book have in their different ways illustrated and explored some of these ideas and concepts as well as indicating the difficulties which the concept of career poses for women's working lives. This final chapter has two objectives. The first is to highlight some of the issues which have been explored in this collection and which would have to be accommodated if the concept of career is to be de-gendered, that is detached from its association with the patterns of some men's working lives. By focusing on women's careers the short-term objective has been to correct the gender imbalance, but the longer-term objective must be to develop theoretical concepts and explanations which are gender-neutral and inclusive of both men and women. Second, the changes currently under way in work organisations and professions will be referred to as providing new difficulties for women's careers as well as presenting an opportunity for the reconceptualisation of the 'successful' career.

The de-gendering of 'career'

The long-term objective is the construction and development of a theoretical concept of career which enables women's and men's careers to be understood without any implicit assumption that certain types of career are deficient or lacking in essential and important characteristics. The chapters in this book have highlighted at least three substantive issues which pose difficulties for women in achieving promotion in their careers. These issues will need to be addressed if the concept of career is to be de-gendered and disassociated from the unidimensional model of a hierarchical, linear career. It is also possible to see these issues as posing difficulties for men in developing multi-faceted careers. The three issues are listed and then examined in turn:

(i)   the combining of paid and unpaid work responsibilities;
(ii) the unidimensional conception of management;
(iii) the language of careers.

(i) Combining paid and unpaid work responsibilities

The conflict and stress that occur when trying to balance work and family roles has been well documented in Britain and particularly in the USA (Barker and Allen 1976, Finch and Groves 1983, Sharpe 1984, Adams and Winston 1980, Scanzoni 1978, Goldsmith 1989, Ferber *et al.* 1991). In earlier studies this was assumed to be a problem for women (Myrdal and Klein 1968) because of the cultural association between caring and feminine identity. Later studies have confirmed that, although women's careers have been most affected, the way forward is to regard work–family issues as universal, not just as women's concern.

As women form an increasing part of the labour market, they show greater attachment to it in terms of the proportion of their lives spent in paid employment. Young women as school-leavers are becoming better qualified for paid work and are entering a wider range of occupations on more equal terms. Slower and more resistant to change are the private worlds of partnerships and families. But here, too, men as well as women are requiring change. Working fathers and mothers are torn between the conflicting demands of their jobs and the desire to see more of their families. Some men as well as many women would give up salary and promotion to have more family and personal time. Both men and women are affected by work–family concerns on a daily basis and avoid jobs that involve relocation (Scase and Goffee 1989, Thompson *et al.* 1992).

Some work organisations have reported increases in numbers of managers, both male and female, who refuse to relocate even for promotions. A study at Mobil Oil Corporation (reported in Thompson *et al,.* 1992) found that Mobil men were more likely than Mobil women to refuse requests for relocation. This is partly explained by the fact that 80 per cent of the male managers in the study had dependent children while only 10 per cent of the female managers did. It is clear that the men and women of the corporation (Kanter 1977) were differently experiencing, and developing different strategies for resolving, work–family conflicts. Mobil men were experiencing high levels of conflict which for some led to refusal to relocate while the Mobil women were anticipating such conflict and resolving it by postponing or avoiding parenthood (Thompson *et al.* 1992: 62). In a similar way, Scase and Goffee's 'reluctant managers' (1989) were mostly male since there were fewer women and of the minority of women managers more were single and/or childfree. It is important to emphasise, therefore, that women who are successful so far in promotion and career terms are perhaps a particular group of women, namely women who have rejected or limited the demands which private, family lives make on careers. But this is to present women and men with an impossible choice. For both women and men to succeed in career terms they must severely curtail the demands of personal and family lives. We must do much better than this if we are to make best use of human capital, both male and female, in the contexts of both work and the family.

These issues are not easy to resolve and solutions have not been forthcoming. The chapters in this book on legislation and social policy directives (Chapters 1, 2 and 3) have demonstrated how limited are political and legislative directives in producing attitudinal and social change. In the very different ideological climate of the USA where individuals and organisations are left to cope with conflict and stress without state or federal regulation, the case for change has been justified in economic terms, as the best way of 'enhancing the productivity and profitability of organisations' (Sekaran and Leong 1992: xi). What is needed, therefore, for both women's and men's careers is some new way of reconciling the experiences of the unpaid and paid work aspects of careers to the benefit of both women and men. Women have so far been underrepresented in the promotion positions of paid work but they have almost monopolised the caring experiences of parenthood. Men have been over-represented in the senior management positions of careers but have denied themselves or been denied the pleasures as well as the responsibilities of full partnership and parenthood.

There are some signs of change. Men are now recognising and having to reconcile work and family demands. When it comes to the division of labour in the home, however, despite some optimistic forecasting (Young and Willmott 1973), most research suggests that women still do the large majority of tasks associated with housework and childcare (Edgell 1980, Moss and Fonda 1980, Sharpe 1984, Yeandle 1984). Thus while men are increasingly making career decisions with their partners and families in mind, nevertheless most men do not do their share of household and childcare tasks. This makes it more difficult for most women to be serious contenders in the competition for promotion in the career.

There have also been some signs of change in the way work organisations operate. In the competitive market place, organisations cannot change unilaterally, and all changes have to be justified in terms of economic efficiency rather than social justice. Thompson *et al.* (1992: 63) have described some of these organisational initiatives in the USA which they list as programmes for (i) dependent care, (ii) parental leave, (iii) spouse relocation, and (iv) alternative work schedules such as flexitime, job-sharing and part-time work. In Britain some of the problems associated with initiatives such as these have been examined by Cockburn (1991), and Kristinsdóttir (Chapter 7) has commented on the limitations of such schemes in Sweden when it is only or predominantly women who participate. Where such initiatives assume or imply that the man is the main career-builder, then the difficulties for women's careers continue.

It is necessary, therefore, to alter the imagery and the culture associated with the 'successful' career. The careers of successful women and men have tended to be unidimensional. Those on the fast track in organisations and the professions have been required to concentrate exclusively on the job. They have been required to act as if they had no other loyalties and certainly no family life (Kanter 1977). The de-gendering of career requires a more positive attitude to the multifaceted career where the management of different identities can be recognised and rewarded with career progress and development. In order to achieve this shift, however, we must also consider the second career problem for both women and men, the unidimensional conception of management.

(ii) Conceptions of management

In one sense experiences of career are experiences of promotion, that is of movements upwards through hierarchically organised job positions. In this sense, experiences of career are experiences of movements into management, of changes in work from doing the job, to the managing and administration of others who are doing the job. This conception has always applied in organisational careers where hierarchies of posts and positions have constituted promotion structures and individuals have developed linear careers through such structures. Increasingly this conception is also relevant to professional careers. Many professionals have in any case always worked in large scale organisations, and for those professionals working in smaller group practices, issues of advancement and progress are increasingly influencing career choices and decisions. Management has come to represent career progress for large numbers of professional workers.

There are, however, considerable gender differences in the distribution of management, hence promotion, positions. The proportion of women who hold management, executive or administrative positions has been rising consistently since the 1970s. These women hold lower-level posts, however, and are concentrated in positions with less authority and responsibility than men (see Introduction and Chapters 3 and 13). One explanation lies in the nature of management itself. Powell (1988) described how the job of manager has been defined as masculine with men seeing themselves and being seen by promotion panels as more suited for it than women. Powell examined the influence of gender stereotyping which suggests that men are more appropriate for hierarchical leadership roles than women and find the intense competition for such positions more conducive. Other researchers have sought the explanation in the nature of organisations themselves (Hearn *et al*. 1989) and in the general patriarchal system which diverts and resists attempts to introduce change in organisations (Marshall 1984, Cockburn 1991).

Gender differences in management styles have been a preoccupation of researchers. Following a review of research into managerial behaviour Powell (1988: 165) concluded that the sex differences that have been found were few and tended to cancel each other out. For Powell the only significant difference between managerial men and women were the environments in which they operated, with sex imbalances contributing to stereotypical preconceptions and cultural dilemmas for managerial women (see Chapter 11 of this volume). However, at the British Psychological Society Conference in January 1992, contributors were still arguing that there were fundamental differences in the qualities which men and women brought to management (Clement 1992a, 1992b). As a result women experienced a contradiction between their formal managerial authority and their feminine identities which militated against the practice of that authority.

It is certainly the case that *beliefs* about sex differences have a great impact on careers in organisations. Promotion in the career depends on organisational representatives, assessors and appraisers, evaluating the suitability of candidates for merit awards and promotion. Managers evaluate the performance of their subordinates. Promotion decisions are based on evaluations of past performance, future potential and comparison between candidates for promotion. Promotion is inevitably competitive since in hierarchical pyramidal career structures there are only a modest number of middle-ranking managerial positions and very few at the top. In such a structure others' evaluations materially affect the progress of an individual in an organisation. Evaluations are based on beliefs about what an individual is like and gender continues to influence such evaluations. Stereotypical beliefs that women are more expressive while men are more task-orientated and better leaders have a marked impact on promotion decisions about managerial posts. Beliefs about gender differences have a continuing effect on managerial careers.

Proposals and recommendations for equalising career opportunities in management have been forthcoming, largely determined by where the explanation for gender imbalance is seen to lie. Those who see the problem as being discrimination in organisations have proposed stronger equal opportunities legislation, the setting of recruitment and promotion targets and the notion of a 'qualifications lever' (Crompton and Sanderson 1990) whereby the qualifications and qualities required for promotion posts are specified, thereby enabling women, as well as men, to seek to acquire them. Those who explain the gender imbalance in management by reference to gender stereotypes have suggested the idea of androgynous management which 'blends behaviours previously deemed to belong exclusively to men or women' (Sargent 1981: 2). Powell has argued (1988: 170) that 'if an androgynous manager is defined as one who has the capability to be either high or low in both task-orientated and people-orientated behaviour, most management theorists would agree that better managers are androgynous'. It is also argued that androgynous managers are actually higher in behavioural flexibility and adaptability and thereby better fitted to organisational needs which increasingly require managers who are adaptable and multi-functional. The new manager will have to decide, therefore, to be more task-orientated or people-orientated depending on an evaluation of subordinates' needs and situational factors such as the firm's general economic circumstances and the organisation's climate.

In general, then, it seems that we need to change and to broaden and extend our conceptions of management if we are to de-gender the concept of career. For individuals, both men and women, there is more to life than career. Obsession with promotion and getting ahead has resulted in a particular conception of management which is aggressive, independent, competitive, ambitious, unemotional and self-confident. This in turn has resulted in a mono-dimensional interpretation of career. By changing our conception of management to include an ability to express feelings and form empathic relations with others, we might also begin to change our understanding of the good manager as well as of the good career. When individuals achieve a balance in their lives between career, family and other interests, then career as well as management might prove to be a work goal worth pursuing. Organisations as well will benefit substantially from the extension of management and career opportunities to a larger pool of managerial and administrative talent.

(iii) The language of careers

It is also necessary to recognise that the language used to describe careers and career development and success is not gender-neutral. In this collection, Coates has demonstrated the link between discourse and career in her paper on language in the professions. In addition, Aldridge has questioned the appropriateness of the language of career in the clerical profession where the concepts of 'vocation' or 'calling' supposedly provide substitutes in the sacred context of the Church. King has examined the power of cultural stereotypes in reputation-building in science. Several other contributors have also recognised in their papers the constraints which the language of career imposes on their interpretations of women's experiences.

The concepts of merit and promotion are interpreted and operationalised according to a particular model of career success. Merit payments are awarded to those making a distinctive, active contribution to the goals of the work group. Holding particular offices, contributing to professional or organisational development, having specific expertise and needing to be retained are the characteristics which are deemed worthy of merit awards. Other sorts of characteristics such as stability, long service, organisational loyalty and doing a good job are not in themselves deserving of merit. Women *can* earn such awards in the same way as men if they accept the appropriateness of the merit-earning characteristics. However, several reports have demonstrated that merit schemes generally favour men. The trade union representing top civil servants (Association of First Division Civil Servants) has claimed that statistics for the first four years of a new performance-related pay scheme had shown clear sex bias (Whitfield 1991). There was a consistent pattern of men on the same grade and with the same seniority being paid more than women. The decision to award performance-related pay was based on an annual review. People scoring high enough marks were eligible for extra cash but the number actually receiving an award was rationed to a certain percentage of the grade. In competition for such awards, management discretion was the final arbiter and women received fewer awards than men. In a similar way the Equal Opportunities Commission has argued that even the most 'objective' systems of merit pay and appraisal are likely to apply more readily to jobs performed by men (IRS 1992). Performance assessments of women's occupations often focused on subjective assessments of attitudes and behavioural characteristics and casual judgments by line managers (Clement 1992b). In these ways the operationalisation of merit schemes is not gender-neutral.

In a similar way the operationalisation of promotion procedures is also designed to reward only one, unidimensional model of career. There is an assumption in appraisers' and assessors' minds of a linear career track. Frequently there is an assertion of gender-neutrality, an emphasis on 'objective' characteristics and an underlining of the openness of competition. In the rational-legal organisation the focus in promotion decisions is on the human capital characteristics (qualifications, experience) among candidates which are deemed to be appropriate. In the open competition for promotion posts the individualistic attributes of candidates are assessed and compared. Past experience is judged and future potential is estimated. But in striving to emphasise achievement characteristics rather than ascription, certain attributes are deemed 'appropriate' whereas others are assumed to be inappropriate. Thus certain pursuits (national service, community position holders) are rated highly in career terms where others (raising children, managing households, caring for dependents) count for little. In addition it is also difficult if not impossible for those on promotion panels to separate the job performance from the job holder. Past achievements in jobs will be defined and assessed in relation to the person, male or female, doing the work. Similarly future potential will be appraised in terms of the person. In all these ways gender will intrude in promotion decisions.

As the contributors to this book have made clear, women have so far not been successful in their achievements in hierarchical, linear, competitive career structures. It seems that in developing the language of career we have a choice. Either women who want career success must adapt and adjust and focus their working lives on the achievement of merit and promotion as currently culturally conceived. Or, alternatively, women can strive to redefine notions of merit and of career in order to encompass a wider variety of career success. Again, the de-gendering of the concept of career *success* would seem the prime requisite.

Change in career contexts

It is necessary to end with a recognition of the changes currently under way in work organisations and professions which will inevitably affect the contexts in which careers are constructed. The concept of 'enterprise culture' has come to represent such changes. According to Keat (Keat and Abercrombie 1991: 1) there has been a radical programme of economic and institutional reform which 'appeals to the efficiency of markets, the liberty of individuals and the non-interventionist state'. Keat went on to summarise some of the main institutional changes as: the transfer of state-owned industries to the private sector; the reorganisation of publicly funded bodies in areas such as education and health; and the application of market principles to the conduct of the professions. The operation of the market in the professions has involved an intensification of competition, with professional services becoming purchasable commodities; the adoption of the techniques of marketing and advertising; the reconstruction of all institutions as commercial enterprises; and the replacement of terms such as client, patient, student with the term 'consumer' as the mode of organisation.

For professionals themselves, whether working in industrial organisations or professional practices, new vocabularies or 'discourses' have been introduced by means of which practitioners explain and account for their careers. The notion of accountability is now commonplace. Professional workers accept appraisal and assessment as a normal part of career development. At (annual) appraisal interviews personal goals are identified, according to organisational objectives, and progress towards such goals are monitored and assessed. This in the new language of career and promotion in the career.

Other changes in the enterprise culture of the professions also have consequences for professional careers. The model of the commercial enterprise has increased the numbers of short-term professional contracts. This has increased the segmentation of professional labour markets, sometimes increased the 'casualness' of contracts and augmented the diversity of professional careers. Thus professional researchers, lawyers and accountants can be employed for a fixed period in order to complete a task or job of work. In the professions of nursing and teaching there are a wide variety and diversity of contracts of employment ranging from full-time, part-time and supply but also with different 'employers' such as in public, private and agency sectors.

With such changes in the professions and work organisations currently under way, the time is appropriate for a revision, a broadening and a reconceptualisation of 'successful' career. We need to recognise the wide diversity of careers and of ways of combining paid work and unpaid work aspects of careers. The 'successful' career is not only the linear career, the achievement of high-ranking promotion positions in hierarchical organisational structures. If such careers are mono-dimensional then they have probably been achieved at tremendous cost to personal and family identities and relationships. The language of career, like the language of promotion, merit and success, needs to be broader, wider, more diverse and inevitably more complex. The labelling of types of career as successful should not only depend on the extent and the rapidity of promotion positions gained.

It is necessary to repeat that there is more to life than paid work. Ultimately, a balance between work, career, family and other interests has to be the most successful career. Obsession with getting ahead results in mono-dimensional careers. A focus on a single goal is hazardous both for the individual with thwarted aspirations and for the organisation which could never satisfy all aspirants. On the other hand, giving little thought to career can also lead to a sense of failure, disappointment and frustration. When individuals achieve a sense of balance in their lives, when they have chosen a pattern which suits them and fulfils all aspects of their perceived identities, then the multi-dimensional career will come to be recognised as potentially most satisfying.

It is also important to emphasise that the multi-dimensional career is in the best economic, as well as social, interests of work organisations. So far such organisations have had to select their top managers and professionals from a limited pool of talent, confined to one gender only. Women's careers are beginning to take off. But many women, like some men, will not be content with mono-dimensional careers. Families, children, relationships and wider responsibilities and interests are far too important to be neglected in the competition for linear careers. Organisations will have to do much better if they are to capitalise on the skills of the vast majority of men and women who do not want to be forced into choosing mono-dimensional careers. The 'successful' career is ready for redefinition. In the new conceptualisation, women as well as some men must be incorporated.

References

Adams, C. T. and Winston, K. T. (1980) *Mothers at Work: Public Policies in the US, Sweden and China*, New York and London: Longman.

Barker, D. L. and Allen, S. (eds) (1976) *Dependence and Exploitation in Work and Marriage*, London: Longman.

Becker, H. S. (1963) *Outsiders: Studies in the Sociology of Deviance*, Chicago: Free Press.

Clement, B. (1992a) 'Bias in selection keeps women out of top jobs', *Independent*, 8.1.92, p. 4.

Clement, B. (1992b) 'Merit pay schemes favour men', *Independent*, 8.7.92, p. 2.

Cockburn, C. (1991) *In the Way of Women: Men's Resistance to Sex Equality in Organizations*, London: Macmillan.

Crompton, R. and Sanderson, K. (1990) *Gendered Jobs and Social Change*, London: Unwin Hyman.

Edgell, S. (1980) *Middle Class Couples*, London: Allen & Unwin.

Evetts, J. (1992) 'Dimensions of career: avoiding reification in the analysis of change', *Sociology* **26**: 1–21.

Ferber, M. A., O'Farrell, B. and Allen, La Rue (eds) (1991) *Work and Family*, Washington DC: National Academic Press.

Finch, J. (1983) *Married to the Job*, London: Allen & Unwin.

Finch, J. and Groves, D. (eds) (1983) *A Labour of Love: Women, Work and Caring*, London: Routledge & Kegan Paul.

Goffman, E. (1968) *Asylums*, Harmondsworth: Penguin.

Goldsmith, E. (ed.) (1989) *Work and Family*, London and Newbury Park: Sage.

Gunz, H. (1989) 'The dual meaning of managerial careers: organizational and individual levels of analysis', *Journal of Management Studies*, **26**: 225–50.

Hearn, J. *et al.* (1989) *The Sexuality of Organisations*, London: Sage.

IRS (1992) *Pay and Gender in Britain 2*, London: Industrial Relations Services.

Kanter, R. M. (1977) *Men and Women of the Corporation*, New York: Basic Books.

Keat, R. and Abercrombie, N. (1991) *Enterprise Culture*, London: Routledge.

Marshall, J. (1984) *Women Managers*, Chichester: Wiley.

Moss, P. and Fonda, N. (eds) (1980) *Work and Family*, London: Temple Smith.

Myrdal, A. and Klein, V. (1968) *Women's Two Roles*, London: Routledge & Kegan Paul.

Powell, G. N. (1988) *Women and Men in Management*, Newbury Park and London: Sage.

Sargent, A. (1981) *The Androgynous Manager*, New York: AMACOM.

Scanzoni, J. (1978) *Sex Roles, Women's Work and Marital Conflict*, Lexington, MA: Heath.

Scase, R. and Goffee, R. (1989) *Reluctant Managers*, London: Unwin Hyman.

Sekaran, U. and Leong, F. (1992) *Womanpower: Managing in Times of Demographic Turbulence*, Newbury Park and London: Sage.

Sharpe, S. (1984) *Double Identity*, Harmondsworth: Penguin.

Taylor, L. and Cohen, S. (1972) *Psychological Survival*, Harmondsworth: Penguin.

Thompson, C. A., Thomas, C. C. and Maier, M. (1992) 'Work–family conflict: reassessing corporate policies and initiatives', in U. Sekaran and F. Leong, *Womanpower*, Newbury Park and London: Sage.

Whitfield, M. (1991) 'Civil servants claim sex bias in pay system', *Independent*, 4.9.91, p. 5.

Yeandle, S. (1984) *Women's Working Lives*, London: Tavistock.

Young, M. and Willmott, P. (1973) *The Symmetrical Family*, London: Routledge & Kegan Paul.

INDEX